OXFORD LEGAL PHILOSOPHY

Series editors: Timothy Endicott, John Gardner, and Leslie Green

A Theory of Legal Personhood

OXFORD LEGAL PHILOSOPHY

Series editors: Timothy Endicott, John Gardner, and Leslie Green

Oxford Legal Philosophy publishes the best new work in philosophically oriented legal theory. It commissions and solicits monographs in all branches of the subject, including works on philosophical issues in all areas of public and private law, and in the national, transnational, and international realms; studies of the nature of law, legal institutions, and legal reasoning; treatments of problems in political morality as they bear on law; and explorations in the nature and development of legal philosophy itself. The series represents diverse traditions of thought but always with an emphasis on rigour and originality. It sets the standard in contemporary jurisprudence.

ALSO AVAILABLE IN THE SERIES

Law and Morality at War
Adil Ahmad Haque

Ignorance of Law
A Philosophical Inquiry
Douglas Husak

Reason and Restitution
A Theory of Unjust Enrichment
Charlie Webb

Allowing for Exceptions
A Theory of Defences and Defeasibility in Law
Luís Duarte d'Almeida

The Ends of Harm
The Moral Foundations of Criminal Law
Victor Tadros

Corrective Justice
Ernest J. Weinrib

Conscience and Conviction
The Case for Civil Disobedience
Kimberley Brownlee

The Nature of Legislative Intent
Richard Ekins

Why Law Matters
Alon Harel

Imposing Risk
A Normative Framework
John Oberdiek

A Theory of Legal Personhood

Visa A.J. Kurki

OXFORD
UNIVERSITY PRESS

OXFORD
UNIVERSITY PRESS

Great Clarendon Street, Oxford, OX2 6DP,
United Kingdom

Oxford University Press is a department of the University of Oxford.
It furthers the University's objective of excellence in research, scholarship,
and education by publishing worldwide. Oxford is a registered trade mark of
Oxford University Press in the UK and in certain other countries

First Edition published in 2019

Published in the United States of America by Oxford University Press
198 Madison Avenue, New York, NY 10016, United States of America

British Library Cataloguing in Publication Data
Data available

Library of Congress Control Number: 2019941482

ISBN 978–0–19–884403–7

Series Editors' Preface

In this exciting book, Visa Kurki resolves dilemmas in the theory of legal personhood. On what he calls the 'orthodox view', legal personhood is an all-or-nothing matter of the legal capacity, determined by law, to be the subject of legal rights and duties. Kurki unpacks the variety and the flexibility of the ways in which the law might treat you—and might treat a corporation, or a fish—more or less as a person. And he points out that the law may do so for one purpose and not for other purposes. An all-or-nothing notion of legal personhood, Kurki concludes, is not well adapted to the variety of the law's purposes.

His first move to resolve the dilemmas is to point out the variety of incidents of legal personhood. They include your capacity to own property, your insusceptibility to being owned, the protection of your life and person by the law of tort, and the fact that you count as a victim for the purpose of criminal law. Those are 'passive incidents', and Kurki's second move is to point out the importance of the distinction between them and the active incidents—responsibilities and competences such as criminal liability and the capacity to form contracts or to hold offices. The combination of passive and active incidents explains fully-fledged membership in a legal system, yet the passive incidents can make someone—such as a human infant—a legal person.

These two steps yield the central insights of the book: that it is an array of interconnected active and passive incidents that makes sense of describing you as a legal person. That complex array of incidents of legal personhood reflects the complexity of human beings in their life in communities. So this book concerns the nature of human beings, as well as the related question of the law's proper relation to human beings and non-human beings.

You—if the law of your community is in good shape—are a paradigm legal person. It is a pleasure to offer you Visa Kurki's book about that aspect of your personality.

T.A.O. Endicott
J. Gardner
L. Green

Preface

Very few legal concepts have lately received such widespread attention as legal personhood. Lawsuits initiated by animal rights advocates to endow chimpanzees and other great apes with legal personhood have attracted attention around the world. Other widely publicized topics include the putative extension of legal personhood to natural objects, such as rivers; the question of whether artificial intelligences could be endowed with legal personhood; and the (primarily American) debate over whether foetuses should be defined as legal persons. In addition, the status of corporations as legal persons remains topical.

Interest in these topics has been re-emerging among scholars working in law, philosophy, and other fields. However, most of these scholars have merely applied existing accounts of legal personhood to these new cases. Few have questioned the underlying definition of legal personhood, which I call the Orthodox View. The Orthodox View comes in many forms, but its most popular formulations equate legal personhood with either the holding of legal rights and/or duties, the capacity to hold legal rights and/or duties, or the capacity to be a party to legal relations.

The origins of this book can be traced back to a puzzlement with the Orthodox View that I experienced when acquainting myself with Finnish animal law scholarship in the early 2010s. Virtually everyone writing on the legal status of animals endorsed a fundamental premise: even though animals are protected by the law, they do not hold any legal rights because they are not legal persons. At first, I took this premise at face value. I became interested in whether animals could be legal persons and whether they thereby could be endowed with the capacity to hold rights. However, a nagging feeling developed that I was asking the wrong questions. The existing definitions of legal personhood were, frankly, mysterious: if legal personhood means, for instance, the 'legal capacity' to hold rights, then how does the legislator go about endowing an animal with such a capacity? The topic of legal personhood itself seemed to warrant a sustained investigation, in the form of a doctoral dissertation—which eventually became this book.

The book has three main objectives. It (1) surveys the historical background of why jurists define a legal person as a subject of legal rights and duties; (2) criticizes the Orthodox View of legal personhood for being untenable; and (3) offers a new account of legal personhood. Even though I identify several issues with the Orthodox View, its main problem is how hard it is to reconcile with certain widely shared theories and convictions regarding what a right is, and who or what is a legal person. If the Orthodox View is assessed in light of contemporary theories of rights, we run into inconsistencies: these theories either ascribe rights to entities that are not usually classified as legal persons, such as foetuses and nonhuman animals, or deny rights to entities that are ordinarily classified as legal persons, such as human children. We must therefore adjust either our rights theories, our beliefs regarding who or what is a legal person, or our definition of legal personhood. I will, over the course of the book, argue for the last option. Rather than being a black-and-white affair, legal personhood comes in shades of grey—it is a cluster property. A legal person is not simply a right-holder or a duty-bearer; rather, legal personhood consists of divisible but interconnected *incidents of legal personhood*.

The book incorporates some material published earlier in journals and edited volumes. The main argument was first sketched in 'Why Things Can Hold Rights: Reconceptualizing the Legal Person', in Visa A.J. Kurki and Tomasz Pietrzykowski (eds): *Legal Personhood: Animals, Artificial Intelligence and the Unborn*. Furthermore, the book contains minor excerpts from the following articles: 'Legal Competence and Legal Power' in Mark McBride (ed.), *New Essays on the Nature of Rights*; 'Animals, Slaves and Corporations: Analyzing Legal Thinghood', *German Law Journal* (2017) 18: 1069–90; and 'Rights, Harming and Wronging: A Restatement of the Interest Theory', *Oxford Journal of Legal Studies* (2018) 38(3): 430–50.

Acknowledgements

There are numerous natural and artificial persons I would like to thank.

Markku Suksi was a mentor and an academic role model at the tiny Law Department of Åbo Akademi University where I received my LLB; he was also the first person to suggest that I might benefit from an acquaintance with the works of Wesley Newcomb Hohfeld. Ari Hirvonen was an inspiring and engaged master's thesis supervisor, who was also of great help with my PhD applications.

People who have read some or all of what was to become this book include Raffael Fasel, Maija Aalto-Heinilä, Joe Wills, Matija Žgur, Pedro Múrias, Daniel Goldsworthy, Samir Chopra, Nigel Simmonds, Nick McBride, David Ibbetson, Joe Sampson, Nino Guruli, Will Bateman, Jussi Sallila, Birgitta Wahlberg, and Mark McBride. I am grateful for their comments and encouragement. Jeffrey Skopek and William Lucy acted as the examiners of my doctoral dissertation, and provided much guidance on how to develop the dissertation into a book. I would also like to thank the organizers and participants of the numerous conferences and seminars where I have presented; my work has greatly benefited as a result. People who have provided support and advice on academic life include Panu Minkkinen, Kimmo Nuotio, Susanna Lindroos-Hovinheimo, Minna Gräns, Raimo Siltala, and Patricia Mindus.

Joshua Neoh, John Adenitire, and Ya Lan Chang read through my book prospectus and provided some really helpful comments. The two anonymous readers employed by Oxford University Press supplied careful and insightful comments on the proposal as well as the two draft chapters.

I have still not fully fathomed that Timothy Endicott, John Gardner, and Leslie Green decided to include the work in the prestigious Oxford Legal Philosophy series. Furthermore, Endicott asked some highly incisive questions about the project as a whole, which were vital in developing the book in its final form. Jamie Berezin, Eve Ryle-Hodges, Iona Jacob and the rest of the OUP editorial staff oversaw the work through the production process swiftly and efficiently.

This book is based on my doctoral dissertation, and pursuing doctoral studies at Cambridge was made possible by a generous grant from the Kone Foundation. Much of the revisions were undertaken during my postdoctoral research stay at Uppsala University, funded by the *Makarna Granfelts stipendiefond*. I was lucky to be able to finalize the manuscript as a Fellow of the Helsinki Collegium for Advanced Studies, virtually free from administrative and teaching duties.

My utmost thanks go to my PhD supervisor Matthew Kramer, who believed in the project when many others did not and has since provided more support with my academic work than I ever could have hoped for. Through his detailed comments on my work, he has instilled in me the philosophical virtues of rigorousness, clarity, and precision. The responsibility for any instances of sloppiness, ambiguity, and imprecision is of course mine to bear.

I also wish to thank my parents for all their support throughout the years. My father has taught me the value of education and my mother, by not taking the well-trodden path herself, has encouraged me to engage with topics that many of my fellow jurists have found rather obscure and arcane. Finally, I thank my wife Line for her companionship, patience, support, and love. This book is dedicated to her.

Visa A.J. Kurki

Contents

'The tendency—and the fallacy—has been to treat the specific problem as if it were far less complex than it really is; and this commendable effort to treat as simple that which is really complex has, it is believed, furnished a serious obstacle to the clear understanding, the orderly statement, and the correct solution of legal problems.'

Wesley Newcomb Hohfeld, 'Some Fundamental Legal Conceptions as Applied in Legal Reasoning'

'"Really", said Longhorn, without showing any kind of sympathy, in fact teasingly. "So you want everyone to be someone. You want what someone is at the beginning to be what he is at the end."'

Leena Krohn, *Tainaron*

Introduction

The Persons of Law

In December 2014, the New York State Supreme Court, Appellate Division, ruled in a case where the court had been exhorted to 'enlarge the common-law definition of "person" in order to afford legal rights to an animal'.[1] The Nonhuman Rights Project, representing a chimpanzee called 'Tommy', had requested that he be afforded the rights that pertain to the writ of *habeas corpus*. This book will not focus on the verdict, but rather on the underlying notion of legal personhood, or legal personality.[2] In its judgment, the court relied on the orthodox definition of legal personhood that equates X's legal personhood with X's holding of legal rights and/or duties:

> Further, although the dispositive inquiry is whether chimpanzees are entitled to the right to be free from bodily restraint such that they may be deemed 'persons' subject to the benefits of habeas corpus, legal personhood has consistently been defined in terms of both rights and duties.[3]

To support this understanding of legal personhood, the court cited *Black's Law Dictionary*, according to which '[s]o far as legal theory is concerned, a person is any being whom the law regards as capable of rights and duties'. The court also mentioned John Chipman Gray's similar assertion.[4] As chimpanzees are currently not legal persons and as supposedly only persons can hold legal rights, chimpanzees do not hold legal rights. Recognizing them as persons for the purposes of *habeas corpus* would thus entail endowing them with their first legal right. This premise structured much of the court's argumentation. The court made reference to contract theories of rights, asserting that 'the ascription of rights has historically been connected with the imposition of societal obligations and duties. Reciprocity between rights and responsibilities stems from principles of social contract, which inspired the ideals of freedom and democracy at the core of our system of government'.[5] Animals could

[1] *People ex rel. Nonhuman Rights Project, Inc. v Lavery*, No 518336, 2014 WL 680276 (NY App. Div. 4 December 2014; hereafter *People ex rel. Nonhuman Rights Project, Inc. v Lavery*) 1.

[2] I use 'personhood' and 'personality' interchangeably.

[3] *People ex rel. Nonhuman Rights Project, Inc. v Lavery* 6. Emphasis in original.

[4] John Chipman Gray, *The Nature and Sources of the Law* (David Campbell and Philip Thomas eds, Ashgate 1997) 6.

[5] *People ex rel. Nonhuman Rights Project, Inc. v Lavery* 4.

not, according to the court, fulfil any 'social responsibilities' in exchange for rights, which is why it would have been 'inappropriate to confer upon chimpanzees the legal rights—such as the fundamental right to personal freedom, protected by the writ of *habeas corpus*—that have been afforded to human beings'.[6] This is why the court rejected the 'rights paradigm' for animals, even though it hastened to add that animals are protected by various animal welfare statutes.

What if the court had relied on a different definition of legal personhood, according to which X's holding of legal rights[7] and/or bearing of legal duties would not entail X's legal personhood? The court's argumentation would likely have been quite different. I will defend a theory of legal personhood according to which legal nonpersons can hold legal rights. It is perfectly reasonable to say that animal welfare statutes have already established such rights for chimpanzees regardless of their personhood status.

Various legal materials have made reference to 'persons' or 'legal persons' ever since Roman scholar Gaius pronounced his famous trifurcation of all law as concerning persons, things, or actions.[8] Article 6 of the Universal Declaration of Human Rights affirms everyone's 'right to recognition everywhere as a person before the law'; a similar provision exists in the UN Disability Convention.[9] There are numerous examples of situations where human individuals have purportedly not been treated as legal persons. Scholars of American antebellum slavery claim often that a slave was—as Paul Finkelman puts it—'treated as property—a commodity—and not a person'.[10] Married women are another historical example. William Blackstone stated famously that, according to the doctrine of coverture, 'the husband and wife are one person in law: that is, the very being or legal existence of the woman is suspended during the marriage, or at least is incorporated and consolidated into that of the husband; under whose wing, protection, and cover, she performs every thing'.[11] The wife thus lost her separate legal personhood in marriage, according to Blackstone.

[6] *People ex rel. Nonhuman Rights Project, Inc. v Lavery* 4.

[7] I use the word 'right' in an unspecified sense in this Introduction and Chapter 1. From Chapter 2 on, I will be employing the Hohfeldian terminology.

[8] Gaius, *Institutiones or Institutes of Roman Law* (Edward Poste tr. ed., 4th edn, Clarendon Press 1904) § 8.

[9] Universal Declaration of Human Rights (adopted 10 December 1948) UNGA Res 217 A(III) (UDHR) art 6. 'States Parties reaffirm that persons with disabilities have the right to recognition everywhere as persons before the law.' United Nations Convention on the Rights of Persons with Disabilities (adopted 13 December 2006, entered into force 3 May 2008) UNTS 2515 art 12.

[10] Paul Finkelman, 'Slavery in the United States' in Jean Allain (ed.), *The Legal Understanding of Slavery: From the Historical to the Contemporary* (Oxford University Press 2012) 114. The person/property distinction is also employed in, for instance, Andrew Fede, *People Without Rights: an Interpretation of the Fundamentals of the Law of Slavery in the US South* (Garland Publishing, Inc 1992).

[11] William Blackstone, *Commentaries on the Laws of England. Vol. 1* (1765) 442.

One very important example of legal personhood that has fascinated jurists for centuries is, of course, the corporation—a nonphysical entity treated as a person. However, there have been more recent attempts to extend legal personhood to a broader range of physical entities as well. Some US states have redefined foetuses as legal persons for some limited purposes, in a departure from the old 'born-alive' rule of the common law; the Nonhuman Rights Project strives toward the legal personhood of certain animals in the United States; and rivers have supposedly been granted legal personhood in Australia, New Zealand, and India.[12] Jurists who seek to improve the treatment of animals are eager to point out the similarities between human slavery and the current legal status of nonhuman animals: both have involved treating sentient beings as property, not as legal persons.[13]

All of this raises the question: what does it mean to be a legal person, or to be 'recognized' or 'treated' as such? The cases above are not merely instances of employing similar terms and phrases—such as 'person', 'legal person', and 'legal personhood'—in saliently dissimilar circumstances. Rather, all of them actually make reference to a *conceptual scheme* extant in Western legal systems: the person/thing distinction, or as I will call it, person/nonperson distinction.[14] Eric Funkhouser submits that conceptual schemes are 'ways of thinking about things'.[15] He writes:

> Every conceptual scheme [...] involves a classification into kinds. Examples are easy to come by. Biology classifies animals as mammals or reptiles, mathematics classifies numbers as prime or composite, and ethics classifies actions as duties or prohibitions. These classifications are then used to describe situations, make generalizations, advance laws and principles, and the like.[16]

One conceptual scheme that can be employed to understand and categorize the norms of a Western legal system is the person/nonperson distinction. Kaarlo Tuori maintains that the divide between persons and nonpersons is a part of the 'deep structure of law' that is shared by all Western legal systems. He explains that concepts like 'legal subjectivity'—that is, legal personhood—and 'subjective right' are basic

[12] See Lisa McLennan Brown, 'Feminist Theory and the Erosion of Women's Reproductive Rights: The Implications of Fetal Personhood Laws and in Vitro Fertilization' (2005) 13 *American University Journal of Gender, Social Policy & the Law* 87; Steven M. Wise, 'Legal Personhood and the Nonhuman Rights Project' (2010) 17 *Animal Law Review* 1; Elaine G. Hsiao, 'Whanganui River Agreement. Indigenous Rights and Rights of Nature' (2012) 42 *Environmental Policy and Law* 371; and Erin L. O'Donnell and Julia Talbot-Jones, 'Creating Legal Rights for Rivers: Lessons from Australia, New Zealand, and India' (2018) 23 *Ecology and Society* 7.

[13] Such an analogy is offered at the very beginning of Wise (n 12). The status of animals as property is also central for Gary Francione's argument in Gary Francione, *Animals, Property & the Law* (Temple University Press 1995).

[14] However, I do not of course claim that jurists would use these terms and phrases *only* when referring to this conceptual scheme.

[15] Eric Funkhouser, *The Logical Structure of Kinds* (Oxford University Press 2014) 6.

[16] Ibid 1.

legal categories which underpin 'the conceptual space for modern law'.[17] I agree with him that our paradigmatic notions of legal personhood are deeply embedded in Western legal thought; the legal personhood of animals, for instance, is not simply unacceptable but rather unthinkable for many jurists. This book is an attempt to understand the person/nonperson scheme. I will address a number of issues pertaining to the scheme, though the primary question is: what does it mean to be a legal person?

Analytic jurisprudence has devised nuanced accounts of ownership, such as the bundle-of-rights analysis whose most sophisticated formulation has been offered by Anthony Honoré.[18] However, the meaning of legal personhood has not garnered similar attention for a while, with the exception of corporate personhood. A judge or a scholar may not need a theory of legal personhood—any more than a theory of ownership—to solve or comprehend easy cases, but the need for a theory may arise in hard cases. The only theoretical account available then is most likely the Orthodox View. According to the view, legal personhood involves either the holding of rights and bearing of duties or the 'legal capacity' to hold rights and bear duties.[19] This definition of legal personhood is not merely a textbook adage—even though any law student in the civil-law world is likely to come across it, and many students of the common law as well—but is also endorsed and employed by jurists with a profound interest in questions relating to legal personhood. For instance, Steven Wise, the American lawyer and legal scholar who has founded the Nonhuman Rights Project and written numerous articles on the topic, claims that legal personhood equals the 'capacity to hold at least one legal right'.[20] This 'capacity' does not refer to one's natural attributes. According to Wise, animals could very well be the holders of legal rights, but they cannot hold such rights as of now because they are legal things. The Nonhuman Rights Project aims to 'demand that American state high courts declare that a nonhuman animal has the capacity to possess at least one legal right, to declare that she is a […] legal person'.[21] For anyone acquainted with contemporary analytic theories of rights, this seems an odd policy statement. How could one's capacity to hold rights depend on whether one is declared a legal person? The question whether animals could hold legal rights drew me originally to the topic of legal personhood, as many of the chief assumptions of our orthodox understanding of legal personhood seemed to be utterly at odds with the most prominent theories of rights. I have since then come to understand that our conception of legal personhood dates back centuries and is, I hope to show, in need of a reappraisal.

[17] Kaarlo Tuori, *Critical Legal Positivism* (Ashgate 2002) 186–8.

[18] Anthony M. Honoré, 'Ownership' in A. G. Guest (ed.), *Oxford Essays in Jurisprudence* (Oxford University Press 1961).

[19] There are some other formulations of this view as well. I will return to them in Chapter 2.

[20] Wise (n 12) 1. [21] Ibid 5.

The main task I set out to perform in this book is to provide a new, less confused, and less confusing way of understanding the conceptual scheme of legal personhood. My main target is the Orthodox View of legal personhood, which equates X's legal personhood with the holding of legal rights and bearing of legal duties by X. This equation may have worked in the context of nineteenth-century notions of rights and duties, but our understanding of these legal positions has come a long way since then, and the current theory, though alluring in its simplicity, has a number of befuddling implications when viewed from a modern point of view.

I will not abandon the idea that X's legal personhood is connected to the legal positions held by X. I will, however, significantly revise the currently dominant view. A noteworthy difference between the implications of my theory and those of the Orthodox View is that according to my theory one can hold legal positions (rights and duties) without being a legal person; the salient difference between legal persons and nonpersons is not always *whether* one holds legal positions but rather *which* legal positions one holds—though of course some nonpersons, such as rocks, do not hold legal positions at all.

Main Tenets of the Proposed Theory

I will now lay out some of the central features of my new theory—*the Bundle Theory of legal personhood*—without really arguing for them at this point. The main tenets of the proposed new theory are twofold:

1. The legal personhood of X is a cluster property and consists of incidents which are separate but interconnected.
2. These incidents involve primarily the endowment of X with particular types of *claim-rights, responsibilities*, and/or *competences*.

I thus take legal personhood to be a complex disjunctive property, consisting of distinct incidents, just as ownership is often analysed as a bundle of rights. I divide the incidents of legal personhood into two groups: active and passive. In contemporary jurisdictions, infants are endowed only with the passive incidents, whereas adults of sound mind are endowed with both the active and passive incidents. What distinguishes infants (who are passive legal persons) from nonhuman animals (who are not) is that infants are endowed with the following incidents:

- their lives, liberty, and bodily integrity are protected;
- they have standing in courts (though infants need, of course, someone else to represent them);
- they may own property even if they cannot dispose of it independently;
- they are not susceptible to being owned;

– they are protected by criminal law as potential victims (killing a newborn counts as a homicide, which is not the case with foetuses in most jurisdictions);
– they can undergo legal harms (torts) which may lead to restitution or compensation, owed to the infant.

Even infants can be endowed with these incidents, with their administration being taken care of by a guardian or a representative. On the other hand, certain *active* incidents of legal personhood are primarily, though not exclusively, applicable to entities that have mental abilities roughly corresponding to those of an adult human being of sound mind:

– they may enter into contracts and perform other acts-in-the-law;
– their behaviour is regulated, for instance through criminal law, and they are held responsible for their actions.

The threshold between passive and active legal personhood is not clear-cut; it is not at all unusual in contemporary Western jurisdictions that minors are criminally liable to some extent and that they may enter into some contracts (e.g. buying school lunch). However, at a certain age, human beings without mental deficiencies typically become fully fledged members of the legal system and are fully endowed with both the active and the passive incidents.

More generally, there is no clear border between 'full' legal persons and nonpersons; an entity may be a legal person for some purposes but not for others. For instance, stipulating that foetuses are legal persons in the context of homicide law would not have to imply that foetuses could also own property.

Central Features of the Western Doctrine of Legal Personhood

Nigel Simmonds's observation that 'jurisprudential reflection upon law has never been clearly separable from the intelligent development of doctrinal ideas' is very much relevant in the case of legal personhood.[22] Theories of law, of rights, and of legal personhood that were reached in nineteenth-century Germany would have a very profound impact on certain core tenets and taxonomies of legal personhood, which are still endorsed by jurists across the Western world.[23] These include,

[22] N. E. Simmonds, 'Rights at the Cutting Edge' in Matthew H. Kramer, N. E. Simmonds, and Hillel Steiner (eds), *A Debate over Rights: Philosophical Enquiries* (Oxford University Press 1998) 119. Emphasis removed.

[23] For this section, I have looked mainly into English, American, German, and French sources (principally case law and legal scholarship). For Italian and Spanish law, I have primarily relied on Guido Alpa and Vincenzo Zeno-Zencovich, *Italian Private Law*

firstly, the fundamental divide into 'natural persons' (*natürliche Personen*; *personnes physiques*)—denoting human individuals who are legal persons—and 'artificial' or 'juristic persons' (*juristische Personen*; *personnes morales*), meaning any other types of legal persons, such as associations, limited liability companies, and foundations, all of which can own property and enter into contracts in their own names. I use 'corporation' in the British sense, meaning 'artificial person' rather than in the primary American sense of 'large for-profit company'. 'Legal person' is also occasionally used as a synonym for 'artificial person', but I use 'legal person' as an umbrella phrase to refer to both natural and artificial persons. In many other European languages, the corresponding umbrella term or phrase is 'legal subject' or 'subject of law/right(s)' (*Rechtssubjekt*; *sujet de droit*).[24] I will suggest in Chapter 3 that these two phrases could be distinguished.

Public-law organizations, such as states and municipalities, are legal persons as well. Though my theory is applicable to public-law organizations, I will not focus on them here. The offered account would likely have to be amplified to account for the legal complexities that pertain specifically to legal persons with public powers. Marginal examples of nonhumans to which legal personhood has been attributed include the rivers, idols, ships, temples, and others.[25] Some such cases will be analysed in Chapters 4 and 5.

Who is a Natural Person?

I will now offer a very brief sketch of the extensional definition of paradigmatic natural persons in contemporary Western legal systems—*extensional* in that I consider the set of beings who are natural persons rather than what actually qualifies them as legal persons, and *paradigmatic* in that I demarcate the set of individuals whose legal personhood is definitely not in dispute.[26] This demarcation will be central for my methodology, which will be presented shortly.

(Routledge-Cavendish 2007) and Teresa Rodríguez de las Heras Ballell, *Introduction to Spanish Private Law: Facing the Social and Economic Challenges* (Routledge-Cavendish 2010) 34. Though I do not list many Finnish or Swedish sources, I know from my legal education that similar doctrines are present in the Finnish and Swedish legal systems. The claim that these doctrines are shared by Western legal systems is corroborated by Aleck Chloros, Max Rheinstein, and Mary Ann Glendon (eds), *International Encyclopedia of Comparative Law, Volume IV: Persons and Family* (Mohr Siebeck 2007).

[24] South Africa—a mixed jurisdiction—is an exception among Anglophone countries in that even jurists writing in English do use the phrases 'legal subject' and 'legal object' synonymously with 'person' and 'thing', respectively. See Jacqueline Heaton, *The South African Law of Persons* (4th edn, LexisNexis South Africa 2015).

[25] Regarding the legal personality of idols, see Hsiao (n 12) and P.W. Duff, 'The Personality of an Idol' (1927) 3 *The Cambridge Law Journal* 42.

[26] Concepts have an extension and an intension. The former comprises the set of things in the world to which the concept applies, and the latter tells us, roughly put, why those things are within the extension of the concept. WVO Quine used the examples of 'cordate' (creature with a heart) and 'renate' (creature with a liver) to illustrate this: the two concepts have the same extension (because every creature that has a heart also has a liver) but different intensions.

In contemporary Western legal systems, the paradigmatic natural persons are

(1) human beings
(2) who have been born,
(3) who are currently alive, and
(4) who are sentient.

1. Humanity: Only human beings are natural persons.[27] This is often not made explicit but is more of a silent assumption. The German Civil Code is explicit about the humanity condition: 'The legal capacity of *a human being* begins at the completion of birth' (emphasis added).[28] A similar statement is made in the Austrian Civil Code: 'Every *human being* has innate rights that are obvious to reason, and is therefore to be considered a person' (emphasis added).[29] Human rights are, unsurprisingly, also usually applied only to human beings. The humanity condition is challenged especially by animal rights advocates.

2. Having been born: This condition dates back to Roman law. It is widely (though not uniformly and without exceptions) accepted in Western legal systems, in both common-law and civil-law jurisdictions, even if US states have increasingly departed from it.[30] The condition is questioned especially when abortion is discussed.[31] Stillborn children are usually excluded, whereas children born alive may occasionally benefit from the *nasciturus pro iam nato habetur quamdiu agitur de eius commodo* maxim—*nasciturus* for short—that is, 'one who is about to be born is to be

The Orthodox View of legal personhood maintains that the intension of 'legal person' is 'someone or something that holds rights and/or bears duties' whereas I maintain that this intensional definition cannot account for the widely-accepted extension of the concept. See W. V. O. Quine, 'Two Dogmas of Empiricism' (1951) 60 The Philosophical Review 20.

[27] '"Natural person" is the term used to refer to human beings' legal status.' Jessica Berg, 'Of Elephants and Embryos: A Proposed Framework for Legal Personhood' (2007) 59 Hastings Law Journal 369, 373.

[28] '*Die Rechtsfähigkeit des Menschen beginnt mit der Vollendung der Geburt.*' German Civil Code (*Bürgerliches Gesetzbuch*, BGBl. I p. 42, 2909; 2003 I p. 738, last amended on 18 December 2018) § 1.

[29] '*Jeder Mensch hat angeborne, schon durch die Vernunft einleuchtende Rechte, und ist daher als eine Person zu betrachten.*' Austrian Civil Code (*Allgemeines bürgerliches Gesetzbuch für die gesammten deutschen Erbländer der Österreichischen Monarchie*, 946/1811, last amended on 14 August 2018) § 16.

[30] The condition is explicitly recognized in the German Civil Code, as noted above, as well as in Part 1, Section 1 of the Italian Civil Code. In Spanish law, the neonate must live for at least 24 hours outside of the womb in order to be deemed a legal person. See de las Heras Ballell (n 23) 34. Regarding French law, see for example Philippe Malaurie, *Cours de Droit Civil. Les Personnes, Les Incapacités* (5th edn, Éditions Cujas 1999) 27: 'For natural persons, legal personality appears at birth […] and disappears at death […].' (*[P]our les personnes physiques, la personnalité juridique apparaît avec la naissance* […] *et disparaît avec la mort* […].).

[31] An American landmark case, defining foetuses as nonpersons in the context of the 14th Amendment of the Constitution, is *Roe v Wade*, 410 US 113, 158 (1972).

treated as if already born whenever that is to her or his advantage'.[32] This rule presupposes, however, that the foetus is later born alive.

3. **Currently alive**: Dead people are not legal persons, even if their estates may very well be. However, it has been argued that dead people possess some limited rights.[33] Dead people's determinations may also continue to 'exist' *post mortem* in the form of a last will. It should be noted that determining when a person is dead is not uncontroversial; the clinical criterion of brain death is sometimes questioned.

4. **Sentience**: An entity that meets the three preceding criteria but that does not have a sentient mind at all, such as anencephalic infants who do not possess a brain cortex and therefore lack sentience, are not paradigmatic legal persons. For instance, such infants have been deemed legal persons in the US, but this decision has been the subject of controversy, which implies that they are not easy cases.[34]

If these four criteria are met, one is a paradigmatic legal person. However, these criteria are only sufficient for what in civil-law traditions is designated as 'legal capacity' (*Rechtsfähigkeit*; *capacité de jouissance*)—most often defined as the capacity to hold rights and bear duties, or as the capacity to be a party in legal relations—as opposed to 'legal competence' (*Geschäftsfähigkeit*; *capacité d'exercice*), meaning the ability to enter binding contracts and so forth.[35] 'Legal capacity' is an ambiguous phrase in that it can also be used synonymously with 'legal competence'; this usage is prevalent, for instance, among disability scholars.[36] Due to this ambiguity I call these two aspects of legal personhood *passive* and *active legal personhood*.[37] The four criteria above are not sufficient for 'legal competence' or active legal personhood, which is

[32] This is Neil MacCormick's translation of the maxim. Neil MacCormick, *Institutions of Law: An Essay in Legal Theory* (Oxford University Press 2007) 79.

[33] See for example Matthew H. Kramer, 'Getting Rights Right' in Matthew H. Kramer (ed.), *Rights, Wrongs and Responsibilities* (Palgrave 2001).

[34] See Berg (n 27) 377–9. Jörg Neuner analyses anencephalic infants from the point of view of German law and concludes that they are 'full legal persons' because the relevant organs—heart, lungs, and brain—are still functioning. Jörg Neuner, 'Zur Rechtsfähigkeit des Anencephalus' (2013) 31 *Medizinrecht* 647, 651.

[35] See Matthias Lehmann, 'Der Begriff der Rechtsfähigkeit' (2007) 207 *Archiv für die civilistische Praxis* 225.

[36] This is the terminology used in the UN Disability Convention. See also Eilionóir Flynn and Anna Arstein-Kerslake, 'Legislating Personhood: Realising the Right to Support in Exercising Legal Capacity' (2014) 10 *International Journal of Law in Context* 81 as well as Gerard Quinn and Anna Arstein-Kerslake, 'Restoring the "Human" in "Human Rights": Personhood and Doctrinal Innovation in the UN Disability Convention' in Conor Gearty and Costas Douzinas (eds), *The Cambridge Companion to Human Rights Law* (Cambridge University Press 2012).

[37] This is inspired by Neil MacCormick's terminology in MacCormick (n 32) 77–99. Similar categorizations have been propounded by various authors. For instance, Ngaire Naffine employs

> the distinction between those whom the law addresses, adult to adult, those to whom it speaks […] and those who are intended to receive the benefits of law because they are perceived to have particular needs and interests, that is law's beneficiaries, but who are not necessarily parties to law's adult discourse.

generally contingent on one's age and mental abilities. For active legal personhood, Western legal systems typically require that a fifth condition is met.

5. Sufficient rationality and age: For active legal personhood, one must be of a certain age and have mental abilities that roughly correspond to those of an adult human being of sound mind. If one lacks either attribute, one is under the power of a legal guardian and thus *alieni juris* or—in the parlance of disability law—lacking legal capacity.

If one meets criteria 1–4, one is a passive natural person; if one also meets criterion 5, one is an active natural person as well. These criteria only apply to contemporary Western legal systems; for instance, slaves were not natural persons despite meeting these criteria.

Legal Nonpersons and 'Things'

There are also several points of consensus regarding what beings are not, or have not been, legal persons. Obviously, rocks and gusts of wind are not legal persons, but among the theoretically significant cases the most salient one is likely slavery, which involved treating human beings as property rather than as legal persons (even though many scholars agree that slaves were legal persons insofar as they could be subjected to criminal punishments).[38] It is likewise widely accepted that nonhuman animals are currently not legal persons, even if many authors claim that some animals should be accorded legal personhood.[39] The historical subjugated status of women in various Western jurisdictions has also often been regarded as explainable in terms of their lack of (full) legal personhood. The most famous example is likely the above-mentioned common-law doctrine of coverture which meant that a married woman's property was subsumed into that of her husband.[40] Contemporarily, the

Ngaire Naffine, *Law's Meaning of Life: Philosophy, Religion, Darwin and the Legal Person* (Hart Publishing 2009) 66. See also Tomasz Pietrzykowski, *Personhood Beyond Humanism: Animals, Chimeras, Autonomous Agents and the Law* (Springer 2018) 11–16.

[38] Just a few of the scholars classifying slaves as legal nonpersons include Fede (n 10); Hans Kelsen at various junctures such as Hans Kelsen, *General Theory of Law and State* (Transaction Publishers 2006) 95; and Wise (n 12) 1. In his doctoral dissertation, the Scandinavian Realist Karl Olivecrona takes himself to be reporting the received opinion when noting that slaves lack legal personality. Karl Olivecrona, *Studier över begreppet juridisk person i romersk och modern rätt* (Appelbergs 1928) 38. Some historical views will be presented in Chapter 1. See also for instance John W. Cairns, 'The Definition of Slavery in Eighteenth-Century Thinking' in Jean Allain (ed.), *The Legal Understanding of Slavery: From the Historical to the Contemporary* (Oxford University Press 2012).

[39] In addition, some animals were prosecuted in criminal courts during the Middle Ages. See E. P. Evans, *The Criminal Prosecution and Capital Punishment of Animals* (The Lawbook Exchange, Ltd 2010) and Katie Sykes, 'Human Drama, Animal Trials: What the Medieval Animal Trials Can Teach Us About Justice for Animals' (2011) 17 *Animal Law* 273.

[40] Many jurisdictions passed statutes abolishing coverture during the mid nineteenth century. See Joan Hoff-Wilson, 'The Unfinished Revolution: Changing Legal Status of US Women' (1987) 13 *Signs* 7. Married women's legal status in the nineteenth-century US is depicted in Carole Shammas, 'Re-Assessing the Married Women's Property Acts' (1994) 6

Finnish and Swedish doctrines of guardianship (*edusmiehyys* in Finnish, *målsmanskap* in Swedish) allowed for women to retain some of their property but always required a male to represent them legally.[41]

This brings us to a terminological point. Scholars often contrast legal persons (*personae*) with what is taken to be their opposite—legal things (*res*). Legal thinghood can be understood in three main senses.[42] First, 'thing' can refer to anything, or at least any physical object, that is susceptible to being owned.[43] This understanding is reflected in phrases such as 'rights *in rem*' ('rights to things', meaning, crudely speaking, property rights) as opposed to 'rights *in personam*' ('rights in relation to persons', such as contractual rights). Many contemporary civil-law taxonomies define things as physical objects that can be owned. Part II of the German Civil Code is titled 'Things and Animals' (following Part I, 'Persons') and contains rules pertaining to the possession, buying, and selling of goods. (Before 1990, that part was called simply 'Things', but animals have since then been declared as 'not things'—even if the provisions that apply to things apply to animals as well, unless otherwise provided.[44])

Second, *res* was used by Roman scholars to refer roughly to what we could call rights and duties.[45] This sense is still reflected in certain modern usages, such as the common-law phrase 'thing in action' (or 'chose in action'), meaning essentially the right to sue.

Journal of Women's History 9. For a contemporary perspective on the active legal personhood of women in a number of Commonwealth countries, see Marsha A. Freeman, 'Measuring Equality: A Comparative Perspective on Women's Legal Capacity and Constitutional Rights in Five Commonwealth Countries' (1990) 16 *Commonwealth Law Bulletin* 1418. A rather famous case is also *In re Lockwood*, where the US Supreme Court allowed state courts to interpret 'person' as excluding females. *In re Lockwood* 154 US 116 (1894).

[41] Finland was a part of Sweden until 1809 when it became an autonomous Grand Duchy of the Russian Empire. The Law of the Realm of 1734, which contained the provisions on *målsmanskap*, remained valid law in Finland until the 1860s. See Anu Pylkkänen, *Trapped in Equality: Women as Legal Persons in the Modernisation of Finnish Law* (Suomalaisen Kirjallisuuden Seura/Finnish Literature Society 2009) 40ff.

[42] See also Visa A.J. Kurki, 'Animals, Slaves and Corporations: Analyzing Legal Thinghood' (2017) 18 *German Law Journal* 1096.

[43] For example, Jeffrey Nesteruk defines 'thing' as 'the subject of property', writing that '[i]n law, "property" is not a "thing" although "things" are the subject of property'. Jeffrey Nesteruk, 'Persons, Property and the Corporation: A Proposal for a New Paradigm' (1990) 39 *DePaul Law Review* 543, 543.

[44] German Civil Code, § 90a. Saskia Stucki has—when addressing the Swiss Civil Code, which has undergone largely the same relabelling with regard to animals as the German Civil Code—summarized this change in legal taxonomy as follows: '[A]nimals are not treated *as* things but *like* things.' (*Tiere [werden] rechtlich also statt* als *Sachen* wie *Sachen behandelt.*) Saskia Stucki, 'Rechtstheoretische Reflexionen zur Begründung eines tierlichen Rechtssubjekts' in Margot Michel, Daniela Kühne, and Julia Hänni (eds), *Animal Law—Tier und Recht. Developments and Perspectives in the 21st Century* (Dike 2012) 146. Emphases in original.

[45] J. R. Trahan, 'The Distinction between Persons and Things: An Historical Perspective' (2008) 1 *Journal of Civil Law Studies* 9, 11.

Third, in an even broader sense, 'thing' can refer to anything that is not a person.[46] This usage was endorsed by the German nineteenth-century scholar Anton Thibaut, for instance.[47]

Here I shall not be using 'thing' in any specialist sense; I shall refer to entities that are not legal persons as 'legal nonpersons' or occasionally simply 'nonpersons', and to objects that can be owned primarily as 'property'.

I should also briefly address the claim that legal personhood and thinghood are jointly exhaustive categories, meaning that any entity must be either a legal person or a legal thing. This is of course true if by 'thing' is meant 'anything that is not a person'. However, it is not the case that any physical object must be either property or a legal person. For instance, let us assume that the institution of outlawing people for their crimes were still in place. The outlaw would be stripped of all legal protections. However, he or she would still not be susceptible to being owned: even if one could perhaps de facto take an outlaw as a slave, treating him or her as property would not receive legal recognition as in the case of de jure slaves. The sale of a slave would be a legally enforceable contract whereas the sale of an outlaw would not.

Business corporations are often mentioned as examples of entities that are simultaneously property and persons. I do not see anything mystical about this dual status; I shall later argue that paradigmatic corporations are group agents, which have their own intentions that are separate from the individual intentions of the shareholders or the executives. Shareholders partake in the formation of the group intentionality through shareholders' meetings, as their ownership is wielded through an aggregative function by which the corporate intentions are formed. The shareholders' role is, in this regard, similar to that of the members of registered societies, who can exert their influence in annual general meetings. (This analysis obviously does not work for shell companies. They will be addressed in Chapters 4 and 5.)

The Problems of the Orthodox View

This work focuses primarily on the conceptual structure of legal personhood. The main questions to be answered are as follows: (1) What does it mean to be a legal person? (2) Who or what can be a legal person? By contrast, normative questions such as 'Who or what should be a legal person?' will not be central, even if I will provide some tools for answering that question in the final chapter, which will also include a discussion of the role of legal personhood in legal reasoning.

46 Ibid.

47 'By Person is meant whatever in any respect is regarded as the subject of a right: by Thing, on the other hand, is denoted whatever is opposed to person.' Anton Thibaut, *An Introduction to the Study of Jurisprudence* (Nathaniel Lindley tr. and ed., T & JW Johnson 1885) § 101. (Cited in Trahan (n 45) 15.)

I should firstly note that I do not take the Orthodox View of legal personhood to be *empirically wrong*. It is not empirically wrong because it cannot be empirically wrong. It makes no predictive claims that could be empirically refuted. Even though some formulations of the Orthodox View can be rejected on their own terms because of the non sequiturs that they contain, the theory at its barest is purely stipulative and definitional. The problem of the theory is rather that it cannot properly explain and structure the various ongoing debates that are, in some way or another, linked to the concept of legal personhood. Such debates include those over the legal status of animals, foetuses, and corporations. The Orthodox View has implications that obscure the need for legal reasoning and normative argumentation; one such implication is that animals do not, or cannot, currently hold legal rights because they are not legal persons. One of the main goals of the theory offered here is thus to provide a framework that would help in explaining what is at stake in these debates over foetal, corporate, and animal legal personhood.

The problems of the Orthodox View can best be exposed using the method of *reflective equilibrium*.

Reflective Equilibrium

Reflective equilibrium—introduced in its most familiar form by John Rawls in *A Theory of Justice*[48]—is a method that can be used to reach consistency between beliefs about 'particular instances or cases, the principles or rules that we believe govern them, and the theoretical considerations that we believe bear on accepting these considered judgments, principles, or rules'. These elements can be revised 'wherever necessary in order to achieve an acceptable coherence among them'.[49] Rawls articulated the method in the context of moral and political philosophy, but its application is by no means limited to these fields. Norman Daniels, who has developed the method further, sees reflective equilibrium as an attempt to produce coherence in and between three sets of beliefs:[50]

(a) a set of considered (moral) judgements
(b) a set of moral principles
(c) a set of relevant background theories[51]

[48] John Rawls, *A Theory of Justice* (Belknap Press of Harvard University Press 1971). Rawls outlined this method in John Rawls, 'Outline of a Decision Procedure for Ethics' (1951) 60 *The Philosophical Review* 177.

[49] Norman Daniels, 'Reflective Equilibrium' in Edward N. Zalta (ed.), *The Stanford Encyclopedia of Philosophy* (Winter 2013) <http://plato.stanford.edu/entries/reflective-equilibrium/>.

[50] The phrase 'reflective equilibrium' can also refer to the outcome of a successful application of the method, i.e. when a set of beliefs is in a state of equilibrium (coherence).

[51] Norman Daniels, *Justice and Justification: Reflective Equilibrium in Theory and Practice* (Cambridge University Press 1996) 22.

None of these beliefs constitutes an 'Archimedean point', or a foundational belief that could not be questioned and reassessed. Even the beliefs in (c) can be re-evaluated as long as one is engaging in a *wide* reflective equilibrium, as opposed to a *narrow* one which would preclude the critical examination of (c). However, the background theories should meet certain criteria according to Daniels. The *independence constraint* is particularly relevant here. It requires that the background theories have some further merit in addition to merely supporting the moral principles in (b), and that the theories reach 'beyond the range of the considered moral judgments used to "test" the moral principles'.[52] Otherwise, the background theory would be redundant (since the background theory partly justifies the beliefs in (a) and (b), but only these beliefs justify the background theory).

Daniels also distinguishes several levels of background theories, using the Rawlsian theory of justice as an example. The social contract is, according to Rawls, a reasonable device for choosing between different conceptions of justice and thus a background theory that constrains what substantive judgements and principles concerning justice one could reasonably reach. However, Daniels notes that the arguments that Rawls mounts in support of the social contract are founded on some further background theories, such as a theory of the person and a theory of the role of morality in society.[53]

Applying the Reflective Equilibrium to Legal Personhood

The structure of the reflective equilibrium proposed by Daniels is *mutatis mutandis* also suitable as a method for reaching coherent beliefs about legal personhood. First, some central convictions about legal personhood are accepted widely by jurists in the Western world. These convictions are analogous to set (a) of considered moral judgements above. I have gone through many such convictions above; they include (but are not limited to):

(i) human beings who meet the aforementioned four criteria of passive natural personhood (born, sentient, and so on) are legal persons;
(ii) animals and foetuses are not legal persons, and slaves were not legal persons;
(iii) there are some relevant legal differences between the legal personhood of adults of sound mind and that of infants and severely mentally disabled individuals;
(iv) there are artificial persons, such as corporations.

I call these and other similar convictions *extensional beliefs*. Convictions (i)–(iv) are far-reaching and shared by jurists very widely. Some marginal cases of legal personhood are often mentioned with less confidence; such cases include the historical instances of treating ships and idols as legal persons. They will not be central for my

[52] Ibid 23. [53] Ibid.

argument, though I will look at how some of these more peripheral cases can be understood through the new theory that has first been tested with the more central cases. The legal status of women has historically varied quite a bit from jurisdiction to jurisdiction, which is why it will not be a focal case when I assess the problems of the Orthodox View. I should also mention that, when I henceforth advert to foetuses as an example of legal nonpersons, I am primarily referring to those jurisdictions that have not moved toward recognizing foetuses as persons in some contexts such as the law of homicide.

What has usually underlain beliefs (i)–(iv) is the Orthodox View of legal personhood. According to the Orthodox View, one's being a legal person is the same thing as one's holding of legal rights and/or bearing of legal duties, or one's capacity to hold such rights and/or bear such duties. This view is almost always propounded or assumed when legal personhood is discussed.

I will show in Chapter 1 how the Orthodox View became the standard theory of legal personhood during the nineteenth century and how it has not really been revisited since, even though our theories of right-holding have improved in the meantime. In Chapter 2, a more recent background theory—the Hohfeldian analysis of legal relations—is brought to bear on the Orthodox View and the extensional beliefs. If the Orthodox View's equation of legal personhood and right-holding is assessed in light of Hohfeld's theory, many of the widely held extensional beliefs come into conflict with the Orthodox View: modern theories of rights, which are based on the Hohfeldian analysis, either ascribe rights to entities that are not usually classified as legal persons, such as foetuses and nonhuman animals, or deny rights to entities that are ordinarily classified as legal persons, such as human children. Slavery is an obvious example. Slaves are very commonly taken to have been legal nonpersons. This would imply according to the Orthodox View that slaves held no rights and bore no duties, and some scholars, such as Hans Kelsen, assert this explicitly.[54] At least as far as duties are concerned, the claim is simply false.[55] The fact that slaveholding societies commonly held slaves legally responsible for their delicts is for slavery scholar Orlando Patterson reason enough to conclude that the 'common definition of a slave as someone without legal personhood' is a 'fallacy that we can quickly dispose of'. He laments that 'most students of slavery tend to be as knowledgeable about jurisprudence as they are ignorant of law'.[56]

[54] 'That a slave is legally no person, or has no legal personality, means that there are no legal norms qualifying any behavior of this individual as a duty or a right.' Kelsen (n 38) 95. Scholars who define slaves as legal nonpersons have been listed above in footnote 38.

[55] The claim is also false with regard to rights, but not as glaringly false.

[56] Orlando Patterson, *Slavery and Social Death. A Comparative Study* (Harvard University Press 1982) 22. It is interesting that in *Political Liberalism* John Rawls endorses the claim that 'slaves are not counted as capable of having duties or obligations'. However, on the same page he makes reference to Patterson's book, which contains a wholesale rebuttal of that very claim. John Rawls, *Political Liberalism. Expanded Edition* (Columbia University Press 2005) 33. Hillel Steiner makes a similar claim: 'self-enslavement [...] cannot be incurred by a self-owner's

Some beliefs must thus be readjusted in order to render the overall set of beliefs consistent. One could firstly question the Hohfeldian scheme of rights and the theories that build upon it. Hohfeld's analysis is, however, an insightful cornerstone of the modern understanding of rights. Other things being equal, the mere fact that the Hohfeldian analysis is so rigorously precise and so widely used counts as a reason for employing it here, as the concept of legal personhood becomes accordingly connected to wider jurisprudential debates. Hohfeld's theory is also used to address a number of issues that are at most tangentially related to legal personhood; this is why his analysis meets the independence constraint.

Rather than abandoning the Hohfeldian analysis, one could argue for an interpretation according to which Hohfeldian legal relations only obtain between legal persons, as Steven Wise and Jessica Berg maintain (though Berg's treatment of Hohfeld is very brief).[57] Unfortunately, neither author really presents any arguments for this view. Their approach seems tailored to the purpose of maintaining the coherence of the three sets and does not have any independent justification, thus failing to meet the requirements of the independence constraint. Hohfeld did use the designation 'person' in his exposition of the relations, but this does not entail that legal personhood would be conceptually related to the capacity of someone or something to participate in Hohfeldian legal relations. I will in Chapter 2 address the question of the domain of Hohfeldian relations extensively, reaching the conclusion that many legal nonpersons not only hold Hohfeldian claims (i.e. interest-theory rights) but also participate in other Hohfeldian legal relations.

Provided the Hohfeldian framework is not abandoned or revised in a way that would accommodate the Orthodox View and the extensional beliefs, two immediate options remain for making the overall set of beliefs coherent:

(1) the adjustment of a significant number of the widely held extensional beliefs,
(2) the adjustment of the Orthodox View.

These alternatives refer of course only to the first step in making the beliefs cohere, as the method of reflective equilibrium typically involves working 'back and forth'. For instance, after one has adjusted a moral principle to better reflect certain moral judgements, one can then revisit some other moral judgements in light of the increased understanding that the refinement of the moral principle has provided.

transferring (selling or donating) that right [to self-ownership], since such transfers entail that transferrors thereby acquire duties to their transferees, whereas slaves, as things wholly owned by others, must lack duties as well as rights.' Hillel Steiner, *An Essay on Rights* (Blackwell 1994) 232f. Emphasis in original.

57 Steven M. Wise, 'Hardly a Revolution—The Eligibility of Nonhuman Animals for Dignity-Rights in a Liberal Democracy' (1998) 22 *Vermont Law Review* 793, 801; Berg (n 27) 372f. Apart from the topic of corporations, Hohfeld himself addressed the question of who or what can hold Hohfeldian legal positions only indirectly.

Pursuing (1) would mean cashing out the implications of the Orthodox View and the Hohfeldian understanding of rights.[58] Thus, if one adopted the interest theory of rights, one would most likely reach the conclusion that at least some nonhuman animals already hold legal rights, and these animals would consequently be classified as legal persons. In contrast, adopting the will theory—the main rival of the interest theory—would entail denying the legal personhood of small children and some mentally disabled individuals because of their inability to hold will-theory rights.[59] The whole concept of legal personhood would essentially be assimilated into the broader 'debate over rights', and the meaning of 'legal person' would be very close to the sense in which some moral and political philosophers use the term 'person', signifying a right-holder. There is of course nothing inherently problematic with these results. One could definitely reach a coherent set of beliefs in this manner. However, going down this road would mean disregarding a significant number of the widely held convictions of jurists regarding who or what is a legal person, without offering much explanatory power in return. Consider corporate personhood. I will argue in Chapter 5 that many non-incorporated collectivities hold legal rights and duties. This conclusion and the Orthodox View would jointly entail that these collectivities are legal persons.[60] One would thus have to conclude that the division between legal organization forms that endow organizations with legal personhood and forms that do not is pointless, because even a group of children who have the right to use a public football field once a week could constitute a legal person.[61] Would our understanding of corporations and legal organization forms be enhanced by this conclusion? I cannot see what interesting insights this could offer that would outweigh the explanatory power of the mainstream corporate theories, which usually stress corporations' capacity to sue in their own name, limited shareholder liability (in the case of business corporations), and so on.[62]

Jurists' convictions regarding the extension of legal personhood should of course not be taken as invariably decisive; but they should be taken seriously, and this book will show how taking them seriously and abandoning (or at least significantly revising) the Orthodox View will lead to some very interesting and illuminating

[58] John Chipman Gray seems to endorse this approach in Gray (n 4).

[59] Not all will theorists deny that children hold rights. I will address this issue in Chapter 2.

[60] I will argue for this in Chapter 5.

[61] It is very common to divide legal organization forms into those that confer legal personality and those that do not. In English law, unincorporated associations and partnerships are often mentioned as examples of legal forms without separate legal personhood. For Spanish and German law respectively, see de las Heras Ballell (n 23) 72ff and Karl Larenz and Manfred Wolf, *Allgemeiner Teil des bürgerlichen Rechts* (CH Beck'sche Verlagsbuchhandlung 1997) 182–3. Ulrich Palm's *Habilitationsschrift* is focused on how an organization's legal personality affects its treatment in German income taxation. Ulrich Palm, *Person im Ertragsteuerrecht* (Mohr Siebeck 2013).

[62] See for instance Eric W. Orts, *Business Persons. A Legal Theory of the Firm* (Oxford University Press 2013) 32–51.

insights as well as a theory of legal personhood with more explanatory power than anything that the Orthodox View would offer. I will pursue alternative (2), exploring whether there are other salient features that the entities usually classified as legal persons share and nonpersons lack, features which prompt jurists to endorse and repeat the current extensional beliefs but which are not readily captured by the Orthodox View. This line of thought will prove to be fruitful and will lead to a new theory of legal personhood. With this enhanced understanding of what being a legal person means, it will also be possible to re-examine certain more contentious extensional beliefs, such as those pertaining to the putative legal personhood of rivers, and the theoretical claim that '[a]nything can be a legal person because legal persons are stipulated as such or defined into existence'.[63] Such issues will be discussed mainly in Chapter 4.

I grant that my theory is significantly more complicated than the Orthodox View. However, the simpler explanation is only better all other things being equal, and the Orthodox View fails to appreciate many of the nuances of the topic to the point of being misleading. One could even speculate that the alluring simplicity of the Orthodox View might have contributed to the recent lack of theoretical interest in legal personhood. The concept has seemed to be completely reducible to the more foundational concepts of rights and duties.

To summarize, this work seeks to analyse jurists' extensional beliefs regarding legal personhood in light of analytic philosophy and, in particular, the Hohfeldian understanding of legal relations. This analysis, if successful, should firstly be able to lay out the salient features that newborn children, adults of sound mind, and corporations share but foetuses, nonhuman animals, slaves, and non-incorporated organizations lack or have historically lacked, prompting jurists to classify the former as legal persons and the latter as nonpersons. After the salient features of legal personhood have been determined, certain further questions can be addressed. These include: the scope of legal personhood, that is, who or what can be a legal person; the peculiarities of the legal personhood of corporations, which range from sprawling organizations to shell companies; and more peripheral cases of putative legal personhood, such as the Whanganui River agreement, supposedly endowing the river with legal personhood.

Legal personhood is not treated here as a necessary feature of law but rather as a contingent conceptual scheme, distinctive of Western legal systems. This scheme may or may not be found in other legal systems, but I make no claims that it is.[64] I also seek to explain the scheme only as part of modern law, by which I mean broadly speaking the legal systems of the industrial era. Those systems are characterized by

[63] Ngaire Naffine, 'Who are Law's Persons? From Cheshire Cats to Responsible Subjects' (2003) 66 *Modern Law Review* 346, 351. This is actually Natalie Stoljar's summation of the legalist (or 'P1') position, proposed in private correspondence to Naffine.

[64] I do consider it rather unlikely that every legal system in the world has or has had the notion of a corporation.

the shift from estates and personal jurisdiction (applicability of laws based on estate membership) to formal equality and uniform applicability of laws, at least among white males, and in particular a focus on liberal ownership and transactions.[65] The theory is perhaps applicable to earlier societies as well—and scholars did already start using *persona* in a distinct legal sense during the Renaissance—but the legal systems of such societies are not within the purview of this volume. Relatedly, when I cover slavery as an example of legal nonpersonhood, I only intend the analysis to apply to slavery as found in modern Western societies, primarily in the antebellum US South, rather than to slavery in the ancient world. I do make occasional references to the Roman law of slavery, but this is mainly because the legal form of slavery as practised in the US was strongly influenced by the Roman understanding of slavery as property.

It is somewhat ironic that what Gaius meant by the 'law of persons' was what we would call the law of statuses, whereas the 'law of persons' that this work seeks to analyse is found in Western societies after they had begun abandoning the idea of personal status. However, the Bundle Theory does not presuppose that all legal persons have equal rights. It is a commonplace that corporations do not have all the same rights and duties as natural persons do, and the incident-based understanding of legal personhood is perfectly able to accommodate this. Similarly, the legal personhood of nonhuman animals would likely entail that some, but not all, incidents of legal personhood are extended to animals.[66]

Personhood and Legal Personhood

I will in this section present a number of preliminary distinctions, clarifications, and caveats that will be fundamental for the rest of the work. Many of the issues addressed here are based upon or reactions to Ngaire Naffine's work, in particular her recent book on the topic of legal personhood.[67]

Naffine distinguishes two main approaches that authors have taken to legal personhood. The first group are so-called Legalists, who 'represent the orthodox, technical approach to law's persons', according to whom one's 'legal nature [...] should not be confused with one's nature beyond the confines of law':

> Law's business is the regulation and practical organisation of human affairs and the resolution of human differences which are highly variable and often have nothing to do with these basic existential matters. Although law has a legal subject known as the 'legal person', this is strictly

[65] See Marc Galanter, 'The Modernization of Law' in Myron Weiner (ed.), *Modernization* (Basic Books 1966).

[66] For an interesting discussion of status and legal personality, see David J. Calverley, 'Imagining a Non-biological Machine as a Legal Person' (2008) 22 *AI & Society* 523, 525–7.

[67] Naffine (n 37).

a formal and neutral legal device for enabling a being or entity to act in law, to acquire what is known as a 'legal personality': the ability to bear rights and duties.[68]

This view is contrasted with that of the Realists, according to whom the law does and should 'operate with a natural conception of the person'.[69] Naffine separates three such conceptions:

- Rationalists: (only) rational beings can or should be legal persons
- Religionists: (only) beings with sanctity or dignity can or should be legal persons
- Naturalists: sentient beings, both human and nonhuman, can or should be legal persons[70]

However, it is unclear whether all the authors Naffine groups under these categories are aptly classified under them. The main question of her book is 'Who is the law for?'.[71] This enquiry is then treated more or less interchangeably with the question of who or what should be a legal person, as well as with a number of other questions. Some authors do fit quite comfortably into this setup. John Finnis draws a similar connection between 'law's point' and legal personhood in the essay 'The Priority of Persons', which is an exploration of how (moral) persons figure in law's point in different ways from legal personhood to the rule of law. In the section on legal personhood, Finnis endorses the formulation (contained in the Roman text *Institutes*) that 'all law exists for the sake of persons' and that 'all men are persons', whereas the institution of slavery is a departure from natural law, as the law does not exist for the sake of slaves.[72] This is one of the many junctures where Finnis implies that all persons—understood in his Catholic sense—should be endowed with legal personhood. He condemns the relatively unprotected status that US law accords to foetuses as a 'refusal to take account of the realities of personal existence before birth', deems the Supreme Court judgment that classified corporations as constitutional persons 'a failure', and criticizes Kelsen's distinction between 'man' and '(legal) person'.[73] The connection between law's point and legal personhood is quite clear here: the protection of moral persons is the point of the law, and such persons should therefore be recognized as legal persons.

[68] Ibid 21. [69] Ibid 20.

[70] This is a simplification. Naffine identifies three strands of naturalists:

> Some [...] urge some minimum legal rights for animals. Their primary interest is in the legal status of animals. Others favour greater recognition in law of the moral status of animals, and their fellowship with humans, without the conferral of rights. Still others want *us* to be treated more like animals.

Ibid 124. Emphasis in original. I focus here on the first group of thinkers.

[71] Ibid 1.

[72] John Finnis, 'The Priority of Persons', *Intention and Identity: Collected Essays Volume II* (Oxford University Press 2011) 22–3 and 26–7.

[73] Ibid 27–8.

However, I am not convinced that all of the authors addressed by Naffine fit equally well into her scheme. Denise Meyerson puts the issue as follows:

> Complicating the matter somewhat is the fact that Naffine poses her question in a variety of ways. She does not ask only: Who should be regarded as legal persons? She also asks: Who should be regarded as the bearers of legal rights and duties? Who should law be 'for'? Who should count or matter in law? Who is worthy of law's concern? What image of human beings and human nature should law reflect? Naffine regards these questions as interchangeable but this can be questioned. For instance, will theorists [...] believe that rights protect choices and that babies therefore cannot have rights. But they believe, of course, that babies are worthy of the law's concern and that the law should protect them from mistreatment. Likewise, everyone will agree that the law should concern itself with and protect animals, whether or not they think that animals should also be regarded as legal persons.[74]

I agree with Meyerson. Naffine's reliance on the Orthodox View explains how she can draw the inference that if one endorses the will theory of rights—favoured by many Rationalists—one is then also committed to a Rationalist idea of the legal person. Since the will theory identifies rights as the kind of control over others' duties that only adults of sound mind can exert, infants and mentally disabled individuals cannot hold rights and therefore cannot be legal persons.[75] However, one does not have to accept this conclusion about legal personhood if one rejects the mutual entailment between such personhood and right-holding.

Despite the query just raised, Naffine makes a number of useful distinctions. One of the main differences between Legalists and Realists, according to her, centres on the 'autonomy' of the legal person: whereas Legalists maintain that 'law is fully responsible for the construction of its subject', Realists believe that the legal person is an 'expression of some important defining attribute of human nature', and that 'law finds its subject [i.e. person] beyond the legal realm and is to be judged by its success at finding and rendering this subject faithfully'.[76] The Realist position takes many forms, and can be understood as having both conceptual and normative elements, though these two elements of Realism are often intertwined. I will try to tease out some relevant differences between the two camps here.

Some Realists suggest a conceptual connection between legal personhood and some other form of personhood. Examples can be found in some jurists' implicit or explicit claim that human beings are the 'real' legal persons, even if legal personhood

[74] Denise Meyerson, 'Persons and their Rights in Law and Morality' (2010) 35 *Australian Journal of Legal Philosophy* 122, 123. See also William Lucy, 'Persons in Law' (2009) 29 *Oxford Journal of Legal Studies* 787 and Bryan Thomas, 'A Critical Review of Law's Meaning of Life: Philosophy, Religion, Darwin and the Legal Person' (2011) 38 *Journal of Law and Society* 631.

[75] 'It would seem to follow that [infants, senile people, and comatose people] are not legal persons, for they have neither rights that they can personally enforce, nor responsibilities.' Naffine (n 37) 68.

[76] Ibid 22.

can be extended to corporations through a legal fiction—a consciously false statement. For instance, Friedrich Carl von Savigny claimed that 'the original concept of person [...] must coincide with the concept of human being, and this original identity [...] can be expressed as follows: every individual human being, and only the individual human being, possesses legal capacity [i.e. is a legal person]'.[77] Even if human beings are the 'original identity' of legal personhood, positive law can according to Savigny extend legal capacity to imaginary subjects—corporations—but this is a legal fiction because it does not flow from the concepts of law and personhood embodied in the *Volksgeist*, the 'spirit of the people'.[78] The legal concept of a person should therefore approximate 'real' personhood, just as legal definitions of death often seek to approximate 'real' death. Legalists' claims that legal personhood is a 'neutral legal device' can be understood as a response to this conceptual thesis: when the law treats, say, companies as legal persons, this is according to Legalists simply a distinctive use of the word 'person' rather than any metaphorical or fictional understanding of moral or metaphysical personhood.

Some strands of the debate between Realists and Legalists take a more normative tone. This part of the debate can be understood as pertaining to the *standards of correctness* concerning which entities can, or should, be legal persons. Realists maintain that something can be properly classifiable as a legal person for *intrinsic reasons*. An intrinsic reason for so classifying an entity is that the entity partakes of a set of properties which are central to moral personhood and which are sufficient in themselves to render morally obligatory the recognition of the entity as a legal person in any prevailing system of governance. We can distinguish 'moderate' Realism according to which all persons should be legal persons, and 'strong' Realism according to which all persons, and *only persons*, should be legal persons. A moderate Realist subscribing to the Kantian understanding of personhood—which attributes moral personhood to rational beings that can set their own moral laws—would thus reason as follows. Whether the law recognizes moral persons as legal persons is a question of whether the law recognizes a fundamental fact: the moral freedom innate in every person. Denying legal personhood to a person constitutes a failure to recognize this fact. A strong Realist would also classify as a failure the extension of legal personhood to any entity that does not possess this moral freedom, as with corporations. Finnis is a prime example of strong Realism.

Legalists, in contrast, maintain that there are only *extrinsic* reasons for classifying any beings as legal persons. An extrinsic reason is here any reason that is not an intrinsic reason.[79] For example, let us assume that nonhuman animals are not the kind of moral persons who should, according to Realists, be endowed with legal

[77] Friedrich Carl von Savigny, *System des heutigen Römischen rechts* (Veit 1840) § 60.

[78] Ibid § 85. I will return to this issue in Chapter 1.

[79] Matthew Kramer has proposed this distinction between intrinsic and extrinsic reasons to me in private correspondence.

personhood merely in virtue of their moral personhood. Regardless, if the only way of inclining legal-governmental officials to bestow adequate legal protection on animals is to have animals classified as legal persons within the prevailing system of governance, then there is an extrinsic reason for the recognition of animals as legal persons by that system of governance.

I should briefly try to situate myself within this debate. We can distinguish three points of disagreement: (1) the 'conceptual autonomy' of legal personhood from other forms of personhood; (2) the question whether only persons *can* be legal persons (the 'can' question); and (3) the question whether persons (or only persons) *should* be legal persons (the 'should' question). First, as far as 'conceptual autonomy' is concerned, I side with Legalists. The treatment of corporations as legal persons is not a fiction, nor is it helpful to designate it as such. I will return to this question below as well as in Chapter 5. However, I am firmly opposed to the Legalist claim that legal personhood can be attributed to any entity; I will address this issue in detail in Chapter 4. Finally, although the question of who or what should be endowed with legal personhood will not be central here, I do tend to side with Legalists, especially with regard to collectivities.

One of the reasons why I stress the independence of legal personhood from most conceptions of personhood is that personhood is most likely an *essentially contested concept*. The notion of essentially contested concepts was introduced by W. B. Gallie, who maintained that for some concepts 'there is no one clearly definable general use […] which can be set up as the correct or standard use'. This applies of course to a wide number of concepts, but what is distinctive about essentially contested concepts is that once this heterogeneousness of usages has been exposed, the proponents of the different views are not satisfied with the disambiguation. Rather,

> [e]ach party continues to maintain that the special functions which the term 'work of art' or 'democracy' or 'Christian doctrine' fulfils on its behalf or on its interpretation, is the correct or proper or primary, or the only important, function which the term in question can plainly be said to fulfil.[80]

This diagnosis seems to apply to personhood as well: even though virtually everyone agrees that human adults of sound mind are persons, there is widespread disagreement regarding the salient features that render them persons, as well as the import—moral or otherwise—of personhood. Definitions of 'person' extend from the Kantian idea of beings that can set their own moral laws to the performative conception of Philip Pettit and Christian List, which focuses on what persons *can do* rather than on

[80] W. B. Gallie, 'Essentially Contested Concepts' (1956) 56 *Proceedings of the Aristotelian Society* 168. Regarding the contestedness of 'person', see Susanne Gibson, 'The Problem of Abortion: Essentially Contested Concepts and Moral Autonomy' (2004) 18 *Bioethics* 221 and Ross Poole, 'On Being a Person' (1996) 74 *Australasian Journal of Philosophy* 38.

what they *are*.[81] Obviously these two conceptions have very different moral implications: in the Kantian tradition, persons have dignity, whereas Pettit and List make no such claims regarding the moral import of their conception.[82] Though I rely on Pettit and List's work as a theoretical foundation for my account of the legal personhood of collectivities, I make no claim that theirs would be the correct definition of personhood. The relevant inquiry is simply whether corporations possess certain functional capacities which enable them to own property and act in the law. Such capacities are also possessed by paradigmatic persons but this is not integral to the proposed theory.

It is, however, not implausible to take certain essential features of personhood as necessary criteria for legal personhood. For instance, as I will argue in Chapter 4, one must be able to hold claim-rights (the correlatives of duties) in order to qualify for passive legal personhood—the kind of legal personhood that infants and mentally severely disabled individuals currently possess. Many authors exclude infants from personhood, whereas I include even third-trimester foetuses and sentient nonhuman animals among the beings that can be passive legal persons because we can hold duties towards them (rather than merely pertaining to them). Thus, if one takes fish to be persons because they are sentient, then passive legal personhood is conceptually connected to one's thin conception of personhood. However, most authors do not take fish to be persons, and I make no such claims. I only maintain that fish can be passive legal persons. On the other hand, I will argue that the capacity to perform acts is a necessary condition of active legal personhood. Hence, insofar as Realism is understood as the claim that the category of legal personhood is only properly applicable to certain types of entities—rather than to any entity to which a legal system purports to apply it—then I am indeed a Realist, with regard to both passive and active legal personhood. But I do not claim that only persons can be legal persons.

Finally, let me express some doubts about the strong Realist claim that all persons, and only persons, should be legal persons. I will focus on collectivities here. The question about the appropriateness of attributing legal personhood to a given organization cannot be fruitfully approached by simply focusing on whether the organization meets some criteria of moral or metaphysical personhood. Pettit and List argue that because organized collectivities 'can perform effectively in the space of obligations', they can be persons.[83] But it would be strange to argue based on this that all organized collectivities should be accorded legal personhood. What about criminal organizations? Even with organizations that do not engage in illegal activities,

[81] Christian List and Philip Pettit, *Group Agency: The Possibility, Design, and Status of Corporate Agents* (Oxford University Press 2011). The terminology of 'intrinsicist' and 'performative' conceptions of personhood has been proposed by Victor Muniz-Fraticelli. Victor M. Muniz-Fraticelli, *The Structure of Pluralism* (Oxford University Press 2014) 223.

[82] Peter French, on the other hand, does argue that corporations are moral persons. Peter A. French, 'The Corporation as a Moral Person' (1979) 16 *American Philosophical Quarterly* 207.

[83] List and Pettit (n 81) 173–4.

corporate legal personhood involves important structural matters, such as the fact that the limited liability of business corporations reduces the risks of investors and increases the risks of the creditors of the corporation. Such issues can be obscured by merely focusing on the question whether these organizations are persons. For similar reasons, pointing out that collectivities are *not* persons (according to, say, the Kantian conception of personhood) is not a sufficient argument for concluding that they should not be legal persons.

Value-Neutrality and the Debate over Rights

By mostly excluding from this book the normative questions concerning who or what should be a legal person, I have already implied that I take the distinction between 'law as it is' and 'law as it should be' to be valid. However, I do not claim to be engaging in a purely descriptive project. Any theory presupposes, first, certain evaluative judgements regarding what is interesting and important in the subject matter, but such judgements need not necessarily be ethical in nature.[84] In addition, some ethically evaluative commitments are required for a theory of legal personhood, in particular if such a theory seeks to determine who or what can be a legal person. Ian Carter has made a useful distinction between *value-freeness*—meaning the 'absence of [ethically] evaluative terms in the definition of a concept'—and *value-neutrality*, which 'involves a suspension of judgment about the comparative merits of divergent ethical positions'.[85] The main claims of the Bundle Theory are not value-free, but they are value-neutral with regard to many ethical positions. I will start by situating my theory within the so-called debate over rights and will then address the value-neutrality of the Bundle Theory more generally.

There are two main theories of rights in analytic jurisprudence, which I have already adverted to a number of times: the will theory and the interest theory.[86] Each has a long tradition and a certain historical connection to the topic of legal personhood. The majority of the nineteenth-century German legal scholars who wrote on the topic of legal personhood identified the Kantian ideas of freedom and autonomy as the central concepts of any new, 'formally equal' legal system. Human beings possessed innate moral freedom, which grounded their capacity to hold rights and thus their legal personhood.[87] The minority view, represented by authors such as Rudolf von Jhering in his later period, advocated an interest-based understanding of rights. Most modern analytic theories of rights are still classifiable as either will or interest

[84] See for instance Julie Dickson, *Evaluation and Legal Theory* (Hart Publishing 2001) 38.

[85] Ian Carter, 'Value-freeness and Value-neutrality in the Analysis of Political Concepts' in David Sobel, Peter Vallentyne, and Steven Wall (eds), *Oxford Studies in Political Philosophy, Volume 1* (Oxford University Press 2015) 284–5.

[86] See in general Matthew H. Kramer, N. E. Simmonds, and Hillel Steiner, *A Debate over Rights: Philosophical Enquiries* (Oxford University Press 1998).

[87] See Chapter 1.

theories. Both have highly sophisticated formulations that manage to capture some important intuitions concerning rights, but neither theory can be said to have 'won' the debate.

This volume is largely but not entirely neutral between the will and the interest theories—or, to be more precise, between the most prominent Hohfeldian versions of these theories. (As mentioned above, one of the goals of this book is to understand the conceptual scheme of legal personhood in Hohfeldian terms in order to build a bridge between more general jurisprudential debates and legal personhood. This, in addition to the analytic strengths of the Hohfeldian analysis, is why I will focus on Hohfeldian theories of rights. I will thus mostly exclude certain prominent non-Hohfeldian theories, such as that of Joseph Raz.[88]) I will demonstrate the main problems of the Orthodox View employing both the interest and the will theory. However, this neutrality will have to be qualified somewhat.

I distinguish three levels of value-neutrality here: the framework level, the building-block level, and the concrete level. The *framework level* involves determining the incidents of legal personhood by juxtaposing central cases of legal personhood and nonpersonhood. This will require very few controversial evaluative assumptions. However, one must take on a number of somewhat more controversial evaluative assumptions in order to determine the 'building blocks' of the incidents of legal personhood (*building-block level*), as well as who or what can be a legal person (*concrete level*). Let me take an example.

Equipped with the Hohfeldian analysis and the understanding of legal personhood provided by my theory, I will argue in Chapter 4 that passive legal personhood functions primarily through claims, whereas active legal personhood will be shown to be connected to the capacity to perform acts-in-the-law. Both of these arguments will require certain evaluative assumptions, situated at the building-block level. Claims, or claim-rights, are the correlates of duties; if X can hold claims, this means that duties can be borne *towards* X rather than merely *pertaining to* X. This argument presupposes certain evaluative assumptions. First, it requires a theory of Hohfeldian claims. Hohfeld's own exposition left open the question of how exactly duties and claims are connected. Kramer's interest theory is the most sophisticated account of this connection, which is why I will use it as an account of claim-rights. Thus, there will be a connection between passive legal personhood and Kramer's theory. Furthermore, the argument requires the evaluative assumption that children and mentally severely disabled individuals can hold claim-rights—otherwise their passive legal personhood could not be explained as functioning through claim-rights. This attribution of claims to children and mentally severely disabled individuals is relatively uncontroversial, even if it is rejected by so-called hard will theorists. However, the will theory of rights will be closely associated with the active element

[88] See Joseph Raz, 'On the Nature of Rights' (1984) 93 *Mind* 194.

of legal personhood, as the exercise of will-theory rights consists in the performance of acts-in-the-law. Thus, there will be a certain connection between active legal personhood and the will theory of rights.

The building-block level alone is not sufficient for reaching a full array of conclusions regarding who or what can—and cannot—be a legal person. Can animals or rivers be passive legal persons? To answer this, we must determine whether they can hold claims, and this requires making some further evaluative and normative assumptions. The building-block level must thus be amplified by the assumptions of the *concrete level*. I maintain that X's capacity to hold claims depends on X's status as a being of ultimate value or a collectivity of ultimately valuable beings, and that only sentient beings are of ultimate value—further argumentation for this view will be provided in Chapter 3. Thus, rivers (*qua* bodies of water) cannot be legal persons because they are not sentient and are consequently ineligible to hold claim-rights, whereas nonhuman animals are sentient and can therefore be passive legal persons. Such a view is obviously not compatible with as many ethical positions as the framework and the building-block levels are. Still, even if one disagreed with the evaluative commitments taken at the concrete level, this would not render the theory as a whole useless. A deep ecologist who maintains that claims can appositely be ascribed to rivers could employ the overall framework and simply show how duties can indeed be held towards bodies of water. If duties can be so owed, then such bodies can be passive legal persons. Moreover, even a hard will theorist could employ the incident-based account of legal personhood, though she would also reject the evaluative assumptions made at the building-block level and would therefore also need to reject my claim that passive legal personhood functions through claim-rights.

Book Structure

The book consists of three substantive parts. Part I, entitled 'The Orthodox View', first examines the history of how 'legal person' came to be understood as a synonym for 'subject of rights and duties'. The historical survey is undertaken in Chapter 1. It traces how the Roman notions of personhood inspired Renaissance-era French and German scholars to start using *persona* in a particular sense that would then, in nineteenth-century Germany, develop into a definition of persons as right-holders. This view would be imported into the English-speaking world by John Austin, and would later influence the works of such influential jurisprudents as John Salmond and Wesley Newcomb Hohfeld. This chapter thus offers a new kind of context for how modern legal philosophy, and especially its notions of personhood and rights, developed. Chapter 2 then criticizes the Orthodox View as internally inconsistent—when examined from the point of view of the Hohfeldian analysis of rights—and lacking in explanatory power.

Part II, 'The Bundle Theory', offers the new theory of legal personhood. I argue in Chapter 3 that legal personhood is best understood in terms of disseverable but interconnected incidents. Such incidents include (but are not limited to) the capacity to own property; victim status in criminal law; and the protection of bodily integrity and liberty. The offered view thus resembles the bundle-of-rights analysis of ownership: one can be a legal person for some purposes without being a legal person for all purposes. The account has numerous benefits. It can, first, better explain what exactly is at stake in the relevant contemporary debates—which are in fact focused on very different elements of legal personhood. For instance, the American chimpanzee trials are not about endowing chimpanzees with their first legal right, but rather about a more extensive protection of their bodily liberty. The debate over whether foetuses should be legal persons is, on the other hand, really about whether foetuses should be treated as potential victims in the context of criminal law. No one is proposing, for instance, that foetuses should be able to own property.

The offered account can also help in explaining certain historical phenomena, such as the legal status of slaves—who were legal nonpersons except as potential criminal malfeasors—and the gradually improving status of women towards full legal personhood. The all-or-nothing orthodox account is unable to account for such nuances.

Chapter 4 assesses a popular claim that anything or anyone could be endowed with legal personhood. I argue against such claims, exposing numerous conflations and non sequiturs underlying them. Rather, one must either at least hold interests or have the capacity to act in order to qualify as a potential legal person.

Part III, 'Applying the Theory', focuses on three particular cases. Chapter 5 examines corporate personhood. I argue that even non-incorporated groups, such as a group of friends, can hold legal rights. Chapter 6 focuses on the legal personhood of artificial intelligences (AIs). Finally, Chapter 7 explores the role of legal personhood in normative debates, using the legal status of animals as the most prominent example.

PART I

The Orthodox View

1

A Short History of the Right-Holding Person

Preliminaries

This book is not primarily a work of legal history but rather an attempt to provide a theoretical framework for understanding legal personhood in contemporary Western legal systems. However, personhood in the given legal sense cannot be understood without placing it in its historical context. I will now firstly make some remarks on the ancient origins and medieval development of the concept of personhood, and then show how legal personhood came to be associated with right-holding among Continental jurists starting from the early modern age. Finally, I will track the influence that this conception of legal personhood had on Anglophone jurisprudence in the nineteenth century. These developments did not take place in isolation from more general debates concerning personhood, which I will (cursorily) address as well.

The Ancient World: *Persona* as a Role

The classification of law by the Roman jurist Gaius into that concerning persons (*personae*), things (*res*), and actions (*actiones*) is usually mentioned as the first reference to the person/thing distinction.[1] However, it is not at all obvious that the Romans thought of the distinction in any abstract or systematic way—Roman law was in many ways casuistic, unsystematic, and practically oriented. The origin of the person/thing division lies, however, in Roman law, which has clearly inspired the modern understanding of legal personhood. This is why the Roman law of persons must be addressed.

Gaius presented his trifurcation in his work *Institutes*, which was originally intended as an introductory text for new students of law. *Institutes*, written originally around 160 CE, would later be incorporated with some changes into the major text of Roman law, *Corpus Iuris Civilis*, on which much of Western legal scholarship is based.

[1] Gaius, *Institutiones or Institutes of Roman Law* (Edward Poste tr. ed., 4th edn, Clarendon Press 1904).

Gaius's *Institutes* does not specify what it exactly implies for an entity to be a person (*persona*) or a thing (*res*).[2] One should firstly note the etymology of the word *persona*. That term is probably a translation of the Greek *prosopon* (πρόσωπον, 'face, appearance'). In Latin, it was originally used to denote the masks worn by actors and their characters. This usage was extended to refer to the 'roles' or qualities of human beings. Cicero, for instance, is known partly for his theory of the four *personae* in every human being: one's rationality, personal attributes, status, and profession.[3] However, *persona* also acquired another meaning, which begins to resemble the modern everyday conception of person: that of an individual human being, stripped of his roles. It has been argued that the origins of this semantic change lie in Stoic philosophy.[4] At any rate, developments towards a modern understanding of 'person' can be seen most clearly in debates within the early Christian church, where the notion of *persona* became important when the natures of the Trinity and Christ were debated. The Council of Alexandria had in 362 CE declared that the Father, the Son, and the Holy Spirit were all distinguishable *hypostases* (substances) but shared a single divine nature. *Hypostasis* (ὑπόστασις) was translated into Latin as *persona*. Similarly, the Council of Ephesus affirmed in 431 CE that Christ was one person (*hypostasis*, *persona*) of both divine and human nature.[5] Such pronunciations necessitated philosophical accounts of *persona* that would explain the creed. Around 500 CE, the Roman philosopher Boethius defined *persona* as 'the individual substance of rational nature', a definition that would become very influential.[6] This was also around the time that the *Corpus Iuris Civilis* was issued by the Eastern Roman Emperor Justinian I.

In the *Corpus*, *persona* was used both in the sense 'role' and in the sense 'individual', but not in the technical sense in which a contemporary jurist would use the phrase 'legal person'.[7] First, slaves were indeed *personae*—human beings—even though the legal personhood of slaves has often been questioned. Second, corporations were usually referred to using the word *universitas*, not *persona*.[8] There was also a third term, *caput* (lit. 'head'), which was used to refer to human individuals, but it was

[2] J. R. Trahan, 'The Distinction between Persons and Things: An Historical Perspective' (2008) 1 *Journal of Civil Law Studies* 9, 11–12. Tomasz Pietrzykowski, *Personhood Beyond Humanism: Animals, Chimeras, Autonomous Agents and the Law* (Springer 2018) 95–9.

[3] See Christopher Gill, 'Personhood and Personality: The Four-Personae Theory in Cicero, De Officiis I', *Oxford Studies in Ancient Philosophy: Volume VI* (Oxford University Press 1988).

[4] Marcel Mauss and W. D. Halls tr., 'A Category of the Human Mind: The Notion of Person; the Notion of Self' in Michael Carrithers, Steven Collins, and Steven Lukes (eds), *The Category of the Person: Anthropology, Philosophy, History* (Cambridge University Press 1985) 18.

[5] Matthias Lutz-Bachmann, 'Der Mensch als Person. Überlegungen zur Geschichte des Begriffs der "moralischen Person" und der Rechtsperson' in Eckart Klein and Christoph Menke (eds), *Der Mensch als Person und Rechtsperson* (Berliner Wissenschafts-Verlag 2011) 110–11.

[6] Udo Thiel, *The Early Modern Subject: Self-Consciousness and Personal Identity from Descartes to Hume* (Oxford University Press 2011) 28.

[7] See P.W. Duff, *Personality in Roman Private Law* (Cambridge University Press 1938) 6–25.

[8] Ibid. 24–5.

occasionally used in a sense whose closest translation would be 'legal standing'.[9] In this latter sense, slaves did not possess *caput*. The idea of *caput* is perhaps the closest the Romans got to a concept resembling the modern, technical understanding of legal personhood. It must nevertheless be concluded that, rather than defining who were legal persons in the eyes of the law, the 'law of persons' in Justinian's *Institutes* addresses the different statuses ('roles') of human beings in hierarchical Roman society. There were three primary groups of statuses: *status libertatis* (whether one was free or slave), *status civitatis* (whether one was a Roman citizen or belonged to one of the less privileged groups), and *status familiae* (whether one was legally independent or under the power of one's *paterfamilias*, the head of the household).

The law of things, on the other hand, pertained to how certain human beings (if they possessed the requisite status under the law of persons) could achieve rights pertaining to things that have monetary value, such as material objects and slaves.[10] The category of things also included obligations and 'rights' (*iura*), which the Romans took to be 'incorporeal things'.[11] The Romans did not, however, have the abstract notion of subjective rights that modern jurists employ, nor did they clearly separate substantive claims from procedural remedies.[12]

As already noted, the Romans did invent the idea of a corporation (*universitas*), that is, an organization that could own property and contract in its own name. The first corporations were public bodies, such as cities and states, which owned public property. Later, private corporations could be established as well.[13] It has been argued that a large part of Europe acquired the idea of corporation because the Romans used corporations to organize the administration of their territories. Thus, even English law, which has been less heavily influenced by Roman law than have most Continental legal systems, knew of corporations relatively early.[14]

[9] Ibid. 25–6.

[10] See Andrea Padovani and others, *A Treatise of Legal Philosophy and General Jurisprudence, Volume 7: The Jurists' Philosophy of Law from Rome to the Seventeenth Century* (2005) 22.

[11] Gaius (n 1) 123–4:

> Things incorporeal are intangible; such as those which have an existence simply in law as inheritance, usufruct, obligation, however contracted. For though an inheritance comprises things corporeal, and the fruits of land enjoyed by a usufructuary are corporeal, and obligations generally bind us to make over the conveyance of something corporeal: land, slaves, money; yet the right of succession, the right of usufruct, and the right of obligation are incorporeal. So are the rights attached to property in houses and land.

[12] See for instance Richard Tuck, *Natural Rights Theories: Their Origin and Development* (Cambridge University Press 1979) 5–13, Pavlos Eleftheriadis, *Legal Rights* (Oxford University Press 2008) 2–4, or H. F. Jolowicz, *Roman Foundations of Modern Law* (Clarendon Press 1957) 66–7.

[13] William L. Burdick, *The Principles of Roman Law and Their Relation to Modern Law* (The Lawbook Exchange, Ltd 2004) 281–6.

[14] Ibid. 287:

> Municipal corporations were a very important part in Rome's system of government [...]. By the time of Julius Caesar, practically all the towns of Italy were municipia [...]. In imperial days, after the conquest of Britain, the same system of municipal government was planted there, and upon the models

The details and subtleties of the Roman law of persons are not of concern here. What is more important is how the Roman system was reflected in later authors' works, finally leading to the modern theory of legal personhood as right-holding and duty-bearing. Most of the relevant developments pertaining to legal personhood would take place on the European continent. After the fall of the Roman Empire, the *Corpus* was lost for centuries in the West, but some parts of it—such as the *Digest*, consisting of the legal opinions of eminent jurists—were rediscovered in Bologna in the twelfth century.[15] This would mark the birth of the study of law at universities, and most continental legal scholarship would thenceforth be based on the *Corpus*. Even though Gaius' *Institutes* would only be rediscovered in 1816, the *Digest* contained numerous references to the Gaian tripartite division. The person/thing distinction would become particularly important in the works of certain Continental thinkers and jurists, even if English jurists also made occasional references to the distinction.[16]

The High and Late Middle Ages saw some interesting developments pertaining to personhood in legal contexts. I will only mention a few that are directly relevant to the modern theory of legal personhood. First, many scholars addressed the question of corporations, as the legal statuses of guilds, towns, and so on were important questions.[17] In particular, the rise of monasteries posed problems, since monks and nuns were not allowed to own property or enter into contracts; legally, they underwent a 'monastic death' when taking the cloth.[18] This caused practical problems which were circumvented by allowing monasteries to own property in their own name. The phrase *persona ficta* was coined by Pope Innocent IV to denote such corporations in canon law—the fictitiousness of corporations implied that they could not be, for instance, excommunicated.[19] We can see that the term *persona* was here applied to corporations, which the Romans most likely would not have done.

of these governmental corporations, England, centuries later, built her own public corporations, municipal, ecclesiastical and educational, and, in time, her commercial and industrial corporations.

[15] This 'rediscovery' is the traditional theory. However, Charles M. Radding and Antonio Ciaralli have recently suggested that the *Corpus* was available much earlier but that the eleventh and twelfth centuries saw a change in the academic approach to the text. Charles M. Radding and Antonio Ciaralli, *The Corpus Iuris Civilis in the Middle Ages: Manuscripts and Transmission from the Sixth Century to the Juristic Revival* (Brill Academic Publishers 2006).

[16] For instance, the thirteenth-century English scholar Henry of Bracton employed Gaius' division in his work *On the Laws and Customs of England*, writing that 'all rights are established' for persons, whereas nonhuman animals and slaves were things that were susceptible to being owned, analogous to other objects of ownership. Henry de Bracton, *On the Laws and Customs of England* (Samuel E. Thorne tr. ed., Belknap Press of Harvard University Press 1968) 29. See also Steven M. Wise, 'The Legal Thinghood of Nonhuman Animals' [1996] *Boston College Environmental Affairs Law Review* 471, 517–19.

[17] See Padovani and others (n 10) 181–90.

[18] Matthias Lehmann, 'Der Begriff der Rechtsfähigkeit' (2007) 207 *Archiv für die civilistische Praxis* 225, 228

[19] See for instance John Dewey, 'The Historic Background of Corporate Legal Personality' (1926) 35 *Yale Law Journal* 655, 664–5.

Steps towards the idea of abstract, subjective rights—conceptually separate from legal remedies and from 'right' (*ius*) in the objective sense—were also taken during the Middle Ages. There is no agreement on when exactly scholars started using *ius* in the sense of subjective right, but some historians see steps towards this usage in the works of such medieval scholars as William of Ockham.[20] The concept of right, and its relation to personhood, would become important first among Renaissance humanists; then in the systems of natural law built by Dutch and German scholars such as Hugo Grotius, Gottfried Leibniz, and Christian Wolff during the early modern age; and finally in the German Historical School, mostly known for its primary proponent, Friedrich Carl von Savigny.

The Early Modern Era: the Birth of the Orthodox View

It would seem that the French law professor Hugues Doneau (1527–1591, also known as Hugo Donellus) took the first steps in developing a technical legal concept of personhood. Doneau, a member of the Renaissance humanist movement, studied the *Corpus* critically and attempted to establish the systematic foundations of the law.[21] He uses the word *persona* in a new, technical sense in his main work, *Commentarii in iure civili* ('Commentaries on the Civil Law'). *Persona* is now the point of departure of legal analysis, and any individual that has a positive *status libertatis*, *civitatis*, and *familiae* is a *persona*.[22] There is an analogy here to the original idea of *persona* as a role, as one's legal personhood would now refer to one's legal roles in civil society. Doneau did not yet clearly distinguish between *homo* and *persona*, however. This was done by the German jurist Hermann Vultejus (1555–1634), according to whom *homo* refers to a human being, whereas *persona* is a *homo habens caput civile*—a human being with a civil standing. Vultejus uses the word *caput*, which, as noted, the Roman jurisconsults occasionally used to refer to the kind of legal standing that free men had and slaves lacked.[23] However, Vultejus seems to be the first to have defined these terms clearly,

[20] See Tuck (n 12) 20–4 and Annabel S. Brett, *Liberty, Right and Nature: Individual Rights in Later Scholastic Thought* (Cambridge University Press 1997).

[21] See Ernst Holthöfer and Johanna M. Baboukis, 'Doneau, Hugues' in Stanley N. Katz (ed.), *The Oxford International Encyclopedia of Legal History* (Oxford University Press 2009). Doneau was not the first humanist jurist; he was preceded by several scholars who would start systematizing Roman law in a critical manner. See Peter Stein, 'Systematization of Private Law in the Sixteenth and Seventeenth Centuries' in Jan Schröder (ed.), *Entwicklung der Methodenlehre in Rechtswissenschaft und Philosophie vom 16. bis zum 18. Jahrhundert* (Franz Steiner Verlag 1998) 122–3.

[22] Christian Hattenhauer, '"Der Mensch als Solcher Rechtsfähig": Von der Person zur Rechtsperson' in Eckart Klein and Christoph Menke (eds), *Der Mensch als Person und Rechtsperson* (Berliner Wissenschafts-Verlag 2011) 44–6.

[23] Ibid. 47–9.

and the first to have claimed that slaves lacked legal personhood—that they were not *personae*.

The great seventeenth-century natural lawyers Hugo Grotius (1583–1645) and Samuel Pufendorf (1632–1694) continued on the path paved by Doneau, employing a systematic approach to legal doctrines that would replace 'the disorderly assemblage of formularies, commentaries and glosses characteristic of medieval legal scholarship'.[24] Grotius is of course renowned as a result of his foundational work on the theory of international law, but he also worked on systematizing domestic law in his *Introduction to Dutch Jurisprudence*. J.-R. Trahan claims that Grotius was the first jurist to separate 'personality' and 'humanity', which would later enable the category of person to include collectivities.[25] However, Trahan's claim seems inaccurate. Firstly, Doneau wrote his treatise decades before Grotius wrote the *Introduction*. It seems more likely that Grotius was inspired by Doneau; the influence of Doneau's work on Grotius has been recognized by legal historians.[26] Secondly, in the Dutch original, Grotius uses the word *mensch*, an old spelling of *mens*, 'human being', rather than the Latin derivative *persoon*, even though the English translator R. W. Lee has used the word person.[27] Grotius therefore does not seem to distinguish between 'human individual' (*homo*) and 'person' (*persona*) in the same way as Vultejus had done, and as later authors would do. Grotius did, however, associate personhood and right-holding in a novel way: 'In order to understand rights of persons to things, since law exists between persons, to whom the right belongs, and between things, over which the right extends, we must treat first of the legal condition of persons, secondly of the legal condition of things.'[28] This is already quite close to the modern understanding of legal personhood as right-holding.

The new ethos of legal scholarship, which would involve trying to understand legal materials in terms of general principles and concepts, would be followed by Samuel Pufendorf. He in turn was strongly influenced by Thomas Hobbes's ideas of personhood. Hobbes had distinguished 'man'—a living body with the capacity to reason—from 'person', whose 'words or actions are considered, either as his own, or as representing the words or actions of an other man, or of any other thing to whom they are attributed, whether Truly or by Fiction'.[29] Persons are thus the *authors* of

[24] N. E. Simmonds, 'Grotius and Pufendorf' in Steven Nadler (ed.), *A Companion to Early Modern Philosophy* (Blackwell 2002) 210.

[25] Trahan (n 2) 12.

[26] Holthöfer and Baboukis (n 21) 360.

[27] Hugo de Groot, *Inleydinge tot de Hollandsche rechts-geleertheyt* (Jan Boom 1738) Grotius also uses 'person' in the sense 'human being' in *On the Law of War and Peace*: 'The capacity of the person [*persona* in Latin original] too, with respect to judgment, disposition, age, education, and every other circumstance must be taken into consideration, when we look for resistance, or submission to the suggestions of wicked inclinations.' Hugo Grotius, *On the Law of War and Peace* (A. C. Campbell tr. ed., 1814) 2.20.31.

[28] Hugo Grotius, *The Jurisprudence of Holland* (R. W. Lee tr. ed., Clarendon Press 1926) 15. Trahan (n 2) 12–13.

[29] Thomas Hobbes, *Leviathan* (C. B. MacPherson ed., Penguin Books 1968) 2177. (Cited in Thiel (n 6) 77).

actions, and though some men are not persons (as with 'Children, Fooles and Mad-Men'), they can be 'personated' by guardians.[30] Hobbes was aware of, and in a way reinvigorating, the old understanding of *persona* as a role, as Udo Thiel points out.[31]

Pufendorf, clearly inspired by Hobbes, distinguishes between 'moral person' and 'human being' ('man'). One should note here that Pufendorf uses 'moral' in an archaic sense, meaning 'everything that directly or indirectly depends upon acts of will by some agent' rather than mere physical causation.[32] Persons are, according to Pufendorf, human beings 'considered under a particular aspect or quality'.[33] Pufendorf also allows for 'compound', or 'fictional', persons. Such a person consists of individuals who share a common will; a compound person can be distinguished here because actions can be attributed to the compound person rather than to the individuals.[34] Pufendorf seems here influenced both by the Roman understanding of personhood and by Hobbes, whose theory of personhood focuses on the attribution of actions.[35]

Leibniz and Natural Law: Persons as Subjects of Rights and Duties

The ethos of the Enlightenment and philosophical rationalism of the seventeenth century would lead to a particular type of natural-law scholarship in Germany. Hugo Grotius had still been rooted in the scholastic and humanist traditions, but the natural-law scholarship that would succeed him attempted to depart both from the Christian scholasticism and from Roman law towards a (putatively) 'ahistorical' type of legal scholarship. Legal works of this era can even be described as quasi-mathematical in nature; they were attempts to derive answers to any legal problem from a set of basic axioms.[36] I must here of course mention the great rationalist Gottfried Leibniz (1646–1716), one of whose many projects involved the creation of a civil code for Holy Roman Emperor Leopold I.[37] Leibniz was strongly influenced by Grotius, and employed the Roman trifurcation in his attempt to build a system of private law. Incorporating the basic elements of person, thing, and action, his system defined them respectively as the *subject*, *object*, and *cause* of a *right*. The concept of right would thus serve as the fourth basic concept. He compared these concepts to the basic terms of geometry:

> [B]oth have elements and both have cases. The elements are simples (*simplicia*); in geometry figures, a triangle, circle etc.; in jurisprudence an action, a promise, a sale, etc. Cases are

[30] Hobbes (n 29) 219. [31] Thiel (n 6) 77.

[32] Knud Haakonssen, 'Natural Law and Personhood: Samuel Pufendorf on Social Explanation', *Max Weber Lecture Series* (European University Institute 2010) 1.

[33] Thiel (n 6) 79–80. [34] Ibid. 79. [35] Ibid. 77.

[36] See Franz Wieacker, *A History of Private Law in Europe* (Tony Weir tr. ed., Clarendon Press 1995) 199–278 for a thorough exposition of the legal scholarship of this era.

[37] Robert Berkowitz, *The Gift of Science: Leibniz and the Modern Legal Tradition* (Harvard University Press 2005) 17.

complexions (*complexiones*) of these, which are infinitely variable in either field. Euclid composed the *Elements of Geometry*; the elements of law are contained in the *Corpus Juris* [...]. To us it seems thus: the [simple] terms from whose complexion there arises the diversity of cases in the law are persons, things, acts, and rights.[38]

These four basic terms are, according to Leibniz, present in any particular legal situation. Firstly, subjects (persons)—which can be natural (*naturalia*) or artificial (*artificialia*)[39]—have the capacity to hold rights (*iura*). The holding of a right means that a person has the 'moral power to execute his or her will';[40] a right imposes on some other person 'the moral necessity to forebear some right', which Leibniz terms an obligation (*obligation*). In addition, every right pertains to a thing (an object), and is acquired on the basis of an act or cause.[41] Peter König describes the system as follows: 'When one asks: who against whom?, one is asking about the subject of rights and duties, when one asks: to what?, [one is asking] about the object of a right, and when one asks: on what ground?, [one is referring] to the *causa*.'[42] There are some exceptions to the basic rule that persons are the subjects and things the objects of rights. Things, such as animals, could occasionally own things: for instance, a bridle could be bequeathed to a horse. On the other hand, in family relationships, persons could occasionally be the objects of rights, if a person was under the power of another.[43]

It seems thus that Leibniz was the first to associate (legal) personhood with right-holding *and* duty-bearing, even if nonpersons could occasionally be the subjects of rights. Leibniz's systematic approach greatly influenced the natural-law school that would come to dominate German jurisprudence for most of the eighteenth century. One important figure in this school was the philosopher Christian Wolff (1679–1754). Wolff's philosophical system was essentially a modification of Leibniz's; it also defined a legal person as the subject of rights and duties. However, Wolff distinguishes *homo moralis* and *persona moralis*: the former is the subject of rights and duties, meaning a potential right-holder and duty-bearer, whereas the latter refers to a human being who actually holds specific

[38] Gottfried Wilhelm Leibniz, *Sämtliche Schriften und Briefe, Sechste Reihe, Erster Band* (Berlin-Brandenburgischen Akademie der Wissenschaften/Akademie der Wissenschaften zu Göttingen eds, 2nd edn, Akademie-Verlag 1990) 189. English translation from Latin in Alberto Artosi, Bernardo Pieri, and Giovanni Sartor (eds), *Leibniz: Logico-Philosophical Puzzles in the Law: Philosophical Questions and Perplexing Cases in the Law* (Springer 2013) xxv.

[39] Leibniz (n 38) 189. [40] Berkowitz (n 37) 57. [41] Ibid. 37.

[42] '*Sofern man fragt, wer gegen wen? fragt man nach dem Subjekt des Rechts und der Verpflichtung, sofern man fragt: auf was? nach dem Objekt des Rechts, und sofern man fragt: aus welchem Grund? nach der* causa.' Peter König, 'Das System des Rechts und die Lehre von den Fiktionen bei Leibniz' in Jan Schröder (ed.), *Entwicklung der Methodenlehre in Rechtswissenschaft und Philosophie vom 16. bis zum 18. Jahrhundert* (Franz Steiner Verlag 1998) 156.

[43] Klaus Luig, 'Die Privatrechtsordnung im Rechtssystem von Leibniz' in Günter Birtsch (ed.), *Grund- und Freiheitsrechte von der ständischen zur spätbürgerlichen Gesellschaft* (Vandenhoeck & Ruprecht 1987) 356.

rights and/or duties.[44] Wolff's influence would be felt in the Prussian Civil Code of 1794—the first of the so-called natural-law codes—according to which '[a] human being is referred to as a person insofar as he enjoys specific rights in the civil society'.[45]

We can conclude that Leibniz was the father of understanding legal personhood as right-holding and duty-bearing, even if he was of course already relying on an existing tradition of legal taxonomy. The other two currently influential definitions—which explain legal personhood in terms of the *capacity* to hold rights and/or duties, or as participation in legal relations—were formulated during the next century, when Immanuel Kant had overtaken Wolff as the dominant German philosopher, and when natural-law jurisprudence had given way to the so-called Historical School. The influence of the Historical School in England and the US was also an important reason why Anglophone legal theory started to employ the person/thing distinction that had been developing on the Continent.

Kant, Hegel, and the Historical School

Immanuel Kant's (1724–1804) later philosophy, starting with the *Critique of Pure Reason* (1781), focused on the preconditions for any possible experiences as Kant endeavoured to derive the basic categories of the world. Kant's moral, political, and legal philosophy, expressed in *Groundwork of the Metaphysics of Morals* (1785) and *The Metaphysics of Morals* (1797), would influence the most important German legal scholars from the late eighteenth century onwards.[46]

Kant's moral philosophy is founded on the categorical imperative, the second formulation of which demands that we never treat the humanity in ourselves and in others purely as a means to an end, but always also as an end in itself. However, with 'humanity', Kant does not actually mean any ordinary understanding of the word but rather the rational nature in persons.[47] Only *persons*, or rational agents with the capability to act autonomously in accordance with principles, are ends in themselves: 'that a person subjects himself voluntarily to the moral law by legislating it for

[44] Hattenhauer (n 22) 51–2. In 1803, Anton Thibaut (1772–1840), who was a natural lawyer but also a Roman scholar, propounded a definition identical to Wolff's. Anton Friedrich Justus Thibaut, *System des Pandektenrechts* (Mauke 1803) 141.

[45] '*Der Mensch wird, in so fern er gewisse Rechte in der bürgerlichen Gesellschaft genießt, eine Person genannt.*' Allgemeines Landrecht für die Preußischen Staaten (1 June 1794), pt I, ch 1, § 1. See also Hattenhauer (n 22) 52–6.

[46] The *Groundwork* is more famous, being Kant's most important work in moral philosophy, whereas *The Metaphysics of Morals* (and especially its first part) deals mostly with political and legal philosophy.

[47] Richard Dean, *The Value of Humanity in Kant's Moral Theory* (Oxford University Press 2006) 17–18.

himself […] makes him a moral being and gives him dignity'.[48] *Things*, on the other hand, may be used purely as means. They do not have a value but only a price.[49] One can see a connection to the Roman-influenced person/thing distinction, and this is no coincidence: Kant was familiar with Roman law and took it to be superior to the German law of his time.[50]

Kant's ethical thought is concerned with internal freedom, that is, a rational agent's 'ability to determine her will independently of alien influences'.[51] Kant's political and legal philosophy, in contrast, is founded on the idea of external or negative freedom—a rational agent's 'ability to set and pursue ends for herself without being subject to the choices of others'.[52] Every person's right to external freedom is, according to Kant, the only natural right, and state power is justified only insofar as it protects this freedom.[53] A person would be granted a sphere of external freedom where his or her will would reign supreme, and this sphere would be as large as is compossible with similar spheres of other persons.

An important way in which the law promotes external freedom is by enabling the existence of property rights—what is 'mine' and 'thine'. By property rights, Kant means both rights that pertain to things—granting the possibility to use things for freely chosen purposes—and contract rights, which 'involve the possession by one person of the "deed" of another'.[54] The possessor may thus choose to control the other person's action. However, entering into such a contract was a choice made by the two persons together, which is why it does not involve treating persons only as means. A third kind of right is 'a personal right of a real kind', which essentially involves treating persons as things. Leibniz had simply conceded that persons were occasionally objects of rights, whereas this would have been problematic for Kant's basic premises. Kant circumvented this problem with the proposed third kind of right. He mentions parental rights as an example (translator's additions in square brackets):

> Given their Personality it follows that the children could never be regarded as the property of the parents, although they still belong to the parents' Mine and Yours (inasmuch as they are

[48] Immanuel Kant, *Metaphysical Elements of Justice. Part I of the Metaphysics of Morals* (John Ladd tr., 2nd edn, Hackett Publishing 1999) xvii.

[49] Christine M. Korsgaard, 'Kantian Ethics, Animals, and the Law' (2013) 33 *Oxford Journal of Legal Studies* 629, 631.

[50] Kant (n 48) xxxi.

[51] Louis-Philippe Hodgson, 'Kant on the Right to Freedom: A Defense' (2010) 120 *Ethics* 791, 793.

[52] Ibid. [53] Ibid. 794.

[54] Frederick Rauscher, 'Kant's Social and Political Philosophy', *Stanford Encyclopedia of Philosophy* (Fall 2016) <http://plato.stanford.edu/archives/fall2016/entries/kant-social-political/>. Kant is clearly making reference to the Roman-law distinction between rights *in personam* and *in rem*; this distinction would later be adopted by Anglophone jurists and would then be analysed and criticised by Hohfeld in his second *Fundamental Conceptions* article. Wesley Newcomb Hohfeld, 'Fundamental Legal Conceptions as Applied in Judicial Reasoning' (1916) 26 Yale Law Journal 710.

Table 1.1 Division according to the subjective relationship between the subject who imposes the duty and the subject bound by the duty

1.	2.
The juridical relationship of persons to beings who have neither rights nor duties.	The juridical relationship of persons to beings who have both rights and duties.
Vacat [empty, no entities], since these are nonrational beings that neither bind us nor can we be bound by them.	*Adest* [not empty, contains entities], for this is the juridical relationship of persons to persons.
3.	4.
The juridical relationship of persons to beings who have only duties but no rights.	The juridical relationship of persons to a being who has only rights but no duties (God).
Vacat, since these would be human beings without Personality (serfs, slaves).[1]	*Vacat*, that is, in mere philosophy, because it is not an object of possible experience.[2]

[1]Kant also addresses the lack of slaves' personality elsewhere in *The Metaphysics of Morals*:

> No person in the state can indeed be without any position of dignity at all, inasmuch as he (or she) has at least that dignity adhering to a citizen. The only exception is someone who has lost indeed be without any position of dignity at all, it through his own criminal act, in which case, although he is allowed to stay alive, he is made into a tool of the will of someone else (either of the state or of another citizen). Such a person (and he can become one only through judgment and Law) is a slave (*servus in sensu stricto*) and is owned by someone else (*dominium*). The latter is, therefore, not merely that person's master (*herus*), but also his owner (*dominus*); being the owner, he can sell or alienate him as a thing, can use him as he pleases (but not for ignominious purposes), and can dispose of his abilities and energies, although not of his life or limbs.

Kant, *Metaphysical Elements of Justice. Part I of the Metaphysics of Morals* (John Ladd tr., 2nd edn, Hackett Publishing 1999) 136. Kant also argues on the same page that '[n]o one can bind himself by a contract to the kind of dependency through which he ceases to be a Person'. However, the arguments he offers to support this claim are quite dubious.
[2]Immanuel Kant, *Metaphysical Elements of Justice. Part I of the Metaphysics of Morals* (John Ladd tr., 2nd edn, Hackett Publishing 1999) 26.

possessed by parents similarly to a thing and they can, even against their Will, be brought back to the parents from possession by someone else). It follows also that the parents' right is not completely a real right [*in rem*], for it is not alienable (*ius personalissimum*), but it is also not completely a personal right [*in personam*], instead it is a personal right of a real kind.[55]

Kant refers, somewhat inconsistently, to children as persons here, even though small children actually would not meet Kant's criteria for personhood. He remarks simply that a child is 'a being endowed with freedom'.[56] This was echoed in Savigny's system of private law, as I will show.

As already noted, rights and duties can only exist between persons according to Kant. He considers the potential for rights and duties between persons and three other groups of beings (see Table 1.1).

Only category 2 is *adest*, that is, contains members. Persons are thus the only possible holders of legal rights and bearers of legal duties. Kant also uses the phrase 'juridical relationship' (*rechtliches Verhältnis*) to describe the relationship between a right and its correlative duty: not only are persons the only possible holders of rights and duties, they are also the only possible parties in legal relationships.

[55] Kant (n 48) 93. [56] Ibid. 92.

In addition to Kant's legal philosophy, one must take account of G. W. F. Hegel's (1770–1831) 'philosophy of right', which was strongly influenced by Kant's works. Hegel employed the person/thing distinction to the same extent as Kant had done. Hegel's definition of personhood is famously complicated, and is often summarized by commentators as being an 'individual willing subject'.[57] The will and freedom of persons is thus of fundamental value. In Hegel's work, persons have the 'capacity for right' (*Rechtsfähigkeit*), which he terms the *abstract right*.[58] Again, persons are taken to have rights pertaining to things. However, Hegel considers the Kantian tripartite division of rights confusing, and maintains rather that personality can simply be understood as the abstract basis for the right to things (emphases in original, word in square brackets by translator):

> *[P]ersonality* alone confers a right to *things*, and consequently that personal right is in essence a *right of things*—'thing' [*Sache*] being understood in its general sense as everything external to my freedom, including even my body and my life. This right of things is the right of *personality as such*.[59]

The 'right of personality' is thus the capacity to hold rights to things, and things are anything external to persons. This is related to the idea of a 'sphere of freedom' that persons hold in relation to things that are external to them. Persons can 'place' their will in 'any thing', whereby the thing 'becomes *mine* and acquires my will as its substantial end (since it has no such end within itself), its determination, and its soul'.[60] Animals are also things—which is why they can be owned, as Hegel explicitly notes.[61]

Hegel's idea of the sphere of freedom would be echoed in some German jurists' works. Hegel's general emphasis on the role of history as a process which would realize the freedom of persons and the 'objective spirit' (*Geist*) of a people[62] would also inspire the Historical School of jurisprudence of the late eighteenth century and the first half of the nineteenth century.

[57] Hegel writes, for instance, that (word in brackets by translator, emphasis in original):

> Personality begins only at that point where the subject has not merely a consciousness of itself in general and in some way determined, but a consciousness of itself as a completely abstract 'I' in which all concrete limitation and validity are negated and invalidated. In the personality, therefore, there is knowledge of the *self* as an *object* [*Gegenstand*], but as an object raised by thought to simple infinity and hence purely identical with itself.

G. W. F. Hegel, *Elements of the Philosophy of Right* (Allen W. Wood ed., Cambridge University Press 1991) § 35.

See for instance Paul Redding, 'Georg Wilhelm Friedrich Hegel' in Edward N. Zalta (ed.), *Stanford Encyclopedia of Philosophy* (Sum 2018) <https://plato.stanford.edu/archives/sum2018/entries/hegel/>.

[58] Hegel (n 57) § 36. One should again note that the German word *Recht* can denote both 'a right' and 'law'. *Rechtsfähigkeit* can be translated as 'capacity for right(s)' or 'legal capacity'.

[59] Ibid. § 40. [60] Ibid. § 44. [61] Ibid § 44 (addition).

[62] See Georg Wilhelm Friedrich Hegel, *The Philosophy of History* (J. Sibree tr., Batoche Books 2001).

The Historical School

Gustav Hugo (1764–1844) is credited as being the founder of the Historical School, though Friedrich Carl von Savigny (1779–1861) was its main proponent. Savigny rejected the rationalist natural-law accounts that had been dominating German jurisprudence and claimed that law was a historical phenomenon, an expression of the 'spirit of the people' (*Volksgeist*). Savigny's *Volksgeist* should not be taken as fanciful metaphysics but rather as a reference to the shared cultural attributes of a people (or its elite), and especially its intellectual tradition.[63] According to the Historical School, legal scholars should conduct historical studies in order to distil the inner principles of a particular legal system. After this historical work, these principles could then be developed further into a scientific system.[64] Savigny set about realizing this mission in his magnum opus, *The System of Modern Roman Law*. The historical basis of *The System* rested almost entirely on Roman law. This was somewhat at odds with the mission statement of the Historical School, as Savigny ignored much of Germanic law that had developed after the Roman era. In addition—and of great importance—Savigny focused exclusively on private law.

One highly relevant issue here—following from the basic tenets of the Historical School—was that Savigny took the *Volksgeist* to be the 'original' source of law. That original source would then be manifested in different legal sources, such as customary law and legislation. This law was not originally created by the state, even if the law would only become 'real' once the state started to protect that law as the positive law of the state. The law contained in the *Volksgeist* was an 'organic' whole, which allowed for jurists to systematize it. This organic nature of the *Volksgeist* meant, according to Kaarlo Tuori's interpretation, at least two things: 'the phenomenon at issue consists of *interdependent elements*' and 'it is subject to the *developmental principle* of living nature'.[65] Having said that, the state could also create 'purely positive law' (*rein positives Recht*) which did not give expression to the *Volksgeist* and was not organically connected to the law contained therein.[66] This relates to Savigny's idea that legal institutions could either be *natural* or *artificial*. Tuori summarizes this idea as follows:

> The former possess a 'natural-ethical' foundation which the latter lack. Family law, for instance, includes such natural institutions as marriage, paternal power and kinship, which all possess a natural-ethical foundation. Relationships within such natural institutions as the family can

[63] See Wieacker (n 36) 311–12 and Mathias Reimann, 'Nineteenth Century German Legal Science' (1990) 31 *Boston College Law Review* 837, 853.

[64] Reimann (n 63) 854.

[65] Kaarlo Tuori, *Ratio and Voluntas: The Tension Between Reason and Will in Law* (Routledge 2010) 80 (emphases in original).

[66] Friedrich Carl von Savigny, *System des heutigen Römischen rechts* (Veit 1840) § 16. See also Niilo Jääskinen, *Historiallisen koulun oikeustiedekäsitys* (University of Helsinki 1983) 32.

never be exhaustively governed by the law. By contrast, artificial legal relationships are in their entirety subjected to law; they are 'pure, mere legal relationships'.[67]

According to Savigny's theory, what persons—be they natural or artificial—possess is legal capacity (*Rechtsfähigkeit*), the capacity to hold rights and bear obligations. (Savigny uses the same term as Hegel had used in his philosophy, though Hegel's term is usually translated as 'capacity for right'.) So who are these persons with legal capacity? Human beings who have been born are in Savigny's system the 'original' persons:

> All law exists for the sake of the innate moral freedom that resides in every human being. This is why the original concept of person or legal subject must coincide with the concept of human being, and this original identity of both concepts can be expressed as follows: every individual human being, and only the individual human being, possesses legal capacity.[68]

As children possess legal capacity from the point of birth, it must be concluded that Savigny takes even infants to have 'innate moral freedom'. There seems to be a contradiction here: how can Savigny claim that infants possess innate moral freedom and thus possess legal capacity even though small children do not meet the criteria of personhood in a Kantian or Hegelian sense? Kant did of course assert that children are 'endowed with freedom', but did not really justify this assertion. Savigny's position could perhaps be understood as influenced by Hegel, according to whom a child's will is free 'in itself' but not free 'for itself'; 'it is only the potentiality of reason and freedom', and does not yet have 'freedom as its object'.[69] This 'potentiality of reason and freedom' may explain why Savigny takes even children to have innate moral freedom. Savigny does in any case recognize that newborn children are actually unable to reign over their spheres of freedom provided by the law, which is why he separates legal *capacity* and legal *competence*.[70] Human beings become legal persons at birth and receive thus the legal capacity to hold private-law rights. Children can therefore, for instance, own property. This is, however, not sufficient for entering into contracts and performing other legal transactions, which presuppose

[67] Tuori (n 65) 80. Tuori is here referring to Book I, § 56 in Savigny's *System*; von Savigny (n 66).

[68] von Savigny (n 66) § 60:

> *Alles Recht ist vorhanden um der sittlichen, jedem einzelnen Menschen inwohnenden Freyheit willen. Darum muß der ursprüngliche Begriff der Person oder des Rechtssubjects zusammen fallen mit dem Begriff des Menschen, und diese ursprüngliche Identität beider Begriffe läßt sich in folgender Formel ausdrücken: Jeder einzelne Mensch, und nur der einzelne Mensch, ist rechtsfähig.*

The Savigny citations in what follows are occasionally my translations and occasionally from the nineteenth-century English translations.

[69] Hegel (n 57) § 10.

[70] I stress yet again that the phrases 'legal capacity' and 'legal competence' are ambiguous. However, they are usually employed in this context, which is why I use them here as well. In my theory, I use the phrases 'passive legal personhood' and 'active legal personhood'.

Geschäftsfähigkeit, legal competence.[71] A child would thus need to be represented by someone with legal competence.

In addition, Savigny noted that the 'original', natural legal capacity of all born human beings could, through positive law, be extended, as with juristic persons, or diminished, as with slaves, but these were not natural legal institutions.[72] Regarding the ontology of corporations, Savigny pronounced the famous 'fiction theory', according to which artificial persons do not have any 'real' existence.[73] His fiction theory sparked a profound debate over the nature of corporations that eventually interested not only Continental scholars but also scholars in the Anglophone world, starting again with John Austin.[74] A lot has been written about this debate in English, which is why I will not address it here.[75]

Savigny also developed his own idea of a legal relationship, which is something quite different from how, say, Wesley Newcomb Hohfeld would conceive of his jural relations. One should first note how Savigny distinguishes, in the spirit of Kant and Hegel, the law or 'objective right' (*objektives Recht*) from (subjective) rights (*subjektives Recht*). Here, the law determines the boundaries of persons' external freedom, whereas a right is the power of a person to affect other persons' choices—a will-theory right.[76] This was connected to legal relationships, which Savigny understood as forming private law; the second book of his *System* was even translated into English under the title *Jural Relations; or, the Roman Law of Persons as Subjects of Jural Relations*.[77]

[71] von Savigny (n 66) § 106.

[72] Ibid. § 60 and § 64. This should not be taken to imply that Savigny deemed slavery to be acceptable: it could not be unified with the equal right to freedom, as it involved the reign of one person over another. Reigning over a specific action of another person was, however, possible and acceptable. This belonged to the law of obligations whereas property law involved the complete reign over a thing. See Helmut Coing, *Europäisches Privatrecht, Band II* (C. H. Beck'sche Verlagsbuchhandlung 1989) 270.

[73] von Savigny (n 66) § 85.

[74] See below where John Austin is discussed, and Peter Stein, *The Character and Influence of the Roman Civil Law* (Hambledon Press 1988) 242. Austin would also introduce the phrase 'legal person', a translation of the German phrase *die juristische Person* which was originally coined by Gustav Hugo to denote corporations, foundations, and so on. Gustav Hugo, *Lehrbuch eines civilistischen Cursus* (6th edn, August Molius 1820) 23 and Michael H. Hoeflich, *Roman and Civil Law and the Development of Anglo-American Jurisprudence in the Nineteenth Century* (University of Georgia Press 1997) 19. As should be obvious, I use the phrase 'legal person' in a wider sense than Austin.

[75] A thorough exposition of the various theories propounded in the nineteenth and early twentieth centuries is in Roscoe Pound, *Jurisprudence, Volume IV* (West Publishing Co 1959) 220ff.

[76] von Savigny (n 66) § 53. See also Coing (n 72) 270.

[77] Friedrich Carl von Savigny, *Jural Relations; or, the Roman Law of Persons as Subjects of Jural Relations : Being a Translation of the Second Book of Savigny's System of Modern Roman Law* (William Henry Rattigan tr. ed., Wildy 1884).

To understand what Savigny meant by legal relationships, we should first recall the idea of natural legal institutions, presented above. A natural institution, such as marriage, acted as a 'type' or 'model' for 'life relationships' (*Lebensverhältnisse*) which could also be described as social relationships. If the law chose to give legal recognition to such a relationship, then the relationship and the legal recognition together constituted a legal relationship.[78] Thus, legal relationships are 'organic' only insofar as the life relationships that they recognize are organic. This idea is illuminated with an example:

> The famous law *Frater a fratre* deals with the following case:—Two brothers are under the paternal power. One makes a loan to the other. The borrower repays this loan after the father's death and it is asked whether he can recover this money paid, as money paid under mistake. Here the Judge has simply to decide upon the question whether there is or is not ground for the *condictio indebiti*; but to know this, a complete view of the jural relation must be present to him. The individual elements of this were: the paternal power over the two brothers, a loan of one to the other, a *peculium* which the debtor had received from the father, the inheriting to that father, the discharge of the loan. From these elements, the decision desired from the Judge must proceed.[79]

It is not easy to formulate what exactly Savigny has in mind here. On my reading, he maintains that the law has here given recognition to social relationships, such as paternal power, loan, and so on. As all of these social relationships are interconnected in various ways, a judge must also be aware of these connections in order to reach the correct legal conclusion in the case. At any rate, Savigny's understanding of legal relations is quite different from any modern, analytic view of legal relations, such as that offered by the Hohfeldian analysis.

Finally, before moving on to address the influence of German legal scholarship in the Anglophone world, I should mention that Savigny also introduced the term *Rechtssubjekt* as a synonym for '[legal] person'.[80] *Rechtssubjekt* can be translated—due to the various meanings of *Recht*—as 'subject of law', 'legal subject', or 'subject of right(s)'.[81] The civil-law world, including the Nordic countries, has adopted this

[78] Tuori (n 65) 79–80.

[79] Friedrich Carl von Savigny, *System of the Modern Roman Law, Volume 1* (William Holloway tr. ed., J. Higginbotham 1867) 7.

[80] The first appearance of the term *Rechtssubjekt* (or its nineteenth-century spelling *Rechtssubject*) in the text corpus *Deutsches Textarchiv* is in Savigny's *System*. Yves Charles Zarka claims that Leibniz was the first to use the phrase *subjectum iuris* ('subject of law'). However, Leibniz's use of the phrase was different from the use of it since Savigny, as becomes apparent from the example employed by Zarka: *Deus est subjectum juris summi in omnia*, that is, 'God is the subject of supreme law over all things'. Yves Charles Zarka, 'The Invention of the Subject of the Law' (1999) 7 *British Journal for the History of Philosophy* 245, 258–9.

[81] The word 'subject' should here be understood in opposition to 'object'. It does not carry the sense of 'subordinate' or 'underling' contained for example in the phrase 'the Queen's subjects'. The German word for 'subject' in the latter sense is *Untertan*.

term as a synonym for 'legal person', whereas it is relatively unknown in the English-speaking world.[82]

Savigny's views on personhood would be echoed by his followers, such as Georg Friedrich Puchta, who continued to characterize law as legal relations between persons.[83] Puchta was a Pandectist—that is, a late nineteenth-century scholar of contemporary Roman law who advocated a conceptual jurisprudence in which legal problems are solved by applying predefined concepts. The Pandectist school was very influential in developing the German Civil Code, and the school's system, with personhood as a central concept, became a part of German legal doctrine. The Pandectist school would be challenged by Rudolf Jhering, who was a representative of conceptual jurisprudence and follower of Puchta until the late 1850s, after which he began to criticize his former school of thought.[84] He also developed an early interest theory of rights, defining rights as legally protected interests, but did not depart from the Orthodox View of legal personhood.[85] Jhering's later jurisprudence would serve as an inspiration for the American legal realist movement. However, because I will be focusing not on legal realism but instead on an attempt to bring order to the common law by applying the systems of Savigny and the Pandectists, I will not present Jhering's thought in more depth here.

The Influence of German Legal Scholarship in the Anglophone World

We have seen that the idea of connecting legal personhood with right-holding emerged among Renaissance humanist scholars on the Continent, and was then slowly refined to what Trahan calls the modern theory of Savigny and his disciples. The Roman (or, at least, Roman-influenced) person/thing distinction was then integral in the formation of many civil-law codifications. The common law, on the other hand, is the product of a long and continuous historical process that has primarily been developed through judicial decisions in concrete cases. Roman legal ideas have

[82] On the influence of Savigny's personhood theory on Scandinavian legal scholarship, see Lars Björne, *Brytningstiden: den nordiska rättsvetenskapens historia. Del II, 1815–1870* (Institutet för rättshistorisk forskning 1998) 349–65 and Claes Peterson, 'Fredrik Schrevelius och den moderna personteoriens upptagande i svensk civilrättsdoktrin' in Yrjö Blomstedt (ed.), *Rättsvetenskap och lagstiftning i Norden* (Juristförlaget 1982).

[83] See for instance G. F. Puchta, *Pandekten* (Verlag von Johann Ambrosius Barth 1872) 19–30.

[84] For a good critical assessment of Jhering's thought, see Neil Duxbury, 'Jhering's Philosophy of Authority' (2007) 27 *Oxford Journal of Legal Studies* 23. See also Wieacker (n 36) 355–7 and H. L. A. Hart, 'Jhering's Heaven of Concepts and Modern Analytical Jurisprudence', *Essays in Jurisprudence and Philosophy* (Clarendon Press 1983).

[85] The Orthodox View is more or less an unquestioned assumption in Jhering's main treatment of rights: Rudolf von Jhering, *Geist des Römischen Rechts auf den verschiedenen Stufen seiner Entwicklung, Teil III* (Breitkopf & Härtel 1877).

nevertheless exerted some influence in English law for a longer time. English legal academics were until the nineteenth century primarily students of Roman and canon law, and employed Roman classifications occasionally in their attempts to bring order to the common law.[86] The Romans had also introduced the idea of corporations into English law; the common law could conceive of Cambridge colleges owning property despite the lack of any systematic idea of legal personality until the nineteenth century, when it was imported from Germany.[87]

One should in addition mention slavery in the British North American colonies, which was influenced by the Roman law of slavery. The Continental colonial powers that had 'received' Roman law, especially Spain and Portugal, were quick to establish Roman-style slavery in the New World, whereas this kind of bondage—treating human beings as property—was foreign to the common law.[88] However, Roman law served as an inspiration for the North American law of slavery. John Finkelman has described how the status of Africans deteriorated in the colony of Virginia: they were first treated as indentured servants, with the promise of freedom, but the laws gradually came to treat them on a par with property. A particularly striking example is the adoption of the Roman-law rule *partus sequitur ventrem* ('offspring follows the womb'). In common law, children traditionally had the same status as their fathers. However, this caused problems, which Finkelman describes:

> This would lead to the situation of slave mothers raising their free-born children, while also creating a class of free mixed-race people. [...] In addition, [...] their mixed-race children would have been legally bastards. [...] Applying these rules to the mixed-race children of slave women would lead to huge social problems, as masters—and leaders of the community—might be prosecuted for illicit (and sometimes adulterous) sex with their own slaves.[89]

All these problems were solved by not employing the common-law rule that applied to persons, but rather the Roman-law rule that pertained to property, according to which the offspring of female livestock or slaves would follow the 'status' of their mothers. The children of slave mothers thus became slaves.

Common-law countries, then, employed some legal rules pertaining to the Roman person/thing distinction even before the influx of German jurisprudence.[90]

[86] Hoeflich (n 74) 16.

[87] Ibid. 19. It should be said, though, that some semblance of the idea of *persona ficta* was already received from canon law during the Middle Ages, as F. W. Maitland points out in his introduction to Gierke's *Political Theories of the Middle Age* (at xiv). Otto Gierke, *Political Theories of the Middle Age* (F.W. Maitland ed., Cambridge University Press 1951).

[88] Paul Finkelman, 'Slavery in the United States' in Jean Allain (ed.), *The Legal Understanding of Slavery: From the Historical to the Contemporary* (Oxford University Press 2012) 105–7.

[89] Ibid. 111–12.

[90] Jeremy Bentham also made brief mention of the person/thing distinction when writing that animals 'are downgraded into the class of *things*' because 'their interests were neglected by the insensibility of the ancient jurists' (emphasis in original). Jeremy Bentham, *The Principles of Morals and Legislation* (1780), ch 17 para 1.4.

However, the Continental ideas of legal personhood and thinghood, and concepts such as rights *in rem* and *in personam*, would gain significant traction in English and American legal scholarship from the nineteenth century onwards. The common law was at this time still essentially medieval in nature, functioning primarily with writs of action rather than with the kind of deductive systems that Continental jurists had been developing.[91] Anglo-American scholars were frustrated by the chaotic nature of the common law, and they set out to emulate the systems of German scholars that had been founded on basic legal concepts. At the same time, American scholars became especially interested in Savigny's Historical School and its principal tenet that a legal system must be understood in its historical context.[92]

John Austin seems to have been the first Anglophone legal theorist to have employed the Continental views on personhood in his works. He had studied in Bonn, Germany, and had become acquainted with Roman law and Continental legal scholarship. Bonn was at that time still dominated by natural-law thinking rather than the Historical School, though Austin would become familiar with both schools.[93] He was persuaded by the systematic approach of German jurisprudence and used it in his lectures, which he started delivering at University College London in 1829. Some of his lectures were published during his lifetime as *The Province of Jurisprudence Determined*, which is mainly concerned with expounding Austin's general theory of positive law. However, the end of the book contains an outline of the rest of his lectures wherein he already makes numerous references to persons. He writes for instance (emphases in original):

> There are certain *rights* and *duties*, with certain *capacities* and *incapacities* to take rights and incur duties, by which *persons*, as subjects of law, are variously determined to certain *classes*.[94]

The influence of Continental scholarship is clear in this passage, as can be seen by Austin's identifying persons as 'subjects of law'—assumedly a translation of the German *Rechtssubjekt*. He also introduces the distinction between rights *in rem* and rights *in personam* to Anglophone jurisprudence, and discusses the bifurcation of law into that of persons and that of things.[95]

91 Hoeflich (n 74) 15–16.

92 Ibid. 76. The influence of German, and especially Savigny's, legal scholarship on English and American legal scholarship was profound. See for instance Michael H. Hoeflich, 'Savigny and His Anglo-American Disciples' (1989) 37 *American Journal of Comparative Law* 17; Stefan Riesenfeld, 'The Influence of German Legal Theory on American Law: The Heritage of Savigny and His Disciples' (1989) 37 *American Journal of Comparative Law* 1; Mathias Reimann, 'The Historical School against Codification: Savigny, Carter, and the Defeat of the New York Civil Code' (1989) 37 *American Journal of Comparative Law* 95; and James E. Herget and Stephen Wallace, 'The German Free Law Movement as the Source of American Legal Realism' (1986) 73 *Virginia Law Review* 399.

93 Hoeflich (n 74) 11–12.

94 John Austin, *Province of Jurisprudence Determined* (John Murray, Albemarle Street 1832) xvi.

95 Ibid. xvi ff.

However, most of Austin's remarks about personhood in *Province* are made *en passant*, whereas a whole chapter is dedicated to personhood and related questions in his *Lectures on Jurisprudence*, published posthumously in 1879. He there makes reference to 'the modern Civilians', that is, the Continental jurists of his time (emphases in original):

['Human being'] is the meaning which is given to the term person, in familiar discourse. […] Many of the modern Civilians have narrowed the import of the term person as meaning a physical or natural person. They define a person thus: […] a 'human being, invested with a condition or *status*.' And, in this definition, they use the term *status* in a restricted sense: As including only those conditions which comprise *rights*; and as excluding conditions which are purely onerous or burthensome, or which consist of duties merely. According to this definition, human beings who have no rights are not persons, but things.[96]

Austin, however, dissents from this definition. He uses 'person' in the sense of 'individual', and claims that '*Persons* are invested with rights and subject to obligations, or, at least, are capable of both' (emphasis in original).[97] For Austin, 'person' and 'human being' are virtually the same thing; it just happens that only human beings are capable of holding rights and bearing duties. Some Continental jurists and philosophers denied slaves' personality, but Austin does not use 'person' in this sense. He does, however, recognize that the law can create artificial persons—he is credited with introducing the term 'legal person' into English, in the sense of 'artificial person'[98]—but he claims that such beings are classified as persons only 'for the sake of brevity in discourse'.[99]

Another early example of a German-influenced definition of personhood is by Thomas Holland, an Oxford law professor who mentions in the preface of *The Elements of Jurisprudence* (1880) his acquaintance with Austin and German scholarship, especially the Pandectists.[100] He writes that 'Persons are the subjects of Duties as well as of Rights. In persons rights inhere, and against them rights are available.' In addition, he notes that a '"natural" […] person is such a human being as is regarded by the law as capable of rights and duties',[101] and that slaves are things, being 'Objects of Rights and Duties'.[102]

Many other Anglophone authors would follow suit.[103] In 1888, W. H. Rattigan, acknowledging his debt to Holland, defined 'person' almost identically,[104] as did

[96] John Austin, *Lectures on Jurisprudence: Or, the Philosophy of Positive Law, vol. I* (John Murray, Albemarle Street 1885) 348. I am not certain why Austin claims that civilians would have taken only right-holding to be constitutive of personhood; Wolff and Thibaut, for instance, clearly define persons as the subjects of rights and duties/liabilities (*Verbindlichkeiten*). Thibaut (n 44) 140–1. The Prussian Civil Code of course defined personhood in terms of right-holding, as noted above.

[97] Austin (n 96) 358. [98] Stein (n 74) 242. [99] Austin (n 96) 354.

[100] Thomas Erskine Holland, *The Elements of Jurisprudence* (Clarendon Press 1880) viii.

[101] Ibid. 65. [102] Ibid. 68.

[103] Neil Duxbury provides an overview of the school of analytic jurisprudence of this era in Neil Duxbury, 'Why English Jurisprudence is Analytical' (2004) 57 *Current Legal Problems* 1.

[104] W. H. Rattigan, *The Science of Jurisprudence, Chiefly Intended for Indian Students* (Civil and Military Gazette Press 1888) vii–xii and 14. Rattigan also translated a part of Savigny's *System* into English.

Frederick Pollock in 1896.[105] Six years later, John Salmond wrote: '[s]o far as legal theory is concerned, a person is any being whom the law regards as capable of rights or duties'.[106] In 1909, John Chipman Gray—who was clearly familiar with German legal scholarship, referring to German jurists 58 times in his magnum opus *The Nature and Sources of the Law*[107]—propounded his famous definition which would later be cited by the New York Supreme Court in the *Tommy* case:[108]

> In books of the Law, as in other books, and in common speech, 'person' is often used as meaning a human being, but the technical meaning of a 'person' is a subject of legal rights and duties.[109]

The celebrated Cambridge legal historian Frederick Maitland was also highly interested in legal personhood, and well acquainted with the relevant German literature. He translated a part of Otto von Gierke's four-part history of German associations *Das deutsche Genossenschaftsrecht* into English under the title *Political Theories of the Middle Age*, and many of his writings compared the German and English doctrines of personhood.[110] In the preface of *Political Theories*, he also makes reference to the German distinction between the subjects and objects of a right—'If Styles owns a horse, Styles is the Subject and the horse the Object of the right'—noting this usage to be 'not inconvenient'.[111]

'Person' had thus in the early twentieth century become a fundamental concept that should be defined in a comprehensive work of analytic jurisprudence, much like 'right' or 'duty'. One should mention Alexander Nékám's doctoral dissertation, which is one of the few English-language monographs of this era focusing on legal personhood in general rather than on the nature of corporations.[112] Nékám claimed that talk of personality was confusing and that 'person' or 'legal person' ought to be

[105] Sir Frederick Pollock, *A First Book of Jurisprudence for Students of the Common Law* (Macmillan and Co, Ltd 1896) 105–7.

[106] John W. Salmond, *Jurisprudence or the Theory of the Law* (Stevens & Haynes 1902) 334. That Salmond was familiar with Savigny's work can be seen at 347f.

[107] See Herget and Wallace (n 92) 426.

[108] *People ex rel. Nonhuman Rights Project, Inc. v. Lavery*, No. 518336, 2014 WL 680276 (N.Y. App. Div. Dec. 4, 2014.

[109] John Chipman Gray, *The Nature and Sources of the Law* (David Campbell and Philip Thomas eds, Ashgate 1997) 19.

[110] Gierke (n 87). For many of Maitland's writings on personality, see F. W. Maitland, *State, Trust and Corporation* (David Runciman and Magnus Ryan eds, Cambridge University Press 2003).

[111] Gierke (n 87) xx f.

[112] Alexander Nékám, *The Personality Concept of the Legal Entity* (Harvard University Press 1938). I do not address the corporate personality debate here extensively. Some examples of English-language treatises of corporate personality are Ernst Freund, *The Legal Nature of Corporations* (Batoche Books 2000)—originally published in 1897; Dewey (n 19); Arthur W. Machen, 'Corporate Personality' (1911) 24 *Harvard Law Review* 253; and Frederick Hallis, *Corporate Personality. A Study in Jurisprudence* (Oxford University Press 1930). For an overview, see Alfred F. Conard, *Corporations in Perspective* (Foundation Press 1976) 417–45.

replaced with the phrase 'legal entity'. Except in Nékám's work, legal personhood would mostly be addressed in general, 'all-encompassing' works of jurisprudence, such as Hans Kelsen's *General Theory of Law*—where Kelsen claims that a legal person *is* nothing else than rights and duties[113]—and Roscoe Pound's *Jurisprudence*, of which over 200 pages are devoted to legal personhood.[114] However, personhood largely ceased to interest Anglophone legal theorists during the latter half of the twentieth century; George Paton's *Text-Book of Jurisprudence* seems to be one of the last introductory English-language works of jurisprudence that address legal personality as a separate topic.[115]

Why did jurists and theorists lose interest in legal personhood? Two considerations seem relevant. First, many of the issues that had called for a theoretical explanation of legal personhood were no longer topical. Slavery, coverture, and the so-called civil death of life prisoners[116] were abolished, and the potential legal personhood of animals was not of much interest. Second, the topic of corporate personhood remained controversial but many were likely weary of the debate over the nature of corporations, which seemed to have yielded only a few results. In his inaugural lecture at Oxford, H. L.A. Hart declared that the debate was 'dead' and described the lecture in question as a 'post-mortem' of the debate.[117]

Conclusion

It is relatively clear that the genealogy of the paradigmatic understanding of legal personhood is in the Continental scholarship that I have presented. The predecessors of the contemporary theories of rights—the so-called will and interest theories—were, in a way, developed in symbiosis with the theory of legal personhood: rights were either legally enforceable choices or legally protected interests, and persons were the holders of these rights. However, the contemporary jurisprudential theories of rights are very different from the ones formulated by Savigny and Jhering, as

[113] Hans Kelsen, *General Theory of Law and State* (Transaction Publishers 2006) 93.

[114] Pound (n 75). Pound did not have much original to say on the topic, which is why his views are not addressed in this book.

[115] George Whitecross Paton, *A Text-Book of Jurisprudence* (4th edn, Oxford University Press 1973).

[116] In some US states, life prisoners were as late as in the 1970s considered 'civilly dead', meaning that they could not for instance make legally enforceable contracts or sue or be sued. See Harry David Saunders, 'Civil Death: A New Look at an Ancient Doctrine' (1970) 11 *William and Mary Law Review* 988 and Gabriel J. Chin, 'The New Civil Death: Rethinking Punishment in the Era of Mass Conviction' (2012) 160 *University of Pennsylvania Law Review* 1789.

[117] H. L. A. Hart, 'Definition and Theory in Jurisprudence', *Essays in Jurisprudence and Philosophy* (Oxford University Press 1984) 36 and 47.

right-holding has been of continuous interest in analytic jurisprudence.[118] Theories of legal personhood, on the other hand, have not really changed much.

What's more, it seems that Anglophone jurists have at times been unaware that the Continental theories that associated personhood with right-holding were often articulated in the context of a private-law system. For Leibniz or Savigny, whether one was a legal person determined one's position in the overall scheme: if one was a person, one was a private-law party, with the capacity to own property, enter into contracts, and so on. However, personhood has occasionally been used in English-language jurisprudence in an indiscriminate way, denoting simply any holder of rights and/or duties. This has led to confusion. For instance, some strands of the current animal rights debate, as framed by Steven Wise, focus on the fact that animals are property and not persons; since only persons can hold rights, animals do not currently hold rights.

Having presented the history of the Orthodox View, I will now proceed to assess its viability in the light of our contemporary understanding of rights.

[118] For the rights theories of the nineteenth century, see N. E. Simmonds, 'Rights at the Cutting Edge' in Matthew H. Kramer, N. E. Simmonds, and Hillel Steiner, *A Debate over Rights. Philosophical Enquiries* (Oxford University Press 1998).

2

Rights and Persons—Hohfeldian Analysis

Preliminaries

We have seen how explaining legal personhood in terms of the holding of rights and/or the bearing of duties became the dominant view in much of the Western world during the nineteenth century and the beginning of the twentieth century. When that view is interpreted in light of the contemporary Hohfeldian theories of rights, it is unable to explain the major convictions regarding the extension of legal personhood—what I call *extensional beliefs*. Out of the four extensional beliefs enumerated in the Introduction, this chapter is focused on two:

(i) human beings who have been born are legal persons; and
(ii) animals and foetuses are not legal persons, and slaves were not legal persons.

What has usually underlain these beliefs is the Orthodox View of legal personhood. If that view's equation of legal personhood and right-holding is assessed in light of Wesley Newcomb Hohfeld's theory, many of the widely held extensional beliefs come into conflict with the Orthodox View. Modern theories of rights, which are based on the Hohfeldian analysis, either ascribe rights to entities that are not usually classified as legal persons, such as foetuses and nonhuman animals, or deny rights to entities that are ordinarily classified as legal persons, such as human children.

We can now distinguish five formulations of the Orthodox View. First, some authors, such as John Chipman Gray, define a (legal) person as any entity that holds at least one right or bears at least one duty.[1] I will henceforth use the designation *Rights-or-Duties* position to refer to this view.

Second, scholars subscribing to what I call the *Rights-and-Duties* position maintain that one must hold at least one right *and* bear at least one duty in order to qualify as a legal person.[2] Such a position was invoked by the court in the *Tommy* case—even

[1] John Chipman Gray, *The Nature and Sources of the Law* (David Campbell and Philip Thomas eds, Ashgate 1997).

[2] See David Bilchitz, 'Moving Beyond Arbitrariness: The Legal Personhood and Dignity of Non-Human Animals' (2009) 25 *South African Journal on Human Rights* 38, 42.

though the court actually shirked from the position when acknowledging that children do not bear duties but are legal persons nevertheless.[3]

Third, the *Capacity-for-Rights* position identifies legal personhood as the legal capacity to hold rights and bear duties. Steven Wise claims that legal personhood consists in the 'capacity to hold at least one legal right'.[4] According to the American *Restatement (Third) of Agency*, a 'person' is '(a) an individual; (b) an organization or association that has *legal capacity to possess rights and incur obligations*; (c) a government, political subdivision, or instrumentality or entity created by government; or (d) any other entity that has *legal capacity to possess rights and incur obligations*' (emphases added).[5] Similar definitions are very popular among Continental scholars, too.[6]

A fourth definition, dating back to Friedrich Carl von Savigny, is that of explaining legal persons as the only possible parties of legal, or jural, relations.[7] Savigny conceived of private law as relationships between persons, and this understanding of legal personhood as the capacity to participate in legal relations is still invoked—though often with reference to the scheme of legal relations created by Wesley Newcomb Hohfeld. Wise, for instance, claims that legal things, such as animals, cannot participate in Hohfeldian legal relations.[8] I call this the *Capacity-for-Legal-Relations* view.

Finally, according to a tradition most prominently represented by Hans Kelsen, a legal person is simply (a bundle of) rights and duties. This conception will mainly be addressed in Chapter 4.

Hohfeld's Analysis

Wesley Newcomb Hohfeld (1879–1918) was an American legal scholar who taught mostly at Stanford and Yale universities. He died young, but presented in two seminal articles an analysis of legal relations that has become the most prominent theoretical framework for understanding legal rights and related legal positions, especially in the English-language world. I will now first present the main features of the theory and then discuss whether Hohfeld endorsed or presented a theory of legal personhood. Afterwards I will apply his theory, amplified with more recent theories of rights

3 *People ex rel. Nonhuman Rights Project, Inc. v Lavery*, No 518336, 2014 WL 680276 (N.Y. App. Div. 4 December 2014) 5.

4 Steven M. Wise, 'Legal Personhood and the Nonhuman Rights Project' (2010) 17 *Animal Law Review* 1.

5 *Restatement (Third) of Agency* (American Law Institute 2006) § 1.04.

6 Judith Rochfeld, *Les grandes notions du droit privé* (2nd edn, Presses Universitaires de France 2013) 15; Karl Larenz, *Allgemeiner Teil des deutschen Bürgerlichen Rechts. Ein Lehrbuch* (C. H. Beck'sche Verlagsbuchhandlung 1983) 41.

7 Some authors distinguish between legal and jural relations; I use the phrases interchangeably.

8 Steven M. Wise, 'Hardly a Revolution—The Eligibility of Nonhuman Animals for Dignity-Rights in a Liberal Democracy' (1998) 22 *Vermont Law Review* 793, 801.

that build on the Hohfeldian analysis, to address the prevalent conceptions of legal personhood.

What Hohfeld aimed to show was that many legal terms were used inconsistently by jurists, and this inconsistency led to faulty reasoning. To remedy this problem Hohfeld reduced all legal relations to eight 'atomic' legal positions—atomic in that what lawyers typically understand as legal relations are actually combinations of these basic elements and could therefore be metaphorically described as molecules.

First-order and higher-order Hohfeldian positions are often distinguished. It can roughly be said that the first-order positions define whether a given type of action is required, permitted, or forbidden, whereas higher-order positions pertain to how legal relations can be changed, and thus only indirectly to the permissibility or obligatoriness of physical conduct.

The first-order positions are duty, liberty, claim, and no-right. One's having the *duty* to φ means that φ-ing—which can be any type of conduct—is required under the terms of some legal norm(s). It also entails that at least one party has a *claim* (a *claim-right*) to this conduct.[9] A Hohfeldian duty is thus always held towards someone. In fact, every Hohfeldian position stands in a logical relation to a correlative position. For instance, if I have the duty to pay you £500, then you have the claim-right that I pay you £500. These two positions are correlatives: a duty entails, and is entailed by, at least one claim-right.[10]

Similarly, *liberty* (also known as *privilege*) and *no-right* (occasionally labelled *no-claim*) are correlatives. Mary's having a liberty vis-à-vis John to refrain from φ-ing means that Mary is not duty-bound towards John to φ. Such a liberty is entailed by a *no-right*, that is, a lack of a claim. Thus, John holds a no-right in relation to Mary with regard to Mary's refraining from φ-ing. The concept of no-right is one example of how our everyday language of rights and duties can be misleading. It is not preposterous to say that two boxers each have the 'right' to hit the other during a match. However, in the Hohfeldian terminology, such rights are actually liberties and are only accompanied by the opponent's correlative no-rights rather than duties. Boxer A's liberty-to-hit-her-opponent is not per se correlated with any duty on the part of B. Rather, B simply holds a no-right which entails and is entailed by A's liberty (see Table 2.1).[11]

[9] This is the so-called correlativity axiom of the Hohfeldian system, according to which duties are always accompanied by claims, and vice versa. See Matthew H. Kramer, 'Rights Without Trimmings' in Matthew H. Kramer, N. E. Simmonds, and Hillel Steiner (eds), *A Debate over Rights. Philosophical Enquiries* (Oxford University Press 1998) 22ff.

[10] Hohfeld himself would actually have said that a duty always correlates with exactly one claim-right. I am here employing Matthew Kramer's modification of Hohfeld, according to which a single duty can correlate with multiple claim-rights. This does not affect my argument.

[11] Another often-mentioned example is free speech: X's liberty-to-criticize-the-prime-minister is not correlated with any duties but rather with the prime minister's no-right pertaining to X's criticism.

Table 2.1 For every regulated type of conduct, A has either a duty or a liberty, and B has either a claim-right or a no-right

A's **duty** towards B to φ (A's duty to pay £500 to B)	↔ implies	B's **claim** or **claim-right** that A φ (B's claim-right that A pay B £500)
is the opposite (or contradictory) of		is the opposite (or contradictory) of
A's **liberty** or **privilege** towards B not to φ (A's liberty not to pay £500 to B)	↔ implies	B's **no-right** concerning A's not φ-ing (B's no-right concerning A's not paying B £500)

The higher-order positions also involve four elements: power, disability, liability, and immunity. A *power* consists in the ability to change a legal relation through a volitional act or omission, whereas a *disability* is the lack of such an ability. Similarly, John's having a *liability* towards Mary means that Mary can change at least one of John's legal positions, and an *immunity* implies the absence of such a susceptibility. If Mary has the power-to-make-a-legally-binding-offer-to-John, then John has a liability-to-undergo-some-change-in-his-legal-positions-through-a-legally-binding-offer-from-Mary. On the other hand, if John is a dog, Mary likely cannot make such offers to John. In this case, Mary holds the appropriate disability and John an immunity.

Any particular Hohfeldian position is not necessarily beneficial or detrimental to its holder: Mary's liability, for instance, can be very beneficial: if John has the power-to-endow-Mary-with-ownership-of-some-money-by-donating-the-money-to-her, then Mary has the corresponding liability-to-be-vested-with-ownership-of-the-money-by-being-given-it-by-John.

Before moving on, we should note one feature of the Hohfeldian analysis. I will in Chapter 7 address the fact that legal personhood can act either as a reason or as a conclusion in legal reasoning. The same is true of rights. Abstractly formulated statements about rights in human rights treaties and bills of rights are often so vague that, in order to determine what legal rules they imply, a judge or a doctrinal scholar may for instance have to balance these rights against other rights enumerated in the same instrument. The *outcome* of this legal reasoning can then be modelled on the level of individuals and collectivities using the Hohfeldian analysis.[12] Hohfeldian rights are thus primarily conclusions rather than reasons. Some other theories do define rights

[12] See Andrew Halpin, *Rights and Law—Analysis and Theory* (Hart Publishing 1997) 31–2: 'The [Hohfeldian] legal relation does not present the raw material of the legal sources, statute or whatever, but the net effect of that material on the two persons and one activity in question.' It is debatable whether Hohfeldian higher-order relations are always between

as reasons. According to Joseph Raz, X holds a right if an aspect of X's well-being is a 'sufficient reason for holding some other person(s) to be under a duty'.[13] As I focus in this book on Hohfeldian theories of rights, Raz's theory will not be central—nor will for instance the theory proposed by Neil MacCormick.[14] I will, however, address some features of Raz's theory that are relevant to Hohfeldian interest theories as well.

Hohfeld and Persons

In his treatment of legal relations, Hohfeld was working in and engaging with the German-influenced tradition of jurisprudence that was imported to the Anglophone world by John Austin. Participants in that tradition had sought to bring order and clarity to legal thinking through the definition of fundamental concepts. Hohfeld was clearly familiar with Austin and with many of the subsequent authors who had identified persons as the holders of rights: especially in his second article on legal relations, he makes numerous references to Austin as well as to, say, Holland's *Elements of Jurisprudence* and Salmond's *Jurisprudence*. When addressing rights *in rem*, Hohfeld cites Austin: 'All rights reside in persons, and are rights to acts or forbearances on the part of other persons'.[15] Though he does not wholly agree with Austin's more specific treatment of rights *in rem*, Hohfeld never questions the identification of persons as the only holders of rights and duties, which is apparent in the following passage: 'To say that all rights, or claims, must be against *persons* is, of course, simply another way of asserting that all *duties* must be predicated of persons. The latter is, in truth, no less obvious than the proposition that all rights must be predicated of persons' (emphases in original).[16]

Hohfeld follows in Austin's footsteps in treating only human beings as persons. Like Austin, Hohfeld is critical of the notion of corporations as holders of legal positions.[17] This is most evident at a juncture where he uses 'human being' and 'person' as

two parties, as higher-order relations necessarily involve three parties. See Visa A. J. Kurki, 'Hohfeldian Infinities: Why Not to Worry' (2017) *23 Res Publica* 137, 137–46.

[13] Joseph Raz, 'On the Nature of Rights' (1984) 93 *Mind* 194, 195.

[14] Neil MacCormick, 'Children's Rights: A Test-Case for Theories of Right' (1976) 52 *Archiv für Rechts- und Sozialphilosophie* 305.

[15] John Austin, *Lectures on Jurisprudence: Or, the Philosophy of Positive Law, vol. I* (John Murray, Albemarle Street 1885) 368 (cited in Wesley Newcomb Hohfeld, 'Fundamental Legal Conceptions as Applied in Judicial Reasoning' (1916) 26 *Yale Law Journal* 710, 740).

[16] Hohfeld (n 15) 722f. The phrase 'no less obvious' could of course here be interpreted as meaning that Hohfeld did not take either assertion to be obvious. However, this juncture is part of a section where Hohfeld criticizes the notion that a right *in rem* would be a right 'against a thing' rather than a number of rights against an unspecified number of persons. It is thus clear that Hohfeld takes both statements 'all duties must be predicated of persons' and 'all rights must be predicated of persons' to be obvious.

[17] See in particular Wesley Newcomb Hohfeld, 'Nature of Stockholders' Individual Liability for Corporation Debts' (1909) 9 *Columbia Law Review* 285, 290ff. Hohfeld explicitly endorses Austin's sceptical treatment of corporations at 291f. See also Kramer (n 9) 49–51.

synonyms.[18] He does not seem to address the legal personhood of slaves or women at all, and the only time he mentions animals is when addressing 'tangible objects'. His animal of choice is the horse, which is bought, sold, and wrongfully possessed in his examples.[19]

Exegetically, it seems clear that Hohfeld took only human beings to be legal persons and the holders of legal positions. However, this is not a reason to assume that his scheme, correctly understood, would only include human beings as the parties of legal relations. The matter must rather be analysed carefully. I will return to this matter below.

Rights in the Hohfeldian Scheme

The strength of the Hohfeldian analysis is that it allows for a very precise breakdown of legal concepts. This is why it has been used as a tool in contemporary legal philosophy for pinpointing the meaning of the term 'right'. According to a vague definition—which is, perhaps, most often employed in non-theoretical contexts—a right is any legal position that is beneficial to its holder. In this vague sense, immunities can be rights if they benefit their holder. Such is the case with the US Bill of Rights, which grants several immunities to citizens in relation to the federal government and the states. Hohfeld noted this ambiguity himself: '[T]he term "rights" tends to be used indiscriminately to cover what in a given case may be a privilege, a power, or an immunity, rather than a right in the strictest sense; and this looseness of usage is occasionally recognized by the authorities.'[20] He takes claims to be 'right[s] in the strictest sense', but this definition of rights has not been universally accepted. In addition, Hohfeld's definitions of claims and duties are so vague that even if one accepted claims to be rights, one would have to provide a more fine-grained account of their nature in order to answer some pressing questions surrounding rights, such as whether nonhuman animals hold (or can hold) rights.

Determining the necessary and sufficient conditions of right-holding has been a major topic in analytic legal philosophy for a while now, and most of the theories can be classified as either interest theories or will theories. Not all such theories are based on Hohfeld's framework, but I will here concentrate on theories that are. The most prominent Hohfeldian interest theory is that of Matthew Kramer; will theories have been developed and refined by H. L. A. Hart, Carl Wellman, Nigel

[18] See Wesley Newcomb Hohfeld, 'Some Fundamental Legal Conceptions as Applied in Legal Reasoning' (1913) 23 *Yale Law Journal* 16, 44 (emphases added):

> A change in a given legal relation may result [...] from some superadded fact or group of facts which are under the volitional control of one or more *human beings*. As regards the second class of cases, the *person* (or *persons*) whose volitional control is paramount may be said to have the (legal) power to effect the particular change of legal relations that is involved in the problem.

[19] See for instance Hohfeld (n 15) 733 and 738.

[20] Hohfeld (n 18) 30.

Simmonds, and Hillel Steiner, among others.[21] Both theories hold that a right-holder stands in a special relationship to a duty-bearer, but they differ on the nature of this relationship. Interest theorists maintain, roughly put, that a duty borne by X constitutes a right for Y if Y's interests are typically served by the performance of the duty. This is a relatively extensive conception of rights: it allows for children's rights to, say, be nurtured. It also allows for many criminal-law rights which the will theory denies, such as the right not be murdered.[22] In addition, it encompasses foetuses' and animals' rights. I will return to the scope of interest-theory rights below. The will theories, on the other hand, define Y's holding of a right as Y's control over X's duty: Y can, for instance, choose to demand the enforcement of X's duty. Such control can only be wielded by people with sufficient mental faculties; this is why only adult human beings without mental deficiencies can hold rights according to a typical will theory.

So we have three conceptions of rights: the vague 'anything-beneficial' conception according to which any beneficial legal position is a right, the interest theory, and the will theory. I will not endorse one of them as the correct notion here; I will rather use them all to test the Orthodox View. What I will show is that when each conception is applied, there will be a discrepancy between the central extensional beliefs (regarding who or what is a legal person), and who or what currently holds legal rights or partakes in Hohfeldian legal relations. There are also some Hohfeldian theories that do not fall under any of these three categories, such as Gopal Sreenivasan's hybrid theory and Leif Wenar's several-functions theory.[23] Though I will not be addressing these theories explicitly, they are just as problematic for the Orthodox View. For instance, Wenar's several-functions theory is almost as liberal in its allocation of rights as the anything-beneficial view, and is thus afflicted by many of the latter's problems.

[21] Kramer's interest theory was first articulated in Kramer (n 9), and subsequently refined in several articles, such as Matthew H. Kramer, 'Getting Rights Right' in Matthew H. Kramer (ed.), *Rights, Wrongs and Responsibilities* (Palgrave 2001). For will theories, see H. L. A. Hart, *Essays on Bentham: Jurisprudence and Political Theory* (Clarendon Press 1982); Hillel Steiner, *An Essay on Rights* (Blackwell 1994); N. E. Simmonds, 'Rights at the Cutting Edge' in Matthew H. Kramer, N. E. Simmonds, and Hillel Steiner, *A Debate over Rights. Philosophical Enquiries* (Oxford University Press 1998); and Carl Wellman, *Real Rights* (Oxford University Press 1995).

[22] As one cannot waive or enforce one's claim-right not to be murdered, it cannot be classified as a will-theory right.

[23] Leif Wenar, 'The Nature of Rights' (2005) 33 *Philosophy and Public Affairs* 223 223 and Gopal Sreenivasan, 'A Hybrid Theory of Claim-Rights' (2005) 25 *Oxford Journal of Legal Studies* 257. See also Matthew Kramer and Hillel Steiner, 'Theories of Rights: Is There a Third Way?' (2007) 27 *Oxford Journal of Legal Studies* 281. Wenar classifies his theory as being neither an interest nor a will theory, but Kramer and Steiner contend that Wenar is in fact propounding an interest theory and not a 'third theory'.

Legal Persons as Holders of Rights

Interest Theory and the Legal Person

According to Kramer's interest theory, rights are equivalent to claims.[24] Thus, X holds a right towards Y if Y has a duty towards X, and having a duty *towards* someone (or something) means that such a duty typically is in the interest of the entity in question.[25] However, the mere fact that the performance of a duty typically benefits X does not yet mean that that duty is held towards X. Such a formulation of the interest theory could result in an excessively wide range of right-holders: depending on how one understands 'benefit' and 'interest', the formulation could grant rights to, say, plants. If we want to object to this ascription of rights to plants, we must do it on moral grounds by showing that plants are not the kinds of beings that can hold rights, as both Raz and Kramer have pointed out.[26]

Interest theory and moral evaluation

Claim-rights involve the directedness of duties; they can be held by beings to whom duties can be owed. Most people would probably agree that duties can be owed to children, but animals are already a somewhat more contentious case. What about rocks, idols, rivers, or atoms? Some individuals may hold duties pertaining to the preservation of a river, but how do we determine whether they hold duties *to* the river—rather than, say, to the general public? Or, to use Raz's example, if a group of scientists has the 'duty to preserve certain rare species of plants because they are the only source of a medicine for a rare and fatal disease', are the plants then right-holders?[27] Interest theorists have proposed two main ways of approaching this issue.

Some theorists, such as Joel Feinberg, maintain that the possession of interests is both necessary and sufficient for the capacity to hold rights.[28] Any X that is endowed with interests can hold rights. Such a view is typically connected to a rather narrow view of interests; according to Feinberg, interests are 'compounded out of desires and aims, both of which presuppose something like belief, or cognitive

[24] To be more precise, rights are claims that are accompanied by sundry immunities. I will disregard this detail in the present discussion, as it does not affect my argument in any way.

[25] Which entities can hold interest-theory rights is discussed more extensively in Kramer (n 21).

[26] See Matthew H. Kramer, 'Do Animals and Dead People Have Legal Rights?' (2001) 14 *Canadian Journal of Law & Jurisprudence* 29; Kramer (n 21); and Raz, (n 13).

[27] The example is from Raz (n 13) 205.

[28] I refer here mainly to Feinberg's article 'The Rights of Animals and Unborn Generations', where he propounds an interest theory of rights. Christopher Wellman argues that Feinberg has in his writings inadvertently espoused both an interest and a will theory. See Joel Feinberg, 'The Rights of Animals and Unborn Generations' in William T. Blackstone (ed.), *Philosophy and Environmental Crisis* (University of Georgia Press 1974) and Christopher Heath Wellman, 'Feinberg's Two Concepts of Rights' (2005) 11 *Legal Theory* 213.

awareness'.[29] Rivers or plants do not possess cognitive awareness and cannot have interests, whereas nonhuman animals can. This is, for Feinberg, sufficient reason to conclude that animals can hold rights whereas plants cannot.

According to Raz and Kramer, on the other hand, X's being endowed with interests is a necessary but not a sufficient condition for X's capacity to hold rights. Raz does not offer a definition of interests but equates X's interests with the well-being of X.[30] He also seems to ascribe interests to plants in the example above. Kramer defines interests as follows:

> [T]o say that some interest(s) of X will be advanced through the occurrence of an event or the emergence of a state of affairs is to say that X will benefit in some way(s) from the specified event or state of affairs. That is, the event or state of affairs will improve X's condition or will avert a deterioration therein.[31]

Kramer allows for the interests of trees, rivers, and elegant buildings because their situation can be enhanced or worsened.

In spite of these extensive conceptions of interests, neither Raz nor Kramer ascribes rights to plants. According to Raz, X can only hold rights if X is capable of having rights.[32] He maintains that '[a]n individual is capable of having rights if and only if either his well-being is of ultimate value or he is an "artificial person" (e.g. a corporation)'.[33] I will address artificial persons in Chapter 5; the focus now will be on entities whose well-being is of ultimate value. Raz distinguishes three categories of value: instrumental, intrinsic, and ultimate value. The instrumental value of something derives from 'the value of its consequences, or from the value of the consequences it is likely to have, or from the value of the consequences it can be used to produce'. Intrinsic value is non-instrumental but justified by ultimate value. Raz takes the example of a companion dog: even if one would not take the dog's well-being to be of ultimate value, the relationship between the dog and the owner would have intrinsic value 'in its being a constitutive part of a valuable form of life', which is why the existence of the dog would be of intrinsic value as well. The ultimate value of something, on the other hand, 'does not derive from its contribution to the value of something else'.[34] Raz does not seem to ascribe ultimate value to the dog's well-being, whereas Kramer does, mainly because the dog is a sentient being.[35]

According to Feinberg, the possession of interests and the capacity to hold rights go hand in hand, whereas Raz and Kramer disentangle these two issues. I am sympathetic to Feinberg's account, but I do not aim to take sides here. Feinberg and Kramer both maintain that animals can hold rights, and both take the sentience of

[29] Feinberg (n 28) 52. [30] Raz (n 13) 195. [31] Kramer (n 26) 33.

[32] This capacity is not the same 'capacity for rights' that is often associated with legal personhood and that I will address below; Raz is not referring to a legal status that could be bestowed by the legislator but rather to a moral status.

[33] Raz (n 13) 195. [34] Ibid. 205–6. [35] Ibid. 206, and Kramer (n 26) 36.

those creatures to be of central importance in this determination. The moral justification of this view is quite widely, though not unanimously, accepted in modern secular Western ethics: the sentience of a being is very often taken to be an important (though not perforce necessary or sufficient) condition for what may be termed—depending on the moral theory—the possession of ultimate value, being a moral patient, figuring in the equal consideration of interests, and so on.[36] Sentience matters because—to use Thomas Nagel's phrase—there is 'something it is like to *be*' a sentient being.[37] Sentient beings have an experience of their existence whereas rocks do not. Sentience is thus also integral to an entity's status as a potential holder of interest-theory rights, as it can be said that things *matter* only to sentient beings.

If one accepts that sentient beings can hold rights, the question remains who or what is sentient. It is quite clear that the majority of nonhuman animals, including at least all vertebrates, are sentient.[38] Also human foetuses during the final trimester possess the capacity to be conscious, though whether they actually experience anything is still unclear; preterm infants can, according to one publication, 'reach a minimal level of consciousness'.[39] Issues such as these are far from settled, but they provide sufficient reason for treating foetuses as potential right-holders, at least in the late stages of development.

In the rest of the book, I will proceed from the premise that only sentient beings are of ultimate value and that they can consequently hold claim-rights. (Some collectivities and AIs are eligible to hold claim-rights as well; they will be addressed in Chapters 5 and 6.) Sentient beings include at least born, non-anencephalic humans:, human foetuses during the final trimester; and most vertebrates. This demarcation of the scope of interest-theory right-holders will also be central in Chapter 4, when I discuss who or what can be a legal person.

Before moving on, I should stress two things. In what follows, I do not claim to be propounding purely conceptual truths, as the question of who or what can hold rights according to the interest theory is intimately intertwined with certain moral considerations. In this regard, my appraisal of the Orthodox View of legal

[36] See Agnieszka Jaworska and Julie Tannenbaum, 'The Grounds of Moral Status', *The Stanford Encyclopedia of Philosophy* (Summer 2018) <https://plato.stanford.edu/archives/spr2018/entries/grounds-moral-status/>. A rather good overview of the importance of sentience according to numerous bioethicists (with regard to when a foetus becomes a 'person' with the right to life) is given in Christopher Kaczor, *The Edge of Life: Human Dignity and Contemporary Bioethics* (Springer 2005) 5–39.

[37] Thomas Nagel, 'What Is It Like to Be a Bat?' (1974) 83 *Philosophical Review* 435, 436.

[38] See, for example, The Cambridge Declaration on Consciousness, drafted by Philip Low and signed on 7 July 2012 by conference participants of Francis Crick Memorial Conference on Consciousness in Human and non-Human Animals. It is available at http://fcmconference.org/img/CambridgeDeclarationOnConsciousness.pdf (accessed 9 February 2019).

[39] Hugo Lagercrantz and Jean-Pierre Changeux, 'The Emergence of Human Consciousness: From Fetal to Neonatal Life' (2009) 65 *Pediatric Research* 255.

personhood—as well as my own theory—can be criticized not only on conceptual but also on moral grounds.

Second, determining who or what *can* hold rights is an inquiry distinct from that of *what* rights some potential right-holder should be endowed with. Maintaining that animals can hold rights does not need to imply that animals should be treated on a par with human moral persons. One could, for instance, hold that animals should be protected from some particularly cruel forms of maltreatment for their own sake as sentient beings but that their interests are otherwise overridden by those of human moral persons. Similarly, even if a third-trimester foetus is sentient, there may still be justifications for the termination of pregnancy during this phase of gestation.

Applying the interest theory

Can the Rights-or-Duties position explain the extensional beliefs regarding legal personhood, if we understand 'right' in line with most versions of the interest theory? It cannot, because the interest theory is consistent with the attribution of legal rights to foetuses, nonhuman animals, and slaves, all of which are central examples of legal nonpersons. The protection of foetuses takes place primarily through the regulation of abortions, especially in late stages of pregnancy, whereas animals are protected by animal welfare laws. Such regulations grant protections to foetuses and animals that will be classified as rights under most versions of the interest theory (including Kramer's).

The claim that animals and late-stage foetuses can hold interest-theory rights relies of course on the somewhat contested ethical assumption that these beings are of ultimate value. However, the Rights-or-Duties position is also unable to explain the extensional belief that slaves were not legal persons. If an entity's holding rights or bearing duties constitutes its legal personhood, and being a slave means that one has no rights (or duties) whatsoever—as Hans Kelsen claims explicitly[40]—then granting just one right or duty to a slave would immediately turn the individual into a legal person. However, not only did slaves bear numerous duties but they also held certain limited rights. Section XXXVII of the South Carolina Slave Code of 1740 penalized the wilful killing of slaves (emphases in original):

> And *whereas*, cruelty is not only highly unbecoming those who profess themselves christians [sic], but is odious in the eyes of all men who have any sense of virtue or humanity ; therefore, to restrain and prevent barbarity being exercised toward slaves, *Be it enacted* by the authority aforesaid, That if any person or persons whosoever, shall wilfully murder his own slave, or the slave of another person, every such person shall upon conviction thereof, forfeit and pay the sum of seven hundred pounds [...].[41]

[40] '[T]hat a slave is legally no person, or has no legal personality, means that there are no legal norms qualifying any behavior of this individual as a duty or a right.' Hans Kelsen, *General Theory of Law and State* (Transaction Publishers 2006) 95.

[41] An Act for the Better Ordering and Governing of Negroes and Other Slaves in this Province, South Carolina, May 1740, Section XXXVII. Transcription from David J. McCord

So the slaves of South Carolina even had the interest-theory right not to be killed wilfully, as well as numerous duties.[42] This fact does not depend on contested evaluative assumptions; virtually everyone accepts that adult humans of sound mind are of ultimate value and can hold rights.[43]

To sum up, defining legal personhood as the holding of interest-theory rights cannot explain the extensional beliefs regarding who or what is a legal person because interest-theory rights are held by beings who are very commonly classified as nonpersons. Animals and foetuses hold rights according to most versions of the interest theory, but they are not legal persons. Slaves held both rights and duties, yet they were classified as legal nonpersons. What has been said so far is also applicable to the anything-beneficial conception because the definition of right according to this conception is a more extensive version of the interest theory. If animals and foetuses have interest-theory rights, they most definitely have anything-beneficial rights.

Will Theory and the Legal Person

Probably the most influential Hohfeldian will theory was articulated by H. L. A. Hart, who argued that rights should not simply be reduced to the correlatives of duties. Rather, the distinctive usage of 'right', where the term could not be replaced by some other expression, is where the right-holder can waive or enforce the duty of another.[44] This is why Hart maintained in his early writings that infants cannot hold rights: infants are simply unable to exert the kind of control that right-holding presupposes. Hart did not of course think that infants should be treated like objects; rather, he maintained that 'the moral situation can be simply and adequately described here by saying that it is wrong or that we ought not to ill-treat [infants and animals] or, in the philosopher's generalized sense of "duty", that we have a duty not to ill-treat them'.[45] Many will theorists share the conclusion that infants and animals, as well as severely mentally handicapped individuals, cannot hold rights.[46] Any

(ed), The Statutes at Large of South Carolina. Vol. 7, Containing the Acts Relating to Charleston, Courts, Slaves, and Rivers (A.S. Johnston 1840) 397.

[42] Slaves could be prosecuted in criminal trials; see subsection 'Onerous legal personhood' in Chapter 4. More generally regarding the legal protection of slaves in the antebellum South, see Thomas D. Morris, *Southern Slavery and the Law, 1619–1860* (University of North Carolina Press 1996) 182–208.

[43] One could also claim that chattels cannot hold legal rights. I will address this matter below after addressing the will theory.

[44] H. L. A. Hart, 'Are There Any Natural Rights?' (1955) 64 *The Philosophical Review* 175, 181:

> If common usage sanctions talk of the rights of animals or babies it makes an idle use of the expression 'a right', which will confuse the situation with other different moral situations where the expression 'a right' has a specific force and cannot be replaced by the other moral expressions which I have mentioned.

[45] Ibid.

[46] Carl Wellman, among others, insists that infants cannot hold rights, even if he admits to having 'suffered a period of intellectual and emotional crisis' after realizing this implication of his will theory. Wellman (n 21) 114.

theory accepting this conclusion is unable to explain some central extensional beliefs regarding legal personhood: infants and mentally disabled individuals figure among the central cases of legal personhood but they do not hold will-theory rights.

However, Hart himself later revised his position on the (legal) rights of children. In *Essays on Bentham*, he wrote:

> Where infants or other persons not *sui juris* have rights, such powers and the correlative obligations are exercised on their behalf by appointed representatives and their exercise may be subject to approval by a court. But since (a) what such representatives can and cannot do by way of exercise of such power is determined by what those whom they represent could have done if *sui juris* and (b) when the latter become *sui juris* they can exercise these powers without any transfer or fresh assignment; the powers are regarded as belonging throughout to them and not to their representatives, though they are only exercisable by the latter during the period of disability.[47]

Hart's treatment is very brief and leaves undetermined exactly whom he intends to include among potential right-holders in this extension of the will theory. Phrases such as 'when the latter become *sui juris*' and 'period of disability' suggest that Hart is mainly thinking of cases where an individual is *alieni juris* for a period of time before becoming *sui juris* (children of sound mind, individuals with temporary mental disorders, and so on). Let us call this alternative WT1. This interpretation would exclude individuals who can never attain the requisite mental status to exercise their rights, such as mentally severely disabled individuals. The Rights-or-Duties position and WT1 would thus jointly entail that such individuals would not be legal persons—a conclusion which would once again run counter to the extensional beliefs.

WT1 is likely the correct interpretation, but it is of course possible that Hart intended even permanently mentally disabled individuals to be included among right-holders, even if his criterion (b) is inapplicable to these individuals. I call this version WT2. If we adopt WT2, it is rather difficult to see why nonhuman animals could not also hold legal rights, given that the appointed representative clearly cannot represent the *will* of the principal but only his, her, or its *interests*. The representative is thus, roughly put, a trustee rather than an agent of the principal.[48] In fact, WT2 and the Rights-or-Duties position would entail that some animals are already legal persons in certain jurisdictions. In a great number of US states, pets can be the beneficiaries of trusts.[49] It follows quite straightforwardly that such pets hold WT2 rights: they

[47] Hart (n 21) 184. Simmonds endorses Hart's approach in Simmonds (n 21) 226f.

[48] The distinction between these two types of representation has been highlighted by Carl Wellman. Wellman (n 21) 114–15.

[49] The *New York Times* wrote in 2005 that twenty-seven states allowed pet trusts. Maryann Mott, 'And to My Dog, I Leave a $10,000 Trust Fund' *New York Times* (22 May 2005) <http://nyti.ms/1KUmJ9T> accessed 9 February 2018. The fact that pets can be the beneficiaries of trusts is of course relevant when determining whether they are legal persons. However, it is simplistic to claim that such trusts alone would constitute legal personality *tout court* for their canine and feline beneficiaries.

hold an equitable title to property, and the relevant 'powers and the correlative obligations are exercised on their behalf by appointed representatives', to use Hart's choice of words. Any argument denying that these animals already hold WT2 rights would need to be a moral argument.[50]

All of the aforementioned versions of the will theory also ascribe some rights to slaves, given that slaves in the antebellum US South had the right to appeal criminal convictions.[51]

To conclude, our extensional beliefs regarding legal personhood cannot be explained in terms of the holding of will-theory rights. Will theories that do not ascribe rights to children and mentally disabled people leave out a great number of individuals who are widely taken to be legal persons. Hart's later will theory does solve some of these problems but instead attributes rights to legal nonpersons or—depending on the interpretation—denies rights to legal persons.

Can Chattels Hold Rights?

The modern Hohfeldian theories of rights either ascribe rights to individuals and creatures that are widely taken to be legal nonpersons, or declare some putative legal persons to be incapable of holding rights. I cannot address every possible objection to the proposed theories of rights, but I will briefly discuss an argument by Gary Francione which relates particularly to legal personhood.

Francione claims that being an object of ownership and having rights are inherently irreconcilable. If he is right, the range of right-holders according to the interest theory does indeed correspond to the extensional beliefs much better. He writes:

> To say that a chattel can have rights requires that the instrumental status of the chattel be altered fundamentally. To say that an item (or animal) is a chattel is to say that it has no inherent value and that its value is exclusively instrumental. […] Although certain legal prohibitions (such as an absolute ban on using animals in burn experiments) may recognize that at least some animal interests are not subject to being 'balanced' away, the regulation of animal treatment under legal welfarism assumes that all animal interests are, at least in theory, subject to sacrifice.[52]

This is an interesting argument and, if it is correct, one could possibly use it to claim that the holding of rights according to the interest theory is a necessary and sufficient condition for legal personhood because slaves and animals would not be able

[50] Hart did seem to think that duties cannot be owed to animals: 'It is an incidental, though substantial merit of [the will theory] that it provides an intelligible explanation of the fact that animals, even though directly protected by the duties of the criminal law prohibiting cruelty to them, are not spoken or thought of as having rights.' Hart (n 21) 185.

[51] See for example Judith Kelleher Schafer, 'Long Arm of the Law: Slave Criminals and the Supreme Court in Antebellum Louisiana' (1985) 60 *Tulane Law Review* 1247. The slaves—and not their masters—were also formally the accused parties of these lawsuits.

[52] Gary Francione, *Animals, Property, and the Law* (Temple University Press 1995) 102.

to hold rights. The resulting range of right-holders would then correspond relatively well with the extensional beliefs. Francione's claim may very well be true of certain conceptions of rights where rights are considered non-overridable; Francione mentions Ronald Dworkin's idea of rights as 'trumps' against utilitarian policy considerations.[53] Such notions of legal rights generally offer rights as *reasons* for reaching certain legal conclusions—indeed, Francione seems to chiefly think of rights as either exclusionary, overriding, or overtopping reasons.[54] Constitutional and fundamental rights have such a role in legal reasoning. However, I am here focused on Hohfeldian rights, which *are conclusions* of the interpretation of the relevant legal material. Francione does also discuss Hohfeldian rights, but his discussion is hampered by the ambiguousness of the Hohfeldian claim-right, unless it is more specified, as in Kramer's interest theory.[55] For example, Francione seems to think that the duty of farm workers to force-feed geese until their livers rupture is correlated with rights held by the geese to be force-fed, which he gives as a reason for discounting the Hohfeldian account. However, the right-holder(s) here should be located in the farm owner(s) or other beneficiaries.[56] Francione takes another example:

> As Professor Joel Feinberg has argued, when we talk about the violation of a duty, we usually mean that the rightholder has herself been wronged. […] A more difficult example would involve regulations that require that researchers not inflict pain on animals unless the infliction is scientifically 'necessary'. Unlike the goose, a laboratory rat may be said to be 'wronged' when the researcher fails to make the 'necessity' determination in a particular case. However, this would be like saying that a woman was wronged—and her right violated—when her husband beat her with a rod that exceeded the width of his thumb. Although both the animal and the woman are wronged, it tugs at our intuitions to say that a woman has a 'right' to be beaten with a smaller rod or that an animal has a 'right' to have pain inflicted only when it is scientifically 'necessary'.[57]

Francione misstates the content of these (claim-)rights: the woman's right, for instance, is not the right-to-be-beaten-with-a-smaller-rod but the right-not-to-be-beaten-with-a-larger-rod. The husband's liberty-to-beat-her-with-a-smaller-rod is correlated with a no-right, not a claim-right. Similar analysis can be applied to the

[53] Ibid.

[54] According to Joseph Raz, an exclusionary reason is 'a second-order reason to refrain from acting for some reason'. Joseph Raz, *Practical Reason and Norms* (Oxford University Press 1999) 39. For a discussion on the difference between 'overtopping' and 'overriding', see Matthew H. Kramer, *Torture and Moral Integrity* (Oxford University Press 2014) 2–12.

[55] Francione (n 52) 97.

[56] One might baulk at this, noting that the geese would die if they weren't fed. However, the geese can be wronged both by overfeeding them and letting them starve. If the farm workers had the duty to feed the geese, and not overfeed them, then it would make sense to talk of the geese's rights-to-be-fed.

[57] Francione (n 52) 97. Francione talks of Hohfeldian claims as rights, which is why I will also use the designation 'right' when discussing claims here.

rat's case. When stated correctly, I consider it clear that both the rat and the woman hold these claim-rights, even if such rights can perhaps only exist in a less than ideal legal system (except as part of more extensive rights: the woman's right-not-to-be-beaten-with-a-large-rod as a part of her right-not-to-be-beaten, and so on). International humanitarian law encompasses similar rules, such as the prohibition on expanding bullets[58]—which entails the right-not-be-shot-at-with-expanding-bullets—and on attacks 'which may be expected to cause incidental loss of civilian life, injury to civilians, damage to civilian objects, or a combination thereof, *which would be excessive in relation to the concrete and direct military advantage anticipated*' (emphasis added).[59] Even the latter example, aiming to minimize the suffering caused by war, produces Hohfeldian claim-rights (which are admittedly somewhat difficult to formulate).

Francione's claim is connected to his more general argument that the so-called welfarist protection of animals in American law is primarily based on the maxim of not 'wasting' property, which he attributes originally to John Locke: the prohibition on gratuitous animal afflictions is merely an example of the 'general tendency of the common law to maximize the value of property'.[60] If this statement is true, then it may of course be argued that the ultimate goal of animal welfare laws is not to protect animals for their own sake but to further certain economic goals. Francione questions, quoting MacCormick, whether it makes sense to talk of the right of turkeys to be fed so that they can be eaten.[61] However, according to Kramer's interest theory, holders of rights are not determined by the purpose of a duty-imposing legal norm but rather by establishing whom the duty in question typically benefits.[62] There is certainly something off-putting about the turkey example, but this does not mean that talk of rights in this case is senseless. The turkey may be the primary beneficiary of the duty to provide food—assuming that the turkey's life as a factory-farmed animal is not, on balance, so painful that a quick death would be more in its interests than a continued existence—though in the long run this serves the interests of the owner. Similarly, it makes sense to talk of the rights of soldiers to be fed properly, even if the purpose of such rights is to ensure their efficiency as combatants, which may lead to their death. It is also fairly clear that business corporations—which are chattels, too—hold rights, even if these rights are typically in place only to ensure that the corporations generate profits for their shareholders.

[58] Hague Convention (II) with Respect to the Laws and Customs of War on Land (adopted 9 July 1899, entered into force September 4 1900) 32 Stat. 1803, Treaty Series 403, declaration III.

[59] Protocol Additional to the Geneva Conventions of 12 August 1949, and relating to the Protection of Victims of International Armed Conflicts (Protocol I) (adopted 8 June 1977, entered into force 7 December 1978) 1125 UNTS 3, Art. 51(5)(b).

[60] Francione (n 52) 32. [61] Ibid. 103. [62] This is a simplification.

So I disagree with Francione: animals do indeed hold (claim-)rights, despite their status as chattels.[63] In fact, an animal could perfectly well have the 'right to be properly owned', as proposed by David Favre.[64]

It should be added that, despite the high level of sophistication of Francione's discussion, it may be partially motivated by tactical reasons concerning the status of animals; this has been pointed out by Bryan Thomas.[65] Francione may be correct in his view that the interests of animals would best be served by abolishing their status as chattels altogether, but this does not alter the fact that animals already hold certain, though limited, interest-theory rights. Francione does in effect admit to this himself when conceding that there are some, though very limited, absolute prohibitions on what one can do to an animal (see quotation at the beginning of this subsection). However, I *do* think that the extent to which one's central interests to life and bodily integrity are not subject to 'sacrifice' or being '"balanced" away'—as Francione puts it—is relevant when determining whether one is a legal person. I will return to this issue in the next chapter.

Summing Up: Legal Persons as Holders of Rights?

It has been established that our extensional beliefs regarding legal persons cannot be explained by the claim that right-holding and legal personhood are mutually entailing. The Rights-and-Duties formulation can also be rejected at this point. Infants are legal persons, yet they bear no duties and thus do not qualify as legal persons according to the Rights-and-Duties view, regardless of whether one employs the interest theory or the will theory of rights. In addition, slaves held both rights and duties yet they were not legal persons. This is also sufficient reason to reject the idiosyncratic view of Arthur Machen, according to whom *only* duty-bearing constitutes legal personality.[66]

What I will do now is focus on an even more abstract question: that of whether legal personhood is equivalent to capacity for participation in legal relations.

[63] For an argument similar to mine, see Cass Sunstein, 'Slaughterhouse Jive' *New Republic* (21 January 2001) 40.

[64] David Favre, 'Living Property: A New Status for Animals Within the Legal System' (2010) 93 *Marquette Law Review* 1021, 1067.

[65] Bryan Thomas, 'A Critical Review of Law's Meaning of Life: Philosophy, Religion, Darwin and the Legal Person' (2011) 38 *Journal of Law and Society* 631, 641. For instance, Francione devotes a part of a later essay to mostly using empirical material in order to show that 'welfarism' is not benefiting animals. See Gary Francione, 'Reflections on "Animals, Property, and the Law" and "Rain without Thunder"' (2007) 70 *Law and Contemporary Problems* 9.

[66] Arthur W. Machen, 'Corporate Personality' (1911) 24 *Harvard Law Review* 253, 263.

Capacity for Rights, Duties, or Legal Relations

Related to (though distinct from) the views presented above is the proposition that legal personhood implies some kind of capacity to hold rights and/or to be a party of legal relations. The Capacity-for-Rights position is taken by Steven Wise, who maintains that legal personhood equals the 'capacity to possess at least one legal right',[67] and by Richard Tur who contends that legal personhood is simply an 'empty slot that can be filled by anything that can have rights or duties'.[68]

As I have shown in Chapter 1, Immanuel Kant was likely the first to propose that only persons can partake in 'juridical relationships', a view that was then developed by Friedrich Carl von Savigny in his *System*. These authors were obviously not employing the Hohfeldian analysis, whereas many similar current views are based on—or at least informed by—Hohfeld's scheme. For instance, Jessica Berg mentions in passing that Hohfeldian legal relations can only exist between legal persons.[69] Steven Wise addresses Hohfeldian legal relations much more extensively, yet he makes on several occasions an unsubstantiated claim: 'Because [Hohfeldian relations] can exist only between two legal persons and one thing, and all nonhuman animals are things, no jural relationships can presently exist between a human being and a nonhuman animal.'[70] This claim is problematic in many ways, but its primary problem pertaining to the discussion at hand is that Wise more or less stipulates that only legal persons could partake in Hohfeldian legal relations. I will return to Wise's position shortly.

The Capacity-for-Legal-Relations position is also advanced by non-Anglophone scholars. In German law, the concept of *Rechtsfähigkeit*—introduced by Savigny—means 'legal personhood', even though it is often translated as 'legal capacity'. *Rechtsfähigkeit* is according to a dictionary definition the 'capacity to be a subject of rights and duties', but it is often also defined as the capacity to participate in legal relations.[71] In addition, these two viewpoints are often offered to clarify each other, implying that they are considered to be synonymous, or almost so.[72]

Can the Capacity-for-Legal-Relations or the Capacity-for-Rights positions, understood in light of the Hohfeldian analysis, cohere with the central extensional beliefs regarding legal personhood? To answer this question, I will now embark upon

[67] Wise (n 4) 1.

[68] Richard Tur, 'The "Person" in Law' in Arthur Peacocke and Grant Gillett (eds), *Persons and Personality. A Contemporary Inquiry* (Basil Blackwell 1988) 122.

[69] Jessica Berg, 'Of Elephants and Embryos: A Proposed Framework for Legal Personhood' (2007) 59 *Hastings Law Journal* 369.

[70] Wise (n 8) 80.

[71] Matthias Lehmann, 'Der Begriff der Rechtsfähigkeit' (2007) 207 *Archiv für die civilistische Praxis* 225, 225. The term is often translated as 'legal capacity', but this is a problematic translation, as the phrase 'legal capacity' often refers to one's ability to perform acts-in-the-law.

[72] For instance Lehmann takes these different definitions to be synonymous. Ibid. 226.

a discussion of the domain (the 'scope') of the Hohfeldian concepts to determine which entities are encompassed by the Hohfeldian legal relations. I have already discussed which entities can be potential right-holders according to the interest theory and the will theory. Rights, as defined in the interest theory, are equivalent to Hohfeldian claims, which is why I will not address them now. However, I will consider the other Hohfeldian categories.[73] Some of the discussion will be quite technical; readers not interested in the intricacies of Hohfeldian analysis may safely skim through the next section or skip it altogether.

The Domains of Hohfeldian Categories

Let us take the Hohfeldian deontic pair of duty and liberty. These two positions are mutually exclusive: one cannot (by definition) both have the duty to φ and the liberty not to φ. However, in relation to every action or omission that is regulated by a legal system, one must either have the duty to φ or the liberty not to φ (and either the duty not to φ or the liberty to φ).[74]

Now, the concept of duty seems to be conceptually restrictive in a certain manner. We do not ascribe duties to every entity in the world. In general, imposing duties on rocks or numbers seems problematic, to say the least. However, does that mean that all of these entities hold liberties? As rocks cannot bear duties, do they hold every possible liberty?

This is a question of the *domain* of Hohfeld's concepts. Because of the different natures of many of the elements, they have to be approached separately. I will start with the higher-order positions (power, liability, and so on) because power is the only category whose domain Hohfeld addressed even passingly. Whether collectivities can hold legal positions will be addressed in Chapter 5; the focus here will be on nonhuman animals as well as on born and unborn children.

Powers and other higher-order positions

The Hohfeldian power is a very wide-ranging concept, perhaps unintuitively wide-ranging for someone not familiar with the Hohfeldian jargon. According to Hohfeld, a power can be identified when 'a change in a given legal relation' can result 'from some superadded fact or group of facts which are under the volitional control of one or more human beings', and 'the person (or persons) whose volitional control is paramount may be said to have the (legal) power to effect the particular change of

[73] Judith Jarvis Thomson makes some remarks regarding who or what can hold Hohfeldian positions in Judith Jarvis Thomson, *The Realm of Rights* (Harvard University Press 1990), for instance on page 49. Kramer addresses this topic in Matthew H. Kramer, *Moral Realism as a Moral Doctrine* (Wiley-Blackwell 2009) 69–85. As mentioned, Wise maintains that only legal persons could partake in Hohfeldian legal relations, though this claim is based solely on a highly problematic understanding of Hohfeld.

[74] This may of course be indeterminate in the case of a particular type of conduct.

legal relations'.[75] Power means, therefore, the ability to cause changes in legal relations through volitional conduct. One does not actually have to intend to cause the legal change in question; it is sufficient that one's conduct causes the change.

The Hohfeldian power is occasionally taken to be a more restrictive concept. For instance, Jordan Curnutt thinks that animals cannot exercise powers because they cannot 'effect a change in another's legal status the way a judge can' or sue to enforce their claims.[76] Curnutt's conception of power is close to the theory of legal powers expounded by Joseph Raz.[77] I call such powers *competences*, and will address them in Chapter 3 as one of the incidents of active legal personhood. However, Hohfeldian powers form a more expansive set. They pertain to changes in legal relations through volitional conduct. Changes in legal relations can of course also be effectuated by non-intentional events. A lightning strike may kill a person, thus causing a myriad of death-related legal consequences.[78] Kramer proposes that this be called *quasi-power*.[79]

Who or what can be endowed with Hohfeldian powers? Hohfeld does use 'human being' and 'person' synonymously in the quotations provided at the beginning of this subsection, but this does not automatically imply that restricting the domain of powers to human beings would be the most appropriate choice. It is possible, for instance, that Hohfeld believed animals to be incapable of volition, perhaps because of the influence of the German tradition according to which nonhuman animals did not possess moral freedom. Whatever his reasons were for excluding nonhuman animals from his definition, science has since then shown that many animals are clearly capable of having intentions and performing volitional actions.[80] Many animals perform actions which effectuate legal changes. If a dog attacks a human being, this has

[75] Hohfeld (n 18) 44. It is rather unclear whether Hohfeld intended to propound such a wide-ranging definition of competences; see Visa A. J. Kurki, 'Legal Competence and Legal Power' in Mark McBride (ed.), *New Essays on the Nature of Rights* (Hart Publishing 2017) 43–4.

[76] Jordan Curnutt, *Animals and the Law. A Sourcebook* (ABC-CLIO 2001) 21–2.

[77] Joseph Raz, 'Voluntary Obligations and Normative Powers' (1972) 46 *Proceedings of the Aristotelian Society* 79.

[78] Andrew Halpin recounts other examples of what he denotes 'mere conditions': 'Water escaping from a reservoir, a person coming of age, moving house, a slate on roof becoming dislodged by a gale—each of these events amounts to the fulfilment of a condition for the emergence of new legal relations (as well as extinguishing old ones).' Halpin (n 12) 61. However, distinguishing between the 'mere triggering' of existing legal positions and genuine changes in legal positions is somewhat complicated; see David Enoch, 'Reason-Giving and the Law' in Leslie Green and Brian Leiter (eds), *Oxford Studies in Philosophy of Law: Volume 1* (Oxford University Press 2011).

[79] Kramer analyses such phenomena in Kramer (n 73) 78–82. He does not, however, use the labels 'quasi-power', 'quasi-liability', and so forth; they have been proposed by him in a private communication. R. W. M. Dias analysed such phenomena earlier, calling this 'subjection'. R. W. M. Dias, *Jurisprudence* (3rd edn, Butterworths 1970).

[80] See for instance The Cambridge Declaration on Consciousness, according to which '[c]onvergent evidence indicates that non-human animals have the neuroanatomical, neurochemical, and neurophysiological substrates of conscious states along with the capacity to exhibit intentional behaviors'.

typically all sorts of legal consequences, such as giving that individual the power to sue the owner of the dog. This is why there is no reason for denying that animals could hold Hohfeldian powers. The matter may become clearer if we look at how powers differ from quasi-powers.

Both powers and quasi-powers can be expressed as if–then statements: if P, then change C in legal relations occurs. However, as regards powers, P is a volitional action or omission of an agent, whereas in the case of quasi-powers, such actions or omissions cannot be located. In fact, locating the cause of a change in legal relations that is not dependent on the use of a power is often difficult. If a bolt of lightning strikes a house and sets it ablaze, should the related legal consequences be traced back to the fire, or to the lightning, or to the electrostatic charge in the clouds? The problem of causation is not only a temporal one, but also a question of level: even if we managed to determine that, say, the relevant cause of the fire-related legal consequences is the events taking place in the thundercloud, we would still need to determine whether to approach the event at the level of electrons, molecules, or clouds.[81] The question of who or what exercised a given power, on the other hand, is in most cases easy to answer. In particular, the aforementioned problem of level usually does not arise, because we treat volitional beings as wholes: whether John or his hand exercised a legal power when signing a contract is a silly question because the hand is not a volitional entity.[82] (There are of course some situations where the volitionality of an action may be truly unclear, or it may be questioned whether a legal change actually is the result of an action or not.)

So where should the line be drawn? Who or what can perform volitional actions and thus exercise Hohfeldian powers? I maintain that any being to which we can attribute motivational states should be considered a potential power-wielder. Let us begin here by noting the three features of agency proposed by Christian List and Philip Pettit:

> First feature. [An agent] has representational states that depict how things are in the environment.
>
> Second feature. It has motivational states that specify how it requires things to be in the environment.
>
> Third feature. It has the capacity to process its representational and motivational states, leading it to intervene suitably in the environment whenever that environment fails to match a motivating specification.[83]

[81] A similar point is made by Christopher Stone: '[W]hen the Nile overflows, is it the "responsibility" of the river? The mountains? The snow? The hydrologic cycle?' Christopher D. Stone, *Should Trees Have Standing? Law, Morality, and the Environment* (3rd edn, Oxford University Press 2010) 17.

[82] Group agents are a special case where there are two levels of volition.

[83] Christian List and Philip Pettit, *Group Agency: The Possibility, Design, and Status of Corporate Agents* (Oxford University Press 2011) 20.

List and Pettit add two more elements—favourable conditions and feasible limits—and reach their final definition:

> An agent is a system that has representational and motivational states such that in favorable conditions, within feasible limits, it acts for the satisfaction of its motivations according to its representations.[84]

The definition is very useful, and sheds light on this issue. It should be applied to entities whose behaviour is best explained by making reference to their representations and intentions; therefore, even relatively simple animals can still be wielding legal powers. However, at some point agency becomes unnecessary in explaining events—even if we may imagine some kind of 'purpose' or 'intention' behind the ways in which plants and bacteria react to their environment, the ascription to them of motivational states is rather meaningless. I am here alluding to three predictive stances, as laid out by Daniel Dennett, which can be employed when predicting the behaviour of an entity: the *intentional stance*, the *physical stance*, and the *design stance*.[85]

When we take the intentional stance, we make reference to an entity's beliefs, desires, and intentions in order to explain and predict its actions, instead of referring to a purely physical explanation. The behaviour of a human being can (in theory) be explained wholly by making reference to his or her physical composition—neurons firing in the brain, and so on—but even if the physical stance could be used for this purpose in practice, it would still be a highly ineffective way of explanation; one could not perform all the calculations in a reasonable time. This is why we primarily use the intentional stance to explain the behaviour of people and many nonhuman animals, even if it can be supplemented by the physical stance in special cases (for instance when a brain tumour leads to odd behaviour). The design stance is in between the two other stances: when using the design stance, we make reference to the 'purpose' or design of an entity to understand and predict its behaviour. Certain authors have argued—correctly, in my opinion—that the design stance actually includes two stances: the intentional designer stance, which makes reference to the intentions of the entity's designer, and the teleological design stance, which merely assumes that the entity has 'parts with functions relative to some purpose'.[86] The intentional designer stance can be used to understand human artefacts, such as a television or a computer, whereas the teleological design stance can explain for instance the functioning of bodily organs as the products of natural selection. See Table 2.2 for a description of the stances.

It is quite natural to conclude that Hohfeldian powers (as opposed to quasi-powers) are readily ascribable only to intentional beings, as only such beings can form volitions—which are central to Hohfeld's definition of power. Human beings

[84] Ibid. [85] Daniel Dennett, *The Intentional Stance* (MIT Press 1987).

[86] Pieter E Vermaas and others, 'The Design Stance and Its Artefacts' (2013) 190 Synthese 1131, 1136–7.

Table 2.2 Four different stances

Stance	Predictions based on
1. Physical stance	The physical make-up of an entity
2a. Intentional designer stance	The intentions of the designer of an entity (e.g. thermostat, computer program)
2b. Teleological design stance	The functioning of an entity (such as bodily organs) in relation to an assumed goal or purpose
3. Intentional stance	The beliefs, goals, and intentions of an entity

and many nonhuman animals are therefore capable of wielding Hohfeldian powers, and I will argue in Chapter 5 that we can also ascribe motivational states to organized human collectivities.

Artificial intelligences (AIs) will chiefly be addressed in Chapter 6, but I should briefly address whether AIs could hold Hohfeldian powers. One should not ascribe intentionality to AI unless one's doing so is the best way to explain its behaviour.[87] This is my point of contention with Pettit and List: they claim that 'a small robotic device' that 'scans the area with its bug-like eyes, then moves about and, using its mechanical limbs, puts any cylinders lying on their side into an upright position' would already qualify as an agent because we can ascribe beliefs, desires, and intentions to it.[88] However, the intentional designer stance would likely be far more suitable. In fact, I am uncertain as to whether there are any robots or software that, as of now, would qualify as subjects of the intentional stance. Robots' behaviour is determined exactly by their programming, which is why the intentional designer stance is *pro tanto* most appropriate in their case. However, this will likely change at some point, especially with the introduction of new ways of programming, such as neural networks that involve letting the program learn 'on its own'. Samir Chopra and Laurence White point out that a 'complex artificial agent could especially aptly be the subject of the intentional stance if even its original programmer or designer, the one with the best knowledge of its innards, would find it a better predictive strategy than any other'.[89] Such an entity would most likely have to be treated as a potential holder of Hohfeldian powers.

Let us conclude our discussion of Hohfeldian powers. These positions can be attributed not only to human beings but also to some nonhuman animals. The domain of disabilities mirrors the domain of powers. Disabilities can only exist in situations where powers can potentially be found. The holders of disabilities must therefore meet the criteria of intentionality that were recounted above.

[87] Samir Chopra and Laurence F. White, *A Legal Theory for Autonomous Artificial Agents* (University of Michigan Press 2011) 12–17.

[88] List and Pettit (n 83) 19.

[89] Chopra and White (n 87) 14.

The other two higher-order jural positions—immunities and liabilities—are not independent categories, as they can only be held in relation to lower-level elements. For instance, if I have the liberty to φ, then I also hold either an immunity or a liability, pertaining to my liberty, towards each potential power-holder. The domains of liabilities and immunities are therefore always dependent on the lower-level categories.

For the sake of completeness, I should briefly address the 'quasi-positions' as well. The domain of quasi-powers and quasi-disabilities—that is, which non-intentional entities are capable of effectuating changes in legal relations—need not be explored in depth here, as such juridical positions are clearly irrelevant with regard to legal personhood. Quasi-liabilities and quasi-immunities must, however, be attributed to Hohfeldian parties.[90] For example, for every individual from whom I will not inherit anything at the event of their non-volitional death, I have a quasi-immunity pertaining to my non-inheritance. (I of course also have an immunity that I will not inherit anything from them in case of volitional death.[91]) Such quasi-positions are, however, dependent on lower-level positions, just like immunities and liabilities.

Duties and liberties

It is very often simply assumed that animals cannot bear legal duties. The main reason behind such assertions is likely that in order for a duty to be reasonable, the duty-bearer must in most cases be able to fulfil and understand the duty. However, this condition is not always met even with human beings: legal systems increase constantly in complexity, and it seems unlikely that all people of sound mind actually understand every duty that concerns them. If they nevertheless bear these duties, one will need to concur that the understanding of duties is not necessarily a precondition for bearing them.[92] If understanding duties is not a precondition for bearing them, then why couldn't certain animals and infants also bear duties?[93]

How could the duty-bearing of animals and infants be approached? We should firstly note the distinction that Kramer makes between nominal and genuine rights, and their counterparts, nominal and genuine duties.[94] Duties are generally enforced

[90] We can of course also think of 'quasi-quasi-liabilities' and 'quasi-quasi-immunities', which are held by non-agent entities in relation to the quasi-powers of non-agent entities. For instance, when a smoke detector detects smoke, it triggers the legal duty for firemen to arrive. Hence, the smoke detector has a quasi-quasi-liability towards the quasi-power of the smoke. The usefulness of these quasi-quasi-positions in legal (or other) analysis is quite doubtful.

[91] This immunity is held towards any potential killers.

[92] There may very well exist legal and moral precepts such as 'ought implies can', but these are not conceptually necessary.

[93] Kramer is one of the few who claim that animals can indeed bear legal duties. Kramer (n 26) and Kramer (n 21).

[94] Kramer (n 9) 9 and Kramer (n 21) 65–73.

through several different means, but genuine duties are legally enforceable. Mark R. Reiff recounts six means of enforcement of restraints:

- physical force,
- strategic power,
- moral condemnation and regret,
- social criticism and the withdrawal of social cooperation,
- automatic sanctions, and
- legal remedies.[95]

Even in the case of nominal duties, some of these means of enforcement can very well be used: one may regret that one has breached one's nominal duty, and the breach may be subject to social criticism. Nominal duties can also be backed up through exercises of various legal liberties—such as the liberties to speak critically—which may be used to pressure the duty-bearer to comply. Obviously, enforcement in these extended senses is not what separates nominal duties from genuine duties; the most important factor is whether legal remedies, backed ultimately by the coercive force of the state, exist.[96] I focus on two types of such legal remedies: forced compliance and punishment.

Forced compliance is at the same time straightforward and difficult. It is straightforward in that animals can obviously be forced to comply with different kinds of requirements: they can be locked in cages, and dogs can be put on leashes to stop them running away. On the other hand, being a potential subject of this kind of physical enforcement does not really seem to serve as a hallmark of a capacity for duty-bearing. If every entity that can be physically enforced to 'comply' were a duty-bearer, then crash-test dummies could have the duty to sit in cars and endure the testing, and marionettes could be obligated to perform in puppet plays. A concept of duty that extends the domain of duty-bearers to inanimate pieces of plastic is not tenable; hence, being potentially subject to forced compliance is not a sufficient condition for inclusion in that domain. However, liability to sanctions is a different matter. Hence, I will use the following method to determine who or what can bear duties. If at least one of the generally accepted rationales of punishment applies to a group of beings, then it is meaningful to hold those beings as potential duty-bearers.

Punishments can be based on backward-looking and forward-looking rationales. The principal form of backward-looking justification of sanctions is retributive: wrongful acts call for just deserts. Sanctions based on retributivist reasoning raise serious moral questions in connection with animals. As animals are generally not

[95] Mark R. Reiff, *Punishment, Compensation and Law: A Theory of Enforceability* (Cambridge University Press 2005) 17–40.

[96] Kramer makes a similar point, as well: 'A genuine right or claim is enforceable. (Unlike a purely moral claim—which is also enforceable in certain ways—a genuine legal claim is enforceable through the mobilizing of governmental coercion, if necessary.)' Kramer (n 9) 9.

considered moral agents, can any ethical theory claim that they would get their just deserts for their non-compliance? Even the retributive punishment of animals can be understandable: human beings can wrongfully but intelligibly decide to punish animals in ways that cannot be founded on consequentalism. For example, a group of hunters may set out to kill a bear that has caused the death of a fellow hunter, even if it is obvious that the bear (living in a remote location) would not pose any danger to the community in the future. In such a situation, the killing could not be grounded on the danger posed by the bear's aggressive nature, or on similar consequentalist justifications. However, one may also wish to commit similar acts of 'retribution' toward inanimate objects, such as a stinging nettle or a sharp rock. Depending on the definition of retribution, 'punishing' inanimate objects is probably a category mistake, as actions cannot even be attributed to them, and the 'punishment' would not matter to them.[97] On the other hand, although the infliction of retributive sanctions on animals may be understandable, it typically is wrongful, as such creatures are generally not morally responsible to the degree required under any modern retributive theory of punishment. Hence, the retributivist rationale for punishment cannot ground the duty-bearing of animals. What about the prospective rationales?

There are two primary rationales that are based on forward-looking reasoning: deterrence and incapacitation.[98] I will focus on deterrence here. A deterrence-oriented punishment is specific (being directed at an entity that has already breached a duty) or general (being directed at duty-bearers at large). Specific deterrence of an animal is feasible if the animal is able to understand the connection between the sanction and the prohibited type of conduct. Any animal trainer knows that sanctions are only effective if the sanction or reward follows shortly after the action or omission in question. It is doubtful that simply the abstract threat of sanctions would have a deterrent effect on animals. General deterrence may regardless work on many nonhuman creatures. An electric fence may keep a flock of animals within their designated area. If the animals learn of this only through personal experience, the deterrence may be called specific, but if they also learn by watching their fellow creatures' spasms of pain, the effect is indeed a rudimentary form of general deterrence.[99]

[97] It could of course be a moral error as well if, for instance, rocks were regularly 'punished' for assault instead of the people who throw them at other people.

[98] Other rationales have also been identified, such as the denunciatory rationale. See Matthew H. Kramer, *The Ethics of Capital Punishment: A Philosophical Investigation of Evil and its Consequences* (Oxford University Press 2011) 155–78.

[99] Social animals also punish each other. See T. H. Clutton-Brock and G. A. Parker, 'Punishment in Animal Societies' (1995) 373 *Nature* 209, 209:

> In social animals, retaliatory aggression is common, individuals often punish other group members that infringe their interests, and punishment can cause subordinates to desist from behaviour likely to reduce the fitness of dominant animals. Punishing strategies are used to establish and maintain dominance relationships, to discourage parasites and cheats, to discipline offspring or prospective sexual partners and to maintain cooperative behaviour.

What of infants and foetuses? Children start to accumulate the capabilities required of a duty-bearer at some point; a clear threshold is probably impossible to determine. At some point—perhaps in toddler years, perhaps earlier—a child starts to be able to react to sanctions and can therefore bear duties to the same degree that animals can bear duties. However, the thresholds of morality and intelligibility are clearly different: it is not unintelligible—but morally highly dubious—to require that 12-year-olds should take care of their alcoholic parents, whereas imposing such a duty on a 2-week-old infant would not make sense at all. This is partly an empirical question; perhaps the infant can understand some sanctions that are imposed upon it, but this seems unlikely. *If* requirements can indeed be communicated to 2-week-olds, then they can perhaps be communicated to sufficiently developed foetuses as well. Why should the threshold be drawn at the moment of birth? Foetuses kick in wombs, which may very well be painful for the gestating women. If it is possible to communicate to them somehow that this conduct is to be eschewed, we can think of foetuses as having duties as well. However, such a prospect is fanciful.

To conclude, it does seem possible to impose duties upon animals and young children, accompanied by deterrence-oriented punishments. This discussion has of course not been comprehensive. However, for present purposes it suffices to state that the idea of genuine legal duties borne by animals and young children is not conceptually absurd, and they should therefore not be ruled out of the domain of legal duties. Of course, even if animals and young children can bear duties, the number of potential duties that they could *reasonably* bear would be considerably lower than the number of duties reasonably borne by adult human beings of sound mind.

The considerations above can be generalized somewhat. A part of the explanation why animals and children can be punished—and can hold legal duties—is that they can perform volitional acts. Legal responsibility is intimately connected with acts: X's criminal and/or civil responsibility may only become actual when X's actions or omissions do not correspond to a standard. There are of course instances of vicarious liability, where one can be held responsible for the acts of one's subordinates. However, one must be a relatively sophisticated agent, capable of performing acts, in order to have subordinates at all. In addition, punishment involves the imposition of some detriment or the withholding of some benefit. Thus, one must be able to benefit and suffer detriment in order to be punished. Finally, there must be a way to communicate the relevant legal requirements to the entity in question. The requirements can be communicated by using language or by the use of sanctions directly.

Liberties—the jural opposites of duties—are about 'the conduct—the act(s) or the omissions(s)—in which the liberty-holder has engaged or in which the liberty-holder is permitted to engage'.[100] A liberty is a permission and hence the negation of

[100] Kramer (n 73) 75.

a duty. A liberty is, consequently, aptly ascribable to an entity only if the negation of that liberty would be aptly ascribable—as a duty—to that entity. The domain of potential liberty-holders is thus coextensive with the domain of potential duty-bearers.

Finally, I will address the jural opposite of claim-right: no-right.

No-rights

As I noted above, claim-rights—or rights, as defined in interest theories—can be attributed to entities that are of ultimate value.[101] However, should the domain of no-rights simply mirror the domain of claim-rights, or should it have an independent domain?

It is not obvious when a lack of claim-rights constitutes no-rights. We should first note that a no-right is not the same thing as the lack of a claim-right. Even if a rock does not hold the claim-right-that-it-not-be-smashed-by-Y, this does not mean that the rock would hold a no-right pertaining to Y's smashing-of-the-rock.[102] The lack of X's claim-right to Y's φ-ing can depend on three different reasons:

1. Y does not have the duty to φ.
2. Regardless of whether Y has the duty to φ, some or all of the other criteria of the interest theory do not obtain (the duty to φ is not/would not be, on balance, in X's interests or Bentham's test is not met, etc).
3. X is not a potential holder of legal claim-rights.

If only condition 1 obtains, then it is relatively straightforward that X has a no-right concerning Y's not φ-ing. If policemen are allowed to shoot citizens at will, then the citizens have a no-right concerning the policemen's shooting them at will. However, the situation is not as obvious in situations where condition 2 obtains. If I am at liberty to take care of my children, does that mean that a person living in a distant part of the world, whom I have never met, has a no-right concerning my taking care of my children? If I do not have the duty to provide for a Japanese child whom I've never met, then does an elephant living in Africa have a no-right concerning my not providing for the child? Well, yes. Even if recounting such relations is usually not necessary for a legal analysis of a given situation, they do follow from Hohfeld's scheme. Just as certain claim-rights are held 'against the world', the same applies to an even greater number of no-rights.

However, condition 3 is the most relevant one here. Who or what can hold no-rights at all? No-rights are ascribable if Y *could* bear the duty-to-φ towards X, but currently does not bear that duty. This is why rocks cannot hold no-rights: as duties cannot be borne towards rocks (because rocks cannot hold claim-rights), there is no need for no-rights as 'placeholders' for potential claim-rights.

[101] Again, there are some exceptions, such as collectivities.

[102] Somewhat more formally, 'X holds a no-right pertaining to Y's φ-ing' is not logically equivalent to 'It is not the case that X holds a claim-right to Y's not φ-ing'.

To sum up, no-rights obtain whenever claim-rights are non-existent but possible, and no-rights can only be held by entities that can hold claim-rights. Determining the domain of no-rights is therefore dependent on ethical conclusions just as with claim-rights. If animals and foetuses can hold claim-rights—as I think they can—then they can also hold no-rights.

Legal Nonpersons and Legal Relations

We have determined the domains of all the Hohfeldian categories. Now we may examine the Capacity-for-Rights and Capacity-for-Legal-Relations doctrines. According to them respectively, only legal persons can occupy either (1) the Hohfeldian positions that are classifiable as rights according to the rights theories examined here, or (2) any of the Hohfeldian positions.

As noted above, certain writers assume that Hohfeldian legal relations only exist between legal persons. Steven Wise in particular has pressed this point. Now that the domains of the Hohfeldian concepts have been determined, we can conclude that this view is not correct, as nonpersons participate in all sorts of legal relations. Indeed, the existence of entities which *can* participate in Hohfeldian relations but *do not* is conceptually impossible: even if a slave is devoid of all claim-rights and duties, she will still hold no-rights and liberties. This makes one question what Wise actually means by his concept of 'legal personhood'. Wise has devised an animal rights pyramid (Figure 2.1) whose first step is 'legal personhood', which is some kind of requirement for actually possessing legal rights:

Legal personhood in Wise's meaning is a highly problematic concept. It precedes right-holding, so Wise does not think right-holding and legal personhood are synonymous. However, neither does it refer to a being's status as a *potential* right-holder, as Wise clearly thinks animals *can* possess legal rights even if they do not. So Wise's legal personhood seems to be some legal attribute that 'makes one count' as a participant in legal relations—an attribute that can be bestowed

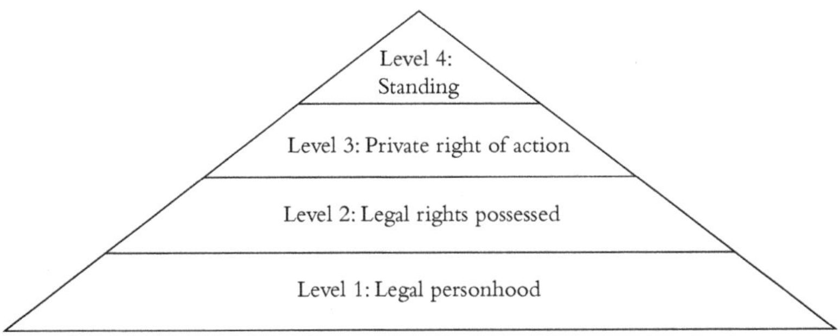

Figure 2.1 The 'animal rights pyramid' according to Steven Wise. (Note: Steven M. Wise, 'Legal Personhood and the Nonhuman Rights Project' (2010) 17 *Animal Law Review* 1, 2).

by the legislator or a judge. As noted, this is conceptually impossible: slaves were parties in Hohfeldian legal relations regardless of whether they were legal persons. However, Wise has an idiosyncratic view of Hohfeldian relations. First, he claims that '[b]ecause [Hohfeldian relations] can exist only between two legal persons and one thing, and all nonhuman animals are things, no jural relationships can presently exist between a human being and a nonhuman animal.'[103] This is a peculiar view of the analysis. It is not supported by an exegesis of Hohfeld's work. Hohfeld did of course use the word 'person' in his writings, but more or less synonymously with 'human being' (see above, subsection 'Hohfeld and Persons'). There is no reason to assume that he would, for instance, have intended to exclude slaves from his scheme. Nor did he claim that every legal relation would obtain between two legal persons and one thing, unless by 'thing' is meant 'conduct'. Overall, it is very unclear what Wise means when insisting that any Hohfeldian relation concerns one thing, given that he also uses 'thing' and 'legal thing' to describe the current legal status of nonhuman animals as chattels. A given Hohfeldian relation may of course pertain to a thing *qua* chattel—as with my duty-not-to-steal-your-wallet—but there are numerous Hohfeldian relations that have nothing to do with chattels, such as my duty-not-to-punch-you.[104] (In addition, higher-level Hohfeldian relations are best understood as obtaining between three or four Hohfeldian parties rather than two. But that is a minor issue that is of no consequence here.)

Second, Wise asserts that all Hohfeldian legal relations involve a beneficiary: '[o]ne of the two persons always has a legal advantage; the other always bears the corresponding legal detriment.'[105] This is misguided, as simply being a party in a Hohfeldian relation does not yet mean that one either benefits or suffers detriment because of this. Hohfeld did of course note that in everyday legal parlance 'a right' can refer to any sort of legal advantage, but this observation is not reflected in his scheme in the way asserted by Wise. One's having a liability, for instance, may be beneficial, detrimental, or neutral: the liability of a criminal to be sentenced to death is detrimental, whereas the liability of a life convict to be paroled is beneficial. In addition, a given legal relation may be beneficial or detrimental to both or all parties. The legal power of a creditor to extend the due date of a debt may be beneficial for both the creditor and the debtor, if the original due date would have caused

[103] Wise (n 8) 80.

[104] Hegel did maintain that all rights pertain to things. He took the Kantian division of rights into the rights of things, rights of persons, and 'personal rights of a real kind' to be mistaken because 'rights of *every* kind can belong only to a person, and seen objectively, a right based on a contract is not a right over a person, but only something external to the person or something which the person can dispose of, i.e. always a thing'. G.W. F. Hegel, *Elements of the Philosophy of Right* (Allen W. Wood ed., Cambridge University Press 1991) 72.

[105] Wise (n 8) 801.

the debtor to run into severe financial difficulties and would thus have undermined his ability to pay the debt.

Wise's nonstandard understanding of Hohfeldian legal relations seems to actually correspond with the anything-beneficial conception of rights that I presented above, according to which any beneficial legal relation is a right. However, animals, foetuses, and slaves *are* parties in beneficial legal relations. They hold numerous claim-rights, and it is of course beneficial for animals that they have immunities against being subjected to the kind of animal trials that were conducted during the Middle Ages. (Someone might baulk at this example, but the immunities are rights according to the anything-beneficial conception.)

Wise's conception of legal personhood is similar to Continental views where legal personhood is explained as the capacity to participate in legal relations. For instance, according to the German Civil Code, children become legal persons at the completion of birth. However, this clearly does not consist in merely endowing the child with the *capacity* to possess 'at least one legal right' (as Wise has put it), but in actually granting numerous legal entitlements to him or her. For instance, the right-to-life of born children is considerably more robust than the right-to-life of third-trimester foetuses—killing a foetus is not a homicide in most Western jurisdictions, whereas killing a newborn typically is.

I maintain—*pace* Wise—that legal personhood *presupposes*, and is not synonymous with, the capacity to participate in Hohfeldian legal relations. This can be illuminated with an example. Think of a society where, because of a very high infant mortality rate, children are not considered viable until their first birthday. Many legal procedures that in our societies are typically undertaken after birth are in this society performed when the child has turned one. Instead of a birth certificate, a viability certificate is issued; the child's records are entered into a population register, and the child becomes a legal person. Would it make sense to say that the child completely lacked the capacity to occupy any Hohfeldian positions before this moment? It would not—not only could many different kinds of legal positions have been extended to the child even before this, but he or she already held such positions, such as liberties and immunities.

However, there is also a sense in which the Capacity-for-Legal-Relations view is appealing. One should here distinguish between two modern senses of 'legal relation'. The phrase can firstly be used to refer to a Hohfeldian, atomic relation. This is a more technical sense that encompasses all areas of law. However, there is also a more everyday sense of 'legal relation', which is used in private law to refer to a bundle of Hohfeldian positions between two or more individuals or corporations, pertaining to a private-law institution. For instance, it is commonplace to talk of *a* contractual relation between two parties, such as a buyer and a seller, even though this relation is from the Hohfeldian perspective typically an array of duties, claim-rights, powers, immunities, and so on. The Capacity-for-Rights and the Capacity-for-Legal-Relations views do indeed have some explanatory power in the field of private law, if we use 'legal relation' in its nontechnical sense. This is consistent with the genealogy of the Capacity-for-Legal-Relations view: Savigny was the first jurist to propose this view in his *System*, which was an exposition of private law.

This non-Hohfeldian view of legal relations can be explicated in terms of Hart's idea of *special rights*, which 'arise out of special transactions between individuals or out of some special relationship in which they stand to each other' and where 'the persons who have the right and those who have the corresponding obligation are limited to the parties to the special transaction or relationship'.[106] A large number of such relations are only recognized and enforced by legal systems if they arise between legal persons. For instance, slaves could typically not enter into legally enforceable contracts, such as marriage. In this sense, the abolition of slavery involved granting the slaves the capacity to hold certain legally enforceable special rights. Here we need to distinguish the *conceptual* and the *legal* capacity to hold special rights. Rocks lack the *conceptual* capacity to hold special rights because they cannot hold any legal positions, and there is nothing the legislator can do about that. Slaves, on the other hand, lacked the *legal* capacity to hold such rights because the legal system did not, for instance, enforce their agreements. But, contrastingly, the legislator could have done—indeed, should have done—something about that.

The idea of special rights connects to what MacCormick calls *passive transactional capacity*, meaning the '[c]apacity to take the benefit or the burden created through a certain transaction'.[107] The capacity to hold special rights is, however, only one element of legal personhood: when slaves were freed, they received not only the powers and liabilities to enter into contracts, but also for instance the rights to life and bodily integrity (held by free people) that they had lacked earlier. I will return to this issue in Chapter 3.

Conclusion

The Hohfeldian analysis shows us that animals and slaves can partake in legal relations in many of the ways that human beings can, and that legal nonpersons can hold rights, or—if one endorses the will theory—that legal persons do not necessarily hold any rights. In order to solve this conflict between the Orthodox View and the widely shared extensional beliefs concerning legal personhood, we must adjust either our theory of legal personhood or our extensional beliefs.

The theory of rights that corresponds best with the extensional beliefs is probably Hart's later will theory, which allowed for children's rights. However, even Hart's account falls short of a perfect correspondence with the extensional beliefs: his

[106] Hart (n 44) 183.

[107] Neil MacCormick, *Institutions of Law: An Essay in Legal Theory* (Oxford University Press 2007) 86.

account either denies rights and thus legal personhood to mentally disabled individuals, or allows that some nonhuman animals are already legal persons—namely those animals that are beneficiaries of pet trusts. Hart's theory would nevertheless probably be the best theory of rights on which to construct a defence of the Orthodox View. However, this brings us to a major problem with that view: it is based on a contested concept. Hart's theory is only one of the numerous theories of rights that have been propounded in analytic jurisprudence. Even if one managed to achieve an account of rights that adequately captures the extensional beliefs regarding legal personhood, the account could be rejected (and would be rejected by many scholars) as faulty on independent grounds.

Relatedly, the positions I criticize often ignore dissimilarities between different areas of law. For instance, the Capacity-for-Rights view does have some application in the field of private law, which it was originally intended to clarify. It does make some sense to say that legal persons are 'empty slots' for private-law rights and duties, to use Tur's expression. However, this explanation is unsuitable as a general theory of legal personhood. To restate one of the many problems of this explanation, foetal personhood amendments do not purport to give foetuses the *capacity* to be empty slots for rights and duties, but rather protect them directly.

One should also mention how the current theory structures legal thought. In everyday legal parlance the term 'right' is often used indiscriminately to refer to both interest-theory and will-theory rights. Very few lawyers or judges would likely deny the existence of the right-not-to-be-tortured, even though it is not a right according to most will theories. However, because animals are not legal persons and because supposedly only legal persons can hold rights, jurists are often hesitant to call similar legal protections that prohibit the torture of animals 'rights'. One thus sees dissimilarity where there is uniformity because of the prevalent theory.

Finally, the simplistic, binary nature of the current theory also obfuscates the fact that an entity can simultaneously be a legal person for some purposes and a legal nonperson for others. Slaves held some rights and bore numerous duties, but is this reason enough to claim that slaves were legal persons *tout court*, without any qualifications? Similarly, if we wish to understand the gradual improvement of women's legal status in various jurisdictions using the conceptual scheme of legal personhood, we cannot rely on a binary account of the scheme—the status of women was in general inferior to that of men, but it was also clearly better than that of slaves and nonhuman animals. Understanding legal personhood as a cluster property, consisting of distinct incidents, allows for a more nuanced picture. That is what the rest of the book sets out to do.

PART II

The Bundle Theory

3

The Incidents of Legal Personhood

Preliminaries

In this chapter, and the rest of the book, I set out to develop a novel way of understanding legal personhood. The Bundle Theory of legal personhood can account for and explain the extensional beliefs regarding legal personhood while at the same time avoiding the pitfalls of the Orthodox View. This chapter will be focused on presenting the individual incidents, whereas Chapter 4 will focus on issues such as the domain of legal personhood and the active/passive distinction.

My theory is—to my knowledge—the first modern and wide-ranging theory of legal personhood that explicitly rejects all the formulations of the Orthodox View. I should regardless acknowledge that some authors have propounded views that are not straightforwardly reducible to that position. For instance, Jonas-Sébastien Beaudry writes:

> The strategy of claiming legal personhood would allow animals to get direct access to the special category of 'persons' which legal systems associate with a plethora of the most robust kinds of protections and rights. [...] Granting legal personhood is fundamentally different from granting 'weak' legal rights, protections or entitlements, insofar as legislators can posit various rules protecting any object without endorsing the idea that these objects are 'persons' or matter for their own sake.[1]

[1] Jonas-Sébastien Beaudry, 'From Autonomy to Habes Corpus: Animal Rights Activists Take the Parameters of Legal Personhood to Court' [2016] *Global Journal of Animal Law* 3, 5–6. Some other authors who tacitly reject the Orthodox View of legal personhood include David Favre and Tomasz Pietrzykowski. Favre writes that 'animals, or at least some animals, already possess limited legal rights', and Pietrzykowski distinguishes 'legal persons' and 'non-personal subjects of rights'. David Favre, 'Living Property: A New Status for Animals Within the Legal System' (2010) 93 *Marquette Law Review* 1021, 1024, and Tomasz Pietrzykowski, 'Beyond Personhood: From Two Conceptions of Rights to Two Kinds of Right-Holders' in Tomasz Pietrzykowski and Brunello Stancioli (eds), *New Approaches to the Personhood in Law* (Peter Lang 2016). See also Tomasz Pietrzykowski, 'The Idea of Non-personal Subjects of Law' in Visa A. J. Kurki and Tomasz Pietrzykowski (eds), *Legal Personhood: Animals, Artificial Intelligence and the Unborn* (Springer 2017).

This is a departure from the Orthodox View, even if Beaudry does not address his divergence from that view. Some other authors have employed the phrase 'personhood rights' as well, while nevertheless subscribing to the Orthodox View.[2]

I bring up yet again the main extensional beliefs that a theory of legal personhood should at least explain:

(i) human beings who meet the criteria of passive natural personality (born, alive, and sentient) are legal persons;
(ii) animals and foetuses are not legal persons, and slaves were not legal persons;
(iii) there are some relevant legal differences between the legal personhood of adults of sound mind and that of infants and severely mentally disabled individuals;
(iv) there are artificial persons, such as corporations.

How can a theory best account for these beliefs? I should first mention one thing Legalists got right: legal personhood is not an intrinsic attribute of an entity; rather, a necessary condition for the legal personhood of any entity is that that entity is treated as a legal person by the prevailing legal system. Whether or not X is a legal person is thus an *institutional fact*. Claiming otherwise would imply that one's legal personhood cannot be changed by legal norms and decisions, and such an account would be unable to explain phenomena such as slavery and corporations, which clearly have to do with legal decisions: slaves can be freed and corporations founded and dissolved. The labels 'natural person' and 'artificial person' can in this regard be misleading because—as Neil MacCormick puts it—'[t]he so-called "natural person" is in its legal personhood necessarily as juristic as the so called "juristic" person'.[3] Natural personhood as a legal category depends on legal decisions just as much as artificial personhood.

There are of course conceivable ways of using the phrase 'legal person' that would not make reference to a legal status. A Kantian theorist could employ 'legal person' to refer to a being that possesses Kantian moral personhood as well as the cognitive and linguistic capacities in order to be able exercise his, her, or its rights legally. 'Legal person' can also plausibly refer to the idea of human beings presupposed by the law or by a branch of law, as in the phrase 'criminal law's person'.[4] One could in this context criticize the law for, say, having too rational an understanding of human beings. I am not saying such usages are wrong, but if we wish to understand the legal

[2] Jessica Berg, 'Of Elephants and Embryos: A Proposed Framework for Legal Personhood' (2007) 59 *Hastings Law Journal* 369, 376f.

[3] Neil MacCormick, 'Persons as Institutional Facts' in Ota Weinberger and Werner Krawietz (eds), *Reine Rechtslehre im Spiegel ihrer Fortsetzer und Kritiker* (Springer 1988) 371.

[4] See for instance Ngaire Naffine, 'Legal Persons as Abstractions' in Visa A. J. Kurki and Tomasz Pietrzykowski (eds), *Legal Personality: Animals, Artificial Intelligence and the Unborn* (Springer 2017) and William Lucy, *Law's Judgement* (Hart Publishing 2017), 35–78.

institutions of slavery and corporate personhood, or if we wish to grasp what the Nonhuman Rights Project is demanding, we must treat legal personhood as a status that can be bestowed and taken away by the legal system.

However, Legalists have provided simplistic accounts of the institutional nature of legal personhood. X's legal personhood cannot be said to depend on any single characteristic; legal personhood is rather a cluster property. This central feature of the Bundle Theory will be addressed next.

Legal Personhood as a Cluster Property

Describing legal personhood as a cluster property is, in fact, rather popular. This description is used by Ngaire Naffine and Richard Tur, among others.[5] However, these accounts typically rely on a nonstandard understanding of what a cluster property is. Naffine writes:

> [L]egal personality is made up of a cluster of things: specifically, it comprises single or multiple clusters of rights and/or duties, depending on the nature and purpose of a particular legal relation. Rights and duties [...] can come in thick and thin bundles, in larger and smaller clusters, which means that we are actually different legal persons in different legal contexts.[6]

What Naffine means by 'contexts' here is for instance that foetuses hold fewer rights than adults. Hence, the cluster-property nature of legal personhood means, according to Naffine, that different legal persons can hold different rights and bear different duties. She then notes that legal personhood in this regard resembles ownership, which can be understood as separate but connected incidents such as possession, liberty to use, and so on.

The legal person of Naffine and Tur is, however, not a cluster property in any ordinary sense. The phrase denotes standardly a property whose extension is determined based on a weighted list of criteria, none of which alone is necessary or sufficient.[7] Ownership according to the bundle-of-rights analysis is a cluster property. For instance, the fact that John is permitted to use a car counts as a reason towards the conclusion that he owns the car, but it is not a sufficient reason to conclude that he owns the car because he could simply have rented it. On the other hand, John's being prohibited from using the car is an insufficient reason to conclude that he

[5] Ngaire Naffine, *Law's Meaning of Life: Philosophy, Religion, Darwin and the Legal Person* (Hart Publishing 2009) 46–7; Richard Tur, 'The "Person" in Law' in Arthur Peacocke and Grant Gillett (eds), *Persons and Personality: A Contemporary Inquiry.* (Basil Blackwell 1988) 121–2. Jens David Ohlin describes legal personality as a cluster concept as well, though he uses 'cluster concept' in a somewhat different sense to Naffine and Tur. Jens David Ohlin, 'Is the Concept of the Person Necessary for Human Rights?' (2005) 105 *Columbia Law Review* 209, 229ff.

[6] Naffine (n 5) 46.

[7] See John R. Searle, 'Proper Names' (1958) 67 *Mind* 166. What *is* necessary and sufficient is a disjunction of certain proper subsets of the set of cluster properties.

does *not* own the car, because he could have rented it out. But the Orthodox View—subscribed to by Naffine and Tur—*does* provide necessary and sufficient criteria for an entity's legal personhood. One is a legal person if and only if one holds legal rights and/or bears legal duties.[8] The mere fact that legal persons are diverse in their instantiations does not mean that legal personhood would be a cluster property in this standard sense of the phrase. The analogy between legal personhood (according to the Orthodox View) and ownership would work if the cluster-property nature of ownership depended on the fact that different persons can own different types of things and different numbers of things. But this is not the reason why ownership is a cluster property.

Legal personhood according to the theory offered here is a cluster property in the ordinary sense, as it consists of interconnected but disseverable incidents. There is no exact border between legal personhood and nonpersonhood. The incidents can, however, be grouped in various ways.[9]

The first relevant distinction in this regard is between active and passive legal personhood: infants and adults are both legal persons, but to different degrees. This bifurcation is very widely recognized. For instance, MacCormick maintains that legal personhood has passive and active elements. He then proceeds to classify the capacities of legal persons into four categories:[10]

- *pure passive capacity*, denoting 'an entity's capability in law to be the beneficiary of some legal provision or provisions, in the sense that these provisions are interpreted as aiming at protecting such an entity from some harm or at advancing some interest or another of that entity';[11]
- *passive transactional capacity*, meaning the '[c]apacity to take the benefit or the burden created through a certain transaction', such as the capability of infants to own property;[12]
- *capacity responsibility*, which 'involves the question whether or not one can be subjected to criminal or civil liability to sanctions for one's acts';
- *transactional capacity, viz.* the capacity to perform acts-in-the-law with valid legal effects.[13]

[8] What follows after 'if and only if' depends somewhat on the specific formulation of the Orthodox View. For Tur, legal persons are 'empty slots' for rights and duties. Tur (n 5) 121.

[9] We can also distinguish legal personhood with regard to a particular incident or a set of incidents from legal personhood *tout court*, without qualifications. This distinction will be addressed later.

[10] The account was first outlined in the 1988 article MacCormick (n 3), which was later republished with some changes in MacCormick's last major work Neil MacCormick, *Institutions of Law: An Essay in Legal Theory* (Oxford University Press 2007) 77–99.

[11] MacCormick (n 10) 86. [12] Ibid. [13] Ibid. 93.

Table 3.1 The passive incidents of legal personhood

Substantive passive incidents	Remedy incidents
- fundamental protections: protection of life, liberty, and bodily integrity - capacity to be the beneficiary of special rights - capacity to own property - insusceptibility to being owned	- standing - victim status in criminal law - capacity to undergo legal harms

MacCormick's account is very insightful and considerably more nuanced than most of the theories presented earlier. It can also be commended for not explicitly subscribing to the tenets of the Orthodox View, even if MacCormick does not explicitly reject that view either. However, his account is lacking in detail, and it leaves out some important elements of legal personhood. I will offer a somewhat different classification.

Passive and Active Incidents

The passive incidents of legal personhood can be divided into two categories, laid out in Table 3.1.

The substantive incidents have chiefly to do with what non-procedural claim-rights and liabilities are held or can be acquired by an entity X. If X's life, liberty, and personal integrity are protected, then the number of duties owed by 'the world' towards X is larger than otherwise. If X has the capacity to be the beneficiary of special rights and the capacity to own property, then X can acquire special rights against determinate parties and ownership-related claim-rights 'against the world'. Finally, even though X *can* simultaneously be the property of someone else and endowed with numerous incidents of legal personhood, a certain tension exists between these two attributes. This tension will be analysed briefly later in this chapter.

The second group has to do with the legal remedies available to X if the duties held towards X are not respected. These include standing, which is (primarily) the capacity to demand the enforcement of one's claim-rights in court; the capacity to undergo legal harms, which may lead to restitution or compensation; and having a victim status in criminal law (comprising both substantive and procedural elements pertaining to criminal law).

In addition, active legal persons (such as adults of sound mind and, to a limited extent, sufficiently developed children) are endowed with incidents that are enumerated in Table 3.2.

Adults of sound mind can exercise legal competences in various legal contexts, whereas legal minors must generally have a representative. In addition, adults'

Table 3.2 The active incidents of legal personhood

Legal competences	Onerous legal personhood
- capacity to administer the other incidents without a representative, e.g. the capacity to enter into contracts	- criminal-law responsibility - tort-law responsibility - other types of legal responsibility

behaviour is regulated, for instance through criminal law, and they are held responsible for their behaviour (*onerous legal personhood*).

Similar features have been identified as central for active legal personhood by numerous legal scholars, including MacCormick and scholars writing in the German tradition.[14] Some legal traditions have also incorporated the active/passive distinction rather neatly into the Orthodox View, which explains legal personhood as the holding of legal rights. For instance, according to French taxonomy, all legal persons including children can 'enjoy' legal rights (*la capacité de jouissance*) whereas adults of sound mind can also 'exercise' their rights (*la capacité d'exercice*).[15] The latter capacity is roughly similar to what I term legal competences.

Before moving on to examine the individual incidents of legal personhood, I should make some general remarks. Despite the clustered nature of legal personhood, it is still not wholly reducible to its individual components. Much as the incidents of ownership together make ownership central to modern capitalist economies, the incidents of legal personhood are interconnected in numerous ways. These connections will be explored later, but I mention here the concept of *legal platform*, which will be salient in Chapter 4. A legal platform is a bundle of legal positions ('rights and duties') that are integrated. The legal positions' being integrated means that they are susceptible to being affected by each other in a certain manner: for instance, if John owns a house but incurs debts due to a contract he has entered, he may end up losing the house. On the other hand, if the debts are incurred by John's single-person corporation, he will likely not lose the house. The corporation and John's *natural legal platform* are thus two separate legal platforms.[16] Legal platforms are primarily administered through acts-in-the-law. Individuals who are *sui juris* take care of the administration themselves—though they may choose to delegate this responsibility—whereas minors are ordinarily represented in this regard by someone else.

[14] See ibid. 89–95, and Matthias Lehmann, 'Der Begriff der Rechtsfähigkeit' (2007) 207 *Archiv für die civilistische Praxis* 225, 226–7.

[15] See Gilles Goubeaux, *Traité de droit civil. Les personnes* (Librairie générale de droit et de jurisprudence 1989) 24

[16] The separation is not absolute, however: if X *qua* natural person has incurred the debts, he may end up losing the ownership of his single-person corporation.

Passive Incidents of Legal Personhood

Protection of Life, Liberty, and Bodily Integrity: Fundamental Protections

I was earlier rather critical of Steven Wise's analysis of legal personhood. Even though his claim that only legal persons can hold legal rights is untenable, I agree with him that the so-called dignity-rights that he is advocating for some nonhuman animals would be central in their legal personhood.

According to Wise, dignity-rights have to do with bodily integrity and bodily liberty. Any dignity-right 'contain[s] a core of fundamental liberty-rights that can be protected either as *in rem* immunity-rights or claim-rights'.[17] Wise claims that '[u]nlike a bare liberty-right, which requires at least an association with a claim-right to be a dignity-right, bare immunity-rights may be dignity-rights in and of themselves; alone they may constitute the most fundamental legal rights, such as bodily integrity and bodily liberty'.[18] Wise has here in mind how constitutional bills of rights often work: they disempower the lawmakers and other officials from passing certain kinds of laws.[19] As the parliament is unable to pass any law that would constitute a violation of someone's bodily liberty, that liberty is accompanied by a corresponding immunity vis-à-vis the parliament, rather than a liability. These are of course important points, but we should be careful when assessing how they relate to the topic at hand.

For instance, nonhuman animals do not bear any duties in the contemporary Western legal systems with which I am familiar. The creatures are therefore in possession of only liberties. Would their legal position be changed significantly—with regard to their legal personhood or otherwise—if, say, a constitutional amendment would disempower the state from imposing duties upon nonhuman animals? In most respects, this change would be quite irrelevant. It would be rather surreal to talk of the animals' dignity-rights to personal liberty when they could still be imprisoned in cages and killed for food. This is why claim-rights, reinforced by immunities, are the

[17] Steven M. Wise, 'Hardly a Revolution—The Eligibility of Nonhuman Animals for Dignity-Rights in a Liberal Democracy' (1998) 22 *Vermont Law Review* 793, 823. I should stress one point: Wise does not only claim that animals currently lack dignity-rights. This is a claim I could mostly agree to. Rather, Wise claims explicitly that animals hold no rights whatsoever. See for instance ibid. 801f.

[18] Ibid. 811.

[19] However, this is not the only way constitutional rights work. According to § 19 of the Constitution of Finland (*Suomen perustuslaki*, 731/1999), '[t]hose who cannot obtain the means necessary for a life of dignity have the right to receive indispensable subsistence and care'. If an individual would, for some reason, 'fall through the gaps' of the social security system and be left without any means of subsistence, he or she could still demand the indispensable subsistence and care by invoking the relevant constitutional section in court.

central component of this incident of legal personhood. Liberties are of course often important as well, but without claim-rights they are usually not enough.

Whether a claim-right is a fundamental protection is determined both by the interests safeguarded and by the hierarchically high status of the claim-right.

First, fundamental protections safeguard the life, personal liberty, and/or bodily integrity of their holder. *Habeas corpus* is a fundamental protection, and the lawsuits initiated by the Nonhuman Rights Project, demanding that nonhuman animals be afforded the writ of *habeas corpus*, are thus mainly focused on this incident. Similarly, the proposed 'personhood amendments' in some American states, which would define foetuses as persons for the purposes of criminal law, also pertain to the fundamental protection of life.[20] The *Roe v Wade* case, which declared state limitations on first-trimester abortions to be unconstitutional, essentially denied fundamental protections to first-trimester foetuses.[21] Furthermore, as I have noted in the preceding chapter, one of the legal ramifications of a slave's being freed was that the slave received numerous robust claim-rights pertaining to his or her life, liberty, and bodily integrity—both against the former owner and 'against the world'.

Second, fundamental protections occupy a high hierarchical status. They are thus close to what Ronald Dworkin calls 'rights as trumps': safeguards that protect individuals against consequentialist policy considerations—even if this protection may not be absolute.[22] Such protections are often codified in a constitution or in other legal sources that are hierarchically superior to ordinary statutes. Protections accorded to nonpersons, on the other hand, are often subject to different kinds of limitations: animal welfare statutes often prohibit the infliction of *unnecessary* suffering on animals. This formulation implies that the animal's interest in not being afflicted with suffering can more easily be subverted by other considerations. However, the difference between persons and nonpersons in this regard is a matter of degree, pertaining to the types of purposes for which one's legally protected interests may be sacrificed. The concrete meaning of the word 'necessary' cannot in this context be understood without asking: 'Necessary for what purpose?' Nonpersons' interests can typically be sacrificed for a wider array of purposes than those of legal persons. For instance, many contemporary legal systems allow for the killing of certain animals for recreation or for economic reasons, whereas the intentional deprivation of human life is allowed for far fewer purposes, typically to protect the fundamental interests of some other natural person(s).[23] Slaves occupied a position similar to that of

[20] Such amendments also pertain to the capacity be a victim of crimes, which I also take to be a hallmark of legal personhood. This is an example of how legal-personhood-related institutions are intertwined and mutually overlapping in various ways.

[21] *Roe v Wade*, 410 US 113.

[22] Ronald Dworkin, 'Taking Rights Seriously', *Taking Rights Seriously* (Harvard University Press 1977).

[23] I have analysed elsewhere the prohibition of inflicting unnecessary suffering in the context of Finnish animal welfare law. I claim that the analysis involves a weighing of the animal's

animals: for instance, Georgia provided in 1816 that masters could be prosecuted for the 'unnecessary and excessive whipping' of their own slaves—many also forbade 'cruelty' towards slaves, much like the so-called animal cruelty laws nowadays.[24]

What I mean by this 'hierarchically high status' is the following. A claim-right has a hierarchically high status if the considerations underlying the claim-right normally prevail against competing considerations and interests, including property interests. I mentioned above that the fundamental protections of legal persons are typically enshrined in legal sources that are hierarchically superior to ordinary statutes. However, this does not have to be the case. It *may* very well be that some extant legal systems can—without the need for any constitutional changes—extend to nonhuman animals protections that prevail against property interests and other important considerations. However, such putative extensions can in many cases pose constitutional problems. A striking example is the infamous *Dred Scott* case, decided by the US Supreme Court in 1858, where the Court ruled that Africans brought over as slaves and their descendants were not, and could not be, citizens of the United States and consequently could not for instance sue in the federal courts.[25] Furthermore, the Supreme Court decided that the Missouri Compromise, which had limited slavery in certain northern states, was unconstitutional because it interfered with the constitutional protection of property:

> [T]he same instrument, which imparts to Congress its very existence and its every function, guaranties [*sic*] to the slaveholder the title to his property, and gives him the right to its reclamation throughout the entire extent of the nation; and, farther, that the only private property which the Constitution has specifically recognised, and has imposed as a direct obligation both on the States and the Federal Government to protect and enforce, is the property of the master in his slave; no other right of property is placed by the Constitution upon the same high ground, nor shielded by a similar guaranty.[26]

interest in being free of suffering against the competing interest which requires such suffering; however, the competing interest can be any 'legally protected purpose', and these purposes include economic benefit but exclude for instance sadistic pleasure. Visa Kurki, 'Förbudet mot åsamkande av onödigt lidande enligt djurskyddslagstiftningen' [2011] *Tidskrift utgiven av Juridiska Föreningen i Finland* 290.

[24] Thomas D. Morris, *Southern Slavery and the Law, 1619–1860* (The University of North Carolina Press 1996) 184. Gary Francione's analysis, which was addressed in Chapter 2, seems to pertain especially to this aspect of the protection of nonpersons: that the legal safeguards of nonpersons can often be overridden or overtopped for other purposes (but not for all purposes, which is why animals typically hold interest-theory rights in Western legal systems).

[25] Only citizens were within the ambit of the US Constitution and its Bill of Rights at the time. However, the 14th Amendment, adopted in 1868, would firstly declare anyone born within the United States a citizen, and secondly forbid each state from denying 'to any person within its jurisdiction the equal protection of the laws'. Citizens and non-citizens would be treated equally, except with regard to voting, running for office, and other similar political institutions. The Supreme Court would later rely on this amendment to extend certain constitutional protections to corporations. See David Cole, 'Are Foreign Nationals Entitled to the Same Constitutional Rights As Citizens?' (2003) 25 *Thomas Jefferson Law Review* 367.

[26] *Dred Scott v Sandford*, 60 US 393 (1857).

This decision did not have much practical import because the Missouri Compromise had already been superseded by the Kansas–Nebraska Act. However, it serves as an example of how constitutional provisions can affect who or what is a legal person in a given legal system. Constitutional provisions that protect property ownership could hinder certain steps towards the legal personhood of animals if, say, a proposed act of parliament would seek to limit severely what animal owners can do with their property.

Certain legal systems have recently included animals in constitutional provisions. Germany, for instance, amended § 20a in its Basic Law in 2002 to include nonhuman animals:

> Mindful also of its responsibility toward future generations, the state shall protect the natural foundations of life and animals by legislation and, in accordance with law and justice, by executive and judicial action, all within the framework of the constitutional order.[27]

This can be seen as a small step towards animal legal personhood, but it should not be exaggerated: the protection of animals in the German constitution is a 'state objective' (*Staatsziel*). State objectives in German constitutional law 'outline a specific program for activities of the state and serve as a guideline for interpreting statutes and administrative rules'.[28] They do not generate directly any (Hohfeldian) rights.[29] However, one important consequence of the 2002 constitutional amendment was that it allowed for the constitutionality of animal welfare statutes even in cases where these would conflict with certain constitutional rights such as the freedom of religion, the freedom of teaching, science and research, and the freedom of artistic expression.[30] So the amendment can be seen as an improvement of the status of animals, as it allows the state to protect animals even in certain situations where this may conflict with the fundamental rights of legal persons. Consequently, if the amendment allows for certain claim-rights held by animals to stay in place despite the fact that they are in tension or conflict with some fundamental rights held by natural or artificial persons, then such claim-rights held by the animals can be said to be fundamental. However, the number of such claim-rights is likely to be small for now.

Capacity to be a Party to Special Rights

What Neil MacCormick has termed *passive transactional capacity* incorporates many of the important features of passive legal personhood. I start with MacCormick's list of examples that he takes to fall under the scope of passive transactional capacity:

[27] Basic Law for the Federal Republic of Germany (*Grundgesetz für die Bundesrepublik Deutschland*, BGBl. III 100-1, last amended on July 13, 2017) § 20a. Translated by Christian Tomuschat, David P. Currie, and Donald P. Kommers.

[28] Claudia E. Haupt, 'The Nature and Effects of Constitutional State Objectives: Assessing the German Basic Law's Animal Protection Clause' (2010) 16 *Animal Law Review* 213, 226.

[29] Ibid. 225–6.

[30] Ibid. 237–56.

When it comes to private law, one may be able to be the beneficiary of a promise albeit incapable of making a binding promise oneself, or even of accepting the terms of a conditional offer. One may be capable of becoming an owner of property by gift, even if incapable of managing it. [...] One may be capable of being the beneficiary of a guardian's or a trustee's duties as such, even though one is incapable of enforcing 'in one's own right' any breaches of duty.[31]

I agree that all of these examples have to do with legal personhood. However, they are quite disparate and should be analysed separately. This heterogeneousness becomes apparent when MacCormick tries to summarize this capacity as the '[c]apacity to take the benefit or the burden created through a certain transaction' and as 'the capacity to be acted upon with legal effect through some form of legal transaction or act-in-the-law, whether the effect be beneficial or detrimental'.[32] These characterizations are rather vague. For instance, slaves and animals can surely take on the 'burden' created through a transaction if they are sold, especially if the seller has treated his slaves or animals relatively well whereas the buyer is cruel towards his. MacCormick specifies what he means by the taking of a burden:

It is a feature of [legal] transactions that not only must the active part in them be taken by some person with appropriate capacity to act in that way, but it must also be the case that the person to whom the performance is directed is endowed with sufficient capacity for the transaction to take its intended effect. The same would apply to transactions the intended effect of which is to effect the imposition of some legal burden on the other party. A burden such as a legal duty can be imposed only on a being that is capable of being a duty-bearer.[33]

There are numerous unclear points here. First, MacCormick's 'burdens' include, but are not limited to, duties. He does not specify what the other types of burdens are. Second, with the 'capability of being a duty-bearer', MacCormick is not referring to the conceptual domain of duties but rather to who or what can, for instance, be bound to a legally enforceable contract. Thus, if the legal representative of a severely mentally disabled individual signs a health-insurance contract in the name of the principal, the principal can come under the burden of the contract in that the insurance fees are to be paid using the principal's money rather than the representative's money.[34] It is, however, somewhat misleading to say that the burden would constitute a *duty* for the principal, given that the principal is not legally required to perform or omit any action because of the contract. Rather, the principal holds a liability and even a claim-right with regard to the payment of the fees, as the representative is duty-bound and empowered to pay the fees on the principal's behalf. I will return to this issue shortly.

There are consequently numerous issues to develop with regard to MacCormick's account. Some issues concerning the representation of passive legal persons will

[31] MacCormick (n 10) 87. [32] Ibid. [33] Ibid.

[34] Another way of making the same point is that the debt is associated with the principal's legal platform.

be discussed in Chapter 4, whereas I will now consider the elements of which MacCormick's passive transactional capacity consists. I maintain that the capacity can be understood in terms of two primary incidents—the capacity to be a party to special rights and the capacity to own property. In addition, these incidents often require the support of numerous other incidents, such as legal standing.

I have already argued in Chapter 2 that the 'capacity to hold rights' that some scholars associate with legal personhood can partly be understood as the capacity to hold what Hart termed *special rights*, which 'arise out of special transactions between individuals or out of some special relationship in which they stand to each other' and where 'the persons who have the right and those who have the corresponding obligation are limited to the parties to the special transaction or relationship'.[35] Another element of this 'capacity to hold rights' is the capacity to own property, which will be discussed in the next section. Property ownership is not a special right according to Hart, because the relevant claims are held against 'the world' rather than merely against the parties to the relationship.

Hart's account of special rights must be qualified in certain ways to make it applicable here. The most important features of special rights as incidents of legal personhood are that these rights must (1) follow from exercises of legal competences and (2) be limited to the parties who perform the transaction and/or to the parties in whose name the transaction is performed. What I mean by legal competences will be outlined later in this chapter. Point (2) pertains chiefly to the being who acquires claim-rights or duties as a result of the transaction. Hart's theory of special rights is based on his early will theory of rights, which does not ascribe rights to children, mentally disabled individuals, or nonhuman animals. I maintain, however, that even such individuals and creatures can be parties to special rights because they can be represented by others, who then have fiduciary duties towards their principals.

Understanding MacCormick's examples in terms of special rights and ownership goes a long way in explaining numerous extensional beliefs regarding legal personhood. Infants and corporations can be the beneficiaries of legally enforceable contracts, whereas animals cannot and slaves could not. Special rights held by passive parties can hence be understood as claim-rights against, say, a promisor, a guardian, or both.[36] I will return to the details of how passive legal personhood works in Chapter 4, when addressing who or what can be a passive legal person.

[35] H. L. A. Hart, 'Are There Any Natural Rights?' (1955) 64 *The Philosophical Review* 175. Though I eschew use of the term 'right' in this work (in an attempt to stay neutral between the interest and will theories), I have retained Hart's original phrase 'special right' here.

[36] The legal claim-right held by a child vis-à-vis a contractor is, of course, distinct from the legal claim-right held by the child vis-à-vis a guardian who is responsible for enforcing or waiving the first-mentioned legal claim-right.

Capacity to Own Property, and Not Being Property

Owning property is a very important hallmark of legal personhood.[37] It ties together numerous incidents of legal personhood: for instance, X's being the beneficiary of special rights that involve the payment of a sum and X's capacity to receive monetary compensation for torts both presuppose the capacity to own property. This capacity is also central to the concept of legal platform, which will be addressed in the following chapter. Yet another important incident is that of not being property, that is, insusceptibility to being owned.

Property ownership also forms an important part of MacCormick's passive transactional capacity. He notes pithily that '[t]hose who doubt [the significance of passive transactional capacity] may wish to reflect on the fact that a gift of property on trust for the benefit of a baby is valid, whereas one for the benefit of a pet dog is not'.[38]

Beings paradigmatically endowed with legal personhood—natural persons and artificial persons—can own property, whereas beings paradigmatically classifiable as nonpersons—animals, slaves, and foetuses—are normally unable to do so. Human children typically gain the capacity to own property at the moment they are born, and artificial persons when they are registered. Animals, slaves, and foetuses, on the other hand, cannot or could not own property.[39] There are some exceptions, however. Many Roman masters enabled their slaves to own property under an arrangement called *peculium*, whereas such an institution did not exist in the North American form of slavery.[40] The fact that pets can be the beneficiaries of trusts in some US states is also a highly interesting development, and a step towards their legal personhood. The case of pet trusts also illustrates why the incidents of legal personhood must be treated separately: even though these animals can be said to own property, causing harm to one of them cannot currently constitute a tort towards the animal; one cannot subsequently be liable to pay the animal compensation.

Yet another incident of legal personhood is that one is not an object of ownership, that is, property. Natural persons cannot be owned, whereas animals and slaves are susceptible to being owned. However, X's legal personhood and X's being an object of ownership are not inherently incompatible—as the example of business corporations illustrates—even if the matter is complicated. There is of course a certain tension between being both an owner and property. Notwithstanding, assuming

[37] Ownership here includes intellectual-property rights such as copyright.

[38] MacCormick (n 10) 87.

[39] Foetuses are of course covered by the *nasciturus* rule, which allows for them in certain contexts to be treated as if they were already born, but only if they are in fact later born alive.

[40] The *peculium* also serves to illustrate the disparate conditions in which Roman slaves lived: whereas household slaves were often treated relatively well and were allowed a *peculium*, slaves working in the mines lived in brutal conditions. Similarly, household pets are typically treated far better than factory-farmed animals today. See Richard Gamauf, 'Slaves Doing Business: The Role of Roman Law in the Economy of a Roman Household' (2009) *16 European Review of History: Revue europeenne d'histoire* 331.

that one accepts the analytic 'bundle' theory of ownership as articulated by Anthony Honoré, there is no reason to assume that objects of ownership cannot also own property.[41] Honoré distinguished eleven 'standard incidents' of ownership. I will list ten of them here as summarized by Hugh Breakey (the eleventh one—the prohibition of harmful use—is often omitted by contemporary scholars, as it is not considered to pertain to ownership *per se* but to conduct in general):

1. The right to possess: to have exclusive physical control of a thing;
2. The right to use: to have an exclusive and open-ended capacity to personally use the thing;
3. The right to manage: to be able to decide who is allowed to use the thing and how they may do so;
4. The right to the income: to the fruits, rents and profits arising from one's possession, use and management of the thing;
5. The right to the capital: to consume, waste or destroy the thing, or parts of it;
6. The right to security: to have immunity from others being able to take ownership of (expropriating) the thing;
7. The incident of transmissibility: to transfer the entitlements of ownership to another person (that is, to alienate or sell the thing);
8. The incident of absence of term: to be entitled to the endurance of the entitlement over time;
9. Liability to execution: allowing that the ownership of the thing may be dissolved or transferred in case of debt or insolvency; and,
10. Residuary character: ensuring that after everyone else's entitlements to the thing finish (when a lease runs out, for example), the entitlements return to vest in the owner.[42]

Honoré did not mean that all of these incidents would be necessary conditions for ownership; he rather intended this as an example of 'full' (liberal) ownership, which would bear more or less resemblance to actual instances of ownership.

The instances can be divided into 'active' (presupposing a relatively sophisticated reasoning capacity) and 'passive' (presupposing only the capacity to enjoy the benefits of property) quite neatly, as shown in Table 3.3.

This can show us why it makes sense to speak of, say, animals' owning property: even though they cannot partake in the active elements of legal ownership, the majority of the elements of ownership can nevertheless be meaningful in the case of animals. It should of course once again be noted that the active/passive classification is not always clear-cut. For instance, talking of animals' right to use money does not really make sense; the primary benefits of having money are the possibility of buying goods and services through the exercise of competences and, for some people, the pleasure one derives from simply having money. Both

[41] Anthony M. Honoré, 'Ownership' in A. G. Guest (ed.), *Oxford Essays in Jurisprudence* (Oxford University Press 1961) 107. For a recent defence of the bundle theory, see Shane Nicholas Glackin, 'Back to Bundles: Deflating Property Rights, Again' (2014) 20 *Legal Theory* 1.

[42] Hugh Breakey, 'Property Concepts', *Internet Encyclopedia of Philosophy* (2012).

Table 3.3 The incidents of ownership classified

Active	Passive
The right to manage	The right to possession
Transmissibility	The right to use
The right to use	The right to the income
	The right to the capital
	The right to security
	Absence of term
	Liability to execution
	Residuary character

presuppose the mental capacity to understand the concept of money, which is why it is not very meaningful to talk of one's right to use money unless one has the mental faculties for this. (The money can of course still be beneficial for animals and infants, if their guardian uses the money to their benefit.) On the other hand, it does make sense to talk of a mentally disabled individual's protected liberty to live in his apartment.

I conclude that even passive legal persons may own property. However, this does not yet answer the question of whether one can be both a subject and an object of ownership. An obvious example of this is business corporations, which serve a double function as both persons and property: they participate in certain legal relations as property, and in others as persons. Their owners may sell or donate their stake in the company, it can be used to cover the owners' debts, and so on. On the other hand, the corporation itself may own property, has standing in courts, and so on. We should now distinguish corporate group agents from other types of business corporations. I will argue in Chapter 5 that many groups can be understood as agents that are separable from their members; the group intentions, beliefs, and desires are formed through collective decision-making. This is also true of most corporations. Business corporations can be understood as a shared project: as exercises of joint intentionality in which the shareholders have a stake. The project is not usually under the sole control of any single shareholder, which is why it makes sense to say that it is a legal person and a legal actor in its own right. The fact that companies are property in fact constitutes the group agency of the company, for the aggregate function through which companies are governed is usually connected to the ownership of stock with voting rights.[43]

[43] Most if not all of the strategic decisions in corporations are of course made by the board or the CEO or other executives, rather than by the owners. Everyday decisions are made by managers and other employees.

On the other hand, not all business corporations really are as described above: in particular, companies that are owned by one human being alone, and where he or she governs the company alone, are not group agents. In this case, the corporation is better understood as merely a separate legal platform, that is, a bundle of legal positions. Such a platform might serve its owner for taxation purposes and—especially in the case of limited-liability corporations—enable devoting assets to a certain goal.[44] Such corporations are under the total control of their single owner, in contrast with group persons; they have no will apart from that of their owner. This is what separates them from slaves. Slaves had a will of their own, even if this will was not recognized in private law, disempowering them from performing acts-in-the-law.[45]

Could slaves have owned property, so that it would not simply have been an extension of their master's property as in the case of companies with a single owner? We should firstly recall the institution of *peculium* that enabled slaves to own property at their master's pleasure. The slave was of course not protected against his or her master, as the master could revoke the *peculium* at any point. However, no logical necessity calls for this revocability; the master could very well be placed under an obligation not to forcefully take the slave's belongings and under a disability to alter this duty. The master's incidents of ownership pertaining to the slave would consequently have been reduced. This is also why it is possible that animals could own property without the abolition of their status as property. In order for such an arrangement to be more than nominal, an animal would need to have a guardian who would take care of the active incidents of ownership, but the animal could still be the beneficiary of the passive incidents. Again, this can only be meaningful if the entitlements of the animal's owner are restricted accordingly.

To sum up, when analysing the relationship between a being's status as a subject of ownership and a being's status as an object thereof, one must distinguish three cases: (1) business corporations *qua* organized human collectivities, (2) business corporations *qua* legal platforms, and (3) individual human beings and animals. In the case of organized collectivities, the group agency of the corporation functions through its being an object of ownership, and this is what enables it to act as a subject of ownership. In case (2), the single-person corporation is merely another 'mask' through which its owner acts legally. Case (3) is different in that the owner and the object of ownership have different wills and/or interests. Regardless, creating some form of limited ownership for the slave or animal is possible.

[44] Katsuhito Iwai analyses this question quite well. See Katsuhito Iwai, 'Persons, Things and Corporations: The Corporate Personality Controversy and Comparative Corporate Governance' (1999) 47 *The American Journal of Comparative Law* 583.

[45] The will of slaves was perhaps given legal recognition in the way that a nonhuman animal's will can be recognized today when animals are bought and sold: if the seller claims, for instance, that the animal or slave he is selling is 'strong-willed', this can increase or decrease the price.

I will return to the topic of property ownership as an incident of legal personhood numerous times over the course of this book.

Standing

Only legal persons are normally recognized as parties of lawsuits. Civil-law jurisdictions are quite explicit about this; for instance, the German Code of Civil Procedure connects legal personhood to *Parteifähigkeit*, 'the capacity of being a party to court proceedings'.[46] French legal scholars have similarly maintained that an animal could only be represented in a lawsuit if it were redefined as a legal person, though such an arrangement would not have to amount to the kind of 'full' legal personhood that natural and artificial persons enjoy.[47] Common-law jurisdictions are slightly more liberal in this regard. American judges in particular have occasionally considered the merits of cases with animal plaintiffs, even if such cases are anomalies.[48] Historically, American slaves generally lacked standing, though some states such as Virginia enabled slaves to sue for their freedom.[49]

Denying someone legal standing can take two different forms, which correspond to two different elements of the concept. Let us start with a dictionary definition:

> Standing is the ability of a party to bring a lawsuit in court based upon their stake in the outcome. A party seeking to demonstrate standing must be able to show the court sufficient connection to and harm from the law or action challenged.[50]

[46] 'Any person having legal capacity shall also have the capacity to be a party to court proceedings.' (*Parteifähig ist, wer rechtsfähig ist.*) German Code of Civil Procedure (*Zivilprozeßordnung*, BGBl. 2005 I p. 3202; 2006 I p. 431; 2007 I p. 1781, last amended on 31 January 2019) § 50(1).) English translation by Carmen von Schöning. However, the same code does allow for the *Parteifähigkeit* of registered organisations that are not legal persons.

[47] 'To permit an animal to be legally represented before a judge is to recognize in the animal some legal rights and thereby the status of a subject of law and even legal personality.' ('*Permettre une représentation juridique de l'animal devant le juge nécessite de reconnaitre à l'animal des prérogatives juridiques, et par là même, un statut de sujet de droit, voire même de personne juridique.*') Lucille Boisseau-Sowinski, 'La représentation des individus d'une espèce animale devant le juge français' (2015) 22 *VertigO—la revue électronique en sciences de l'environnement* 41. Even if the author seems to distinguish 'legal person' and 'subject of law' here, she treats the two concepts as synonymous in most other junctures.

[48] See Cass Sunstein, 'Can Animals Sue?' in Cass R. Sunstein and Martha C. Nussbaum (eds), *Animal Rights: Current Debates and New Directions* (Oxford University Press 2004) 259.

[49] It may seem odd that slaves were empowered to sue for their freedom. A relatively logical explanation is that the legal system wanted to allow for the possibility that the slaves 'were not really slaves at all but, rather, free persons who were illegally held in slavery. The only way to make it possible for such persons to recover their freedom was to allow them to sue for it.' A. Leon Higginbotham Jr and Barbara K. Kopytoff, 'Property First, Humanity Second: The Recognition of the Slave's Human Nature in Virginia Civil Law' (1989) 50 *Ohio State Law Journal* 511, 533.

[50] *US Legal Dictionary*.

Two elements need to be distinguished here:

- the *invested* aspect of standing: *viz.*, the articulated recognition that X has a 'stake in the outcome' which renders enforceable any of X's claim-rights that are affected;[51]
- the *competence-related* aspect of standing: *viz.*, the legal competence of X to pursue the case in court.

The invested element of standing has to do with whether an entitlement of X is recognized by the legal system as enforceable in court. If the legal system does not recognize X's invested standing, then the claims of X are (1) unenforceable in courts or (2) enforced only circumstantially when they happen to coincide with someone else's enforceable rights. Invested standing may also be reflected in administrative procedures. For instance, according to Finnish administrative law, '[a] person has *standing as a party to an administrative matter* where his/her rights, interests or obligations are affected by the matter' (emphasis added).[52] Such parties must be heard before the matter is decided, and they have the standing to challenge in court the decision reached in the matter.

The competence-related element empowers a party to decide whether to pursue the suit or not (and is thus, in fact, an active incident). For example, in criminal cases, the legal system may recognize the victim as someone with invested standing yet without the prerogative to decide whether the case is pursued. There are also various situations where one lacks the competence to pursue a case despite having invested standing. Obvious examples are cases where the legal system denies competence to someone because his or her mental faculties are deemed insufficient for legal competence, such as with children and mentally handicapped people. However, not all cases of denied competence have such justification, as with the now-obsolete common-law doctrine of coverture: 'If the wife be injured in her person or her property, she can bring no action for redress without her husband's concurrence, and in his name, as well her own; neither can she be sued.'[53]

This doctrine recognized the wife's invested standing to a limited extent but did not enable her to take legal action independently. Similar doctrines have been in place in various jurisdictions; for example, the Swedish and Finnish doctrine of guardianship did not exempt women from owning property altogether but provided that

[51] However, X's standing is not a *necessary* condition for the enforceability of X's claim-rights, given that authorities and/or other individuals may have the capacity to enforce certain claim-rights regardless of whether the claim-right-holder has *locus standi*.

[52] '*Hallintoasiassa asianosainen on se, jonka oikeutta, etua tai velvollisuutta asia koskee.*' Administrative Procedure Act (*Hallintolaki*, 434/2003) § 11. The English translation makes use of the pronouns 'his' and 'her', which seems to imply that the section would only cover natural persons; however, artificial persons are included as well.

[53] William Blackstone, *Commentaries on the Laws of England. Vol. 1* (1765) 442.

most legal competences pertaining to the property had to be exercised by the husband or some other male, or could only be exercised by the wife with the man's permission.[54] In such cases, the property was acknowledged as belonging to the wife, giving her invested standing in any lawsuits over the property, yet she was denied the competence to decide whether to pursue any such lawsuits.

In addition, abstract standing and standing *in casu* can be distinguished. Abstract standing is close to the German idea of *Parteifähigkeit*; it concerns whether X has invested and/or competence-related standing at all in a given legal system. Standing *in casu*, on the other hand, pertains to one's standing in a particular case. In a discussion of legal personhood on a general level, abstract standing is more important. A lack of abstract standing often results in the summary dismissal of a lawsuit, and abstract standing could indeed perhaps be described as 'the standing to have one's standing *in casu* seriously considered'. One relevant case is *Citizens to End Animal Suffering and Exploitation, Inc. et al. v New England Aquarium, et al.*, where the organizations named as plaintiffs tried to get a dolphin, Kama, accepted as the plaintiff of the case.[55] The case was dismissed without the consideration of merits—because of lack of standing—in keeping with the denial of legal standing to animals in most modern legal systems. Animals typically lack both invested and competence-related standing even though legal protections are accorded to them.[56]

The enforceability of environmental law has also occasionally been hampered because no-one has had the standing to sue polluters. Different solutions have been devised to address this problem. In the US, courts have resorted to the notion of aesthetic injury, granting human beings the standing to sue 'in virtue of the injuries they incurred as the result of defendants' actions that threatened to significantly diminish the species of animal'.[57] Christopher Stone has argued that even trees could be granted legal standing, and justified his proposal at least partly by the claim that the standing of trees and other natural objects would enhance the enforcement of

[54] See Anu Pylkkänen, *Trapped in Equality: Women as Legal Persons in the Modernisation of Finnish Law* (Suomalaisen Kirjallisuuden Seura/Finnish Literature Society 2009) 40ff and Pirkko K. Koskinen, 'Laki ja tapa naisen aseman määrittäjinä' [2009] *Tidskrift utgiven av Juridiska Föreningen i Finland* 27.

[55] *Citizens to End Animal Suffering and Exploitation v New England Aquarium*, 836 F Supp 45 (D Mass. 1993).

[56] This was recognized in *Tilikum et al*:

> Even though Plaintiffs lack standing to bring a Thirteenth Amendment claim, that is not to say that animals have no legal rights; as there are many state and federal statutes affording redress to Plaintiffs, including, in some instances, criminal statutes that 'punish those who violate statutory duties that protect animals.'

Tilikum et al v Sea World Parks & Entertainment Inc., 842 F Supp 2d 1259 (SD Cal 2012) 7. The court cites *Cetacean Community v Bush*, 386 F.3d 1169 (9th Cir 2004) 1175.

[57] Jeffrey M. Skopek, 'Aesthetic Injuries, Animal Rights and Anthropomorphism' (2009) 122 *Harvard Law Review* 1204, 1208. See also Sunstein (n 48) 257–60.

environmental mandates.[58] In some European countries, the legislator has instead opted to grant certain authorities and/or environmental non-governmental organizations a statutory standing to sue. In these cases, there is typically no requirement that the plaintiff show any personal involvement in the matter; the authority or organization is rather understood to be representing a general interest. It consequently does not have invested standing (because its claim-rights are not directly affected) but is only endowed with the competence-related aspect of standing.

I have here highlighted some of the key features of standing with regard to legal personhood, but some aspects of the multifaceted notion have been left unexplored. For instance, the focus has here been on standing as the 'capacity to sue', but one could also discuss standing as the 'capacity to be sued'. The diplomatic immunity enjoyed by the representatives of foreign nations does not free them from following the laws of their host country, but it does give them immunity from prosecution. However, diplomatic immunity and other similar institutions—often relating to politicians and heads of state—do not have much bearing on the questions that this investigation seeks to understand. They are consequently not addressed further.

Capacity to be Legally Harmed

Tort liability is one important legal institution for remedying certain kinds of harm caused to others. It is restricted by several factors such as causation and culpability, but also by the fact that typically only harm done to a legal person is classified by tort law as harm to a recognizable victim.[59] If an animal is harmed by a human being, this can typically only engender tort liability if the economic interests (or, in the case of subjective valuation, the 'sentiments') of the animal's owner are harmed simultaneously. For instance, if the hoof of a racehorse is tortiously harmed by someone, the owner of the horse may sue the tortfeasor for damages. However, the welfare losses of the horse are not legally recognized; if the owner thinks that having the horse is no longer economically viable, he may decide to have it killed and use the compensation he has recovered for a completely different purpose.[60] Slaves have typically occupied a similar position—only their owners have been able to recover compensation for harm inflicted to the slaves.[61] Foetuses are a different case: they are not

[58] Christopher D. Stone, *Should Trees Have Standing? Law, Morality, and the Environment* (3rd edn, Oxford University Press 2010). Stone will be addressed in Chapter 4.

[59] Austin recognizes this as well: 'A slave (as the subject of property) may be damaged; but (as having no rights) is not himself susceptible of injury.' John Austin, *Lectures on Jurisprudence: Or, the Philosophy of Positive Law, vol. I* (John Murray, Albemarle Street 1885) 349f.

[60] The situation is somewhat different if the owner or the tortfeasor can opt for restitution *in natura*, but the rationale behind this would still not be focused on the animal's interests.

[61] See for instance Andrew Fede, *People Without Rights: An Interpretation of the Fundamentals of the Law of Slavery in the US South* (Garland Publishing, Inc 1992) 100–1:

> [T]he courts held strangers whose violence damaged another person's slave, or caused the owner to lose some free labor, liable to the owner for the economic losses caused by the slave mistreatment. Judges

property, which is why there is no owner who could recover damages. Foetuses that are born alive can typically recover damages for harm that has been caused to them tortiously, in accordance with the 'born alive' rule that is widely in force in many Western jurisdictions.[62] On the other hand, if the foetus perishes before being born, the damages cannot be recovered.

David Favre has made an interesting proposal for a cause of action which would enable a (domestic) animal to be a plaintiff in a tort case. According to the proposal, the plaintiff—an animal represented by a human being—would have to show the following elements in order to be afforded a legal remedy:

1. That an interest is of fundamental importance to the plaintiff animal;
2. That the fundamental interest has been interfered with or harmed by the actions or inactions of the defendant;
3. That the weight and nature of the interests of the animal plaintiff substantially outweighs the weight and nature of the interests of the human defendant.[63]

If these criteria are met, the defendant would be required to provide a tort-law remedy for the plaintiff. In Favre's model, three remedies would exist: money damages, injunctive relief, and title transfer. Money damages would be provided for harm already caused, whereas injunctive relief would be available if the tort is ongoing. Finally, title transfer would involve transferring the creature to a new owner if the current owner is unable to improve the living conditions of the animal.[64] Favre notes correctly that any payment of monetary damages would have to take place through the establishment of a trust for the animal.[65] Favre is writing in the US context where trusts are available, but if his model were applied in civil-law countries that do not know of trusts, the money would likely have to be treated as belonging explicitly to the animal itself.

Capacity to Count as a Victim

Closely related to many of the aforementioned incidents—yet distinguishable from them—is the capacity to count as a victim of criminal offences. Take the fundamentally different statuses of newborn children and foetuses. As Dwight G. Duncan notes, 'a doctor deliberately taking the life of a woman's infant seconds after birth with or without the woman's permission is infanticide, but a doctor deliberately

therefore applied the common law rules of civil liability concerning personal property to cases of non-fatal slave abuses.

[62] Some US states have abandoned this rule, however, as a part of a movement towards foetal personhood.

[63] David S. Favre, 'Judicial Recognition of the Interest of Animals—A New Tort' (2005) *Michigan State Law Review* 333, 353. For a criticism of Favre's position, see Richard L. Cupp Jr, 'A Dubious Grail: Seeking Tort Law Expansion and Limited Personhood as Stepping Stones toward Abolishing Animals' Property Status' (2007) 60 *SMU Law Review* 3.

[64] Favre (n 63) 366.

[65] Ibid.

taking the life of a woman's infant any time before birth is effectuating the woman's constitutionally protected right to abortion'.[66] (Duncan is here referring, hyperbolically, to the US Constitution.) Even though abortions are legally regulated, and some such regulations can be said to generate claim-rights for foetuses, the legal protection of newborn children is considerably more robust; not only are the claim-rights held by the children more numerous, but the sanctions for contraventions of those claim-rights are more severe. Furthermore, foetuses and newborn children have different procedural statuses in the criminal trials of many countries.

Similarly, it would be wrong to say that animals in contemporary Western legal systems and slaves in the antebellum US are not or were not legally protected at all. These individuals and creatures have been defended by criminal-law protections which have typically proscribed at least particularly gratuitous or cruel conduct towards these groups. The safeguards have not necessarily coincided with the interests of the slaves' or the animals' owners. However, the protection of these groups has often been framed as the protection of something other than the welfare of the animals or slaves themselves; for instance, the South Carolina Slave Code of 1740 justified the criminalization of the wilful killing of slaves by adverting to the odiousness of cruelty 'in the eyes of all men who have any sense of virtue or humanity'. Similarly, animal welfare laws are still occasionally claimed to be protecting, for instance, the moral feelings of human beings.[67] Animal welfare crime is not treated in the same way as analogous crimes committed against legal persons. For instance, animal welfare crimes are often treated as victimless crimes; procedural rules pertaining to victims do not usually include animals.[68] In addition—as noted above—the animal typically cannot receive compensation for the harm it has suffered; any monetary sanction or compensation goes to the animal's owner or to the state. Finally, in jurisdictions where being an 'offended party' is a procedural role in criminal trials, the animal cannot be an offended party.[69]

[66] Dwight G. Duncan, 'When is a Human Being Not a Legal Person?: Lethal Ramifications at the Beginning of Life' (2013) 8 *University of St Thomas Journal of Law & Public Policy* 82, 82.

[67] In the animal rights literature, such views are often classified as advocating 'indirect moral duties'. SeeScott D. Wilson, 'Animals and Ethics', *Internet Encyclopedia of Philosophy* <https://www.iep.utm.edu/anim-eth/>, section 1.

[68] The Oregon Supreme Court has delivered two interesting judgments in this regard. In *State v Fessenden/Dicke* (355 Or 759 (2014)) the court affirmed a decision by a lower court, according to which 'animals were included in the class of "persons" that officers may aid without a warrant' (at 763). *State v Nix* (355 Or 777 (2014)) concerned Oregon's anti-merger statute, according to which a given type of conduct that violates only one statute constitutes as many crimes as there are victims. The court ruled that animals are such victims, which is why the defendant could be convicted of twenty counts of animal neglect rather than one.

[69] In Nordic law, the offended party (in Swedish *målsägande,* in Finnish *asianomistaja*, in Norwegian *fornærmede*) is a procedural status in criminal cases; it is typically the same person as the victim, except in homicide cases. An offended party may for instance ask the prosecutor

Summing Up

To conclude, passive legal personhood consists of three substantive incidents—fundamental protections, the capacity to be a party to special rights, and the capacity to own property—and three incidents that have to do with the enforceability of one's substantive incidents, as well as with sanctions that may be applied if the duties pertaining to the substantive incidents are not fulfilled. Before considering the benefits of this new approach as opposed to the Orthodox View, I will present the active incidents as well.

Active Incidents of Legal Personhood

We have so far been focusing on the passive incidents of legal personhood, with which even small children and mentally severely disabled individuals are currently endowed. However, according to one of the main extensional beliefs from which I have proceeded, there are some relevant legal differences between the legal personhood of the just-mentioned individuals and that of adults of sound mind. That difference consists in whether one is endowed with the active incidents of legal personhood. I identify two such incidents: the capacity to perform acts-in-the-law (*legal competences*) and legal responsibility (*onerous legal personhood*). Western contemporary legal systems do not enable toddlers or people with serious mental deficiencies to enter into contracts, nor are such creatures or individuals punished for their wrongdoings in the fora of criminal law.

I should note here that the threshold between being an active and a passive legal person is not clear-cut. For instance, there are usually legal rules that determine an age of majority, but typically even younger people may enter into some contracts and be liable for some of their actions. This is why some scholars distinguish between 'capacity', 'limited incapacity', and 'total incapacity'.[70] I will return to this issue in Chapter 4, as well as to the question of who or what can be a passive and/or active legal person.

Legal Competences

A notion closely associated with legal personhood is that of *will* or *choice*. The concept of will was important in the German philosophy of the eighteenth and nineteenth centuries, and has ever since been central in the will theories of rights. This will has also been connected with legal personhood for a long time. The firmest

to sue for damages during the criminal trial, so that a separate civil suit need not be brought to court. If the offended party is a minor, this power is exercised by his or her representative.

[70] Andreas Heldrich and Anton F. Steiner, 'Capacity', *International Encyclopedia of Comparative Law, Volume IV: Persons and Family* (Mohr Siebeck and Martinus Nijhoff 2007) 2–21.

such connection emerges when legal personhood is taken to be the holding of will-theory rights. Such a conception of legal personhood is not tenable, for reasons laid out in the preceding chapter, but legal personhood and having a legal will are nevertheless closely related.

A rather stark example of the connection between legal personhood and will is the 1858 verdict of the Virginia Supreme Court of Appeals in *Bailey v Poindexter's Executor*.[71] The late slave owner John Lewis Poindexter had in his last will and testament determined that his slaves either be freed—in which case they would need to leave the State of Virginia—or be publicly auctioned. The slaves themselves could choose which option they preferred. (These rather bizarre terms were due to the conditions set out in state legislation, which declared that any manumitted slave would need to leave the state within a year from the manumission or be reenslaved. Thus, emancipation was accompanied by exile.) However, the high court determined—against precedent—that any will granting such a choice to a slave is void. The majority opinion held that Poindexter had 'endeavored to clothe his slaves with the uncontrollable and irrevocable power of determining for themselves whether they shall be manumitted'.[72] The manumission could depend on other types of events but not on slaves' choices, because giving legal recognition to such choices would imply endowing the slaves in question with 'legal capacity'.[73] Similarly, the doctrines of coverture and the Swedish–Finnish guardianship restricted women's capacity to dispose of their property, to sue and so on. All these examples involve restrictions on the *legal competences* of women and slaves.

Defining competence

The term 'act-in the-law' (also 'legal act', 'legal transaction') is used, especially among Continental jurists, to refer to intentional acts that constitute the creation, upholding, or termination of entitlements, particularly in the field of private law. 'Competence' or 'capacity' refers to one's ability to perform acts-in-the-law. Because of the ambiguity of 'capacity', I will use 'competence' here.

I should begin by stressing that legal competences ought not to be confused with Hohfeldian powers. I have already mentioned in Chapter 2 that if a volitional act causes a change in legal relations, this is an exercise of a Hohfeldian power. Not all such acts are acts-in-the-law, however. X's having a Hohfeldian legal power with respect to Y and Z means that X can, through volitional conduct, effect a change in a legal relation that currently obtains between Y and Z. X does not actually have to

[71] *Bailey v Poindexter's Executor*, 55 Va 132, 14 Gratton 132 (1858). See also Colin Dayan, *The Law is a White Dog: How Legal Rituals Make and Unmake Persons* (Princeton University Press 2011) 140–76.

[72] *Bailey v Poindexter's Executor* 99 (cited in Higginbotham Jr and Kopytoff (n 49) 537).

[73] Ibid. 536–7.

intend to cause the legal change in question as long as X's volitional conduct causes the change.

The Hohfeldian power is consequently quite wide-ranging, given that hitting somebody constitutes an exercise of a power because legal relations have been changed through the performance of a volitional action. Thus, a homeless person could commit a crime in order to spend the night in jail, and this would constitute an exercise of a legal power according to Hohfeld's account. For some theorists, this constitutes a counterexample to the Hohfeldian conception, which seems to yield counterintuitive results. Another well-known putative counterexample is moving house, which is an intentional action that has legal consequences but is regarded by many theorists as not an instance of an exercise of a legal power.[74] In any case, the Hohfeldian power is clearly too expansive for our current purposes, as children and even nonhuman animals change legal relations through volitional conduct all the time. The Hohfeldian power is thus not very helpful when distinguishing passive and active legal personhood. The narrower concept of competence, on the other hand, is crucial in this distinction.

The notion of competence has been central in Anglo-American legal philosophy ever since H. L. A. Hart made the famous distinction between power-conferring and duty-imposing rules, though he used the label 'power' instead of 'competence' to refer to the notion. He wrote:

> Legal rules defining the ways in which valid contracts or wills or marriages are made do not require persons to act in certain ways whether they wish to or not. Such laws do not impose duties or obligations. Instead, they provide individuals with facilities for realizing their wishes, by conferring legal powers upon them to create, by certain specified procedures and subject to certain conditions, structures of rights and duties within the coercive framework of the law.[75]

Hart was likely not referring to Hohfeld's conception of a legal power, but rather to a more circumscribed notion that corresponds with the Continental idea of competence. Indeed, Hart himself recognized the relationship between power-conferring rules and competence.[76] I have elsewhere argued for the following definitions of legal competence and act-in-the-law:[77]

Legal competence:

1. X holds the competence C to effect the legal consequence r if and only if X can perform an act-in-the-law to bring about r.
2. If X holds C, any act by X that effects r is an exercise of C.

[74] See Joseph Raz, 'Voluntary Obligations and Normative Powers' (1972) 46 *Proceedings of the Aristotelian Society* 79, 80.

[75] H. L.A. Hart, *The Concept of Law* (Clarendon Press 1964) 27–28.

[76] Ibid 284.

[77] Visa A.J. Kurki, 'Legal Competence and Legal Power' in Mark McBride (ed.), *New Essays on the Nature of Rights* (Hart Publishing 2017).

Act-in-the-law:
Act A, performed by X, constitutes an act-in-the-law if and only if

1. X performs A with the intention to bring about the legal consequence r, and
2. the fact that X has performed A in order to bring about r is an element of a set of actually occurrent conditions minimally sufficient for r.

The definition employs the logical structure of minimal sufficiency. I have already presented the idea of minimal sufficiency in Chapter 2—when discussing Bentham's test—but I will mention its main features here. A set of facts is minimally sufficient for some state of affairs S if and only if (i) the set is sufficient for S and (ii) every element in the set is necessary for the sufficiency of the set. We can contrast minimal sufficiency with joint sufficiency. If my signing a contract is sufficient in order for me to become bound by that contract, then my signing that contract while wearing a green hat is (ordinarily) also sufficient. The signing and the hat-wearing are thus jointly sufficient for the contractual obligations to obtain. However, these two conditions are jointly not *minimally* sufficient, because the hat-wearing is in fact completely irrelevant for the legal consequence. Nor is minimal sufficiency equivalent to the logical structure where certain conditions are individually necessary and jointly sufficient for a state of affairs S to obtain; the elements in a set that is minimally sufficient for *S* might not be individually necessary conditions for S.

To conclude, acts-in-the-law are acts which effect changes in legal relations in virtue of the fact that they have been performed with the intention to effect the change in question. Legal institutions in which participation involves the performance of acts-in-the-law are typically restricted to legal persons: slaves and married women who were for many purposes denied legal personhood could not perform the acts-in-the-law required for, say, a contract. However, one can be unable to perform acts-in-the-law and yet be a legal person, as infants exemplify. In this case, an infant typically needs a representative who performs the acts-in-the-law on the infant's behalf. In addition, being able merely to perform acts-in-the-law while representing someone else is not indicative of legal personhood. Slaves in ancient Rome could perform acts-in-the-law, but they were merely representing their masters. One must hold competences pertaining to one's own legal platform, if the competences are to count as an incident of legal personhood.

Onerous Legal Personhood

Yet another distinction between nonhuman animals and infants on one hand, and adults of sound mind on the other, is the fact that adults of sound mind are held legally responsible for their acts in various ways. Such responsibility functions through *genuine duties*, that is, duties accompanied by the prospect of legal sanctions. I am referring in particular to criminal and civil responsibility: in contemporary Western legal systems, only legal persons can be sued for their wrongdoings, and only they can be subjected to criminal sanctions. I call this element of legal personhood *onerous legal personhood*.

Onerous legal personhood is, of course, not the only way of controlling entities. Most obviously, inanimate beings are controlled through other means than by demanding some type of conduct of them: enacting a legal duty for a bridge not to collapse does not save lives. Though legal systems usually require some kinds of conduct of animals, such requirements are usually understood as the duties of human beings who are legally obligated to take measures in order to ensure that animals under their control do not cause harm to public or other persons' interests. This is not to say that modern legal systems would not impose some punishment-like institutions on animals: for example, dogs that attack human beings may be euthanized because of their aggressiveness. Nevertheless, the institutions of private-law and criminal-law responsibility are not applied to assess the behaviour of nonhuman animals in the same way as that of legal persons. If we leave out the historical curiosity of animal trials, animals are not prosecuted or held tortiously liable for their actions.

The fact that women have historically often occupied a kind of 'grey zone' between full legal personhood and nonpersonhood is also occasionally reflected in their legal responsibility. Blackstone writes:

> But though our law in general considers man and wife as one person, yet there are some instances in which she is separately considered; as inferior to him, and acting by his compulsion. And therefore any deeds executed, and acts done, by her, during her coverture, are void [...]. And in some felonies, and other inferior crimes, committed by her through constraint of her husband, the law excuses her: but this extends not to treason or murder.[78]

Onerous legal personhood again illustrates the interconnectedness of the incidents of legal personhood: for instance, most forms of tort liability are only feasible if one can own property. Corporations are held civilly—and occasionally criminally—liable, which is made feasible by the fact that corporations can own property. However, criminal responsibility has been ascribed to slaves despite their not being legal persons for most other purposes. Considering an adult human being of sound mind a nonperson in the eyes of the criminal law—meaning that he or she could not commit crimes—would often be an impractical choice. It would tend to undermine one of the elements of the minimum content of natural law as set out by Hart, since the ability of humans to harm one another would not be fully recognized by one of the primary legal institutions that the society uses to control behaviour.[79] Andrew Fede explains why slaves could be accused of crimes in the antebellum US:

> [W]hy did the law not treat the slave like property that could not be criminally liable? The answer lies just below the surface of the various colonial codes. Slaves were, biologically, people who could commit crimes against third parties. When a master's slave injured a third party's

[78] Blackstone (n 53) 775. [79] See Hart (n 75) 193–9.

> right, somebody had to be held criminally responsible. There were only two alternatives—the master and the slave. The former was unacceptable under all theories of common law jurisprudence. The slave had to be the candidate for criminality.
>
> [...]
>
> The law had to recognize the fact [...] that slaves could commit crimes that endangered the public peace and implicated the purposes of criminal law. [...] Slaves, moreover, violently attacked persons and committed property crimes that impaired the rights of third parties in society. [...] This conflict of interests was easily solved by the criminal law of slavery.[80]

The fact that slaves were criminally liable shows also why Hans Kelsen's claim—'that a slave is legally no person, or has no legal personhood, means that there are no legal norms qualifying any behavior of this individual as a duty or a right'[81]—does not accurately depict the institution of slavery. Some aspects pertaining to this incident will be discussed in Chapter 4, which is why I will not address legal responsibility further here.

Assessing the Bundle Theory

This chapter has laid out the incidents of legal personhood. I have shown through examples how paradigmatic legal persons are typically endowed with these incidents whereas paradigmatic nonpersons typically lack these incidents. My account will be further developed in Chapter 4, which will be focused on numerous questions about active and passive legal personhood. I will now consider some benefits of my approach over the Orthodox View, and then discuss the connections between legal personhood and other personhood conceptions.

First, my approach is consistent with the central extensional beliefs regarding legal personhood. Second, it avoids the most glaring pitfalls of the Orthodox View. As legal personhood is not treated as a strictly binary concept here, I can account for the fact that slaves held some claim-rights but were not legal persons, and that women's path to 'full' legal personhood was a matter of gradual change over time. The fact that slaves were legal nonpersons in general but could nevertheless be sentenced in criminal trials is hard to explain if legal personhood is defined as the holding of any rights and/or the bearing of any duties. This difficulty is exemplified by Kelsen's assertion that slaves did not bear any duties. Similarly, claims such as 'women were not legal persons in England in the nineteenth century' may be correct, but clearly wrong is any suggestion that English women of that time held no legal positions that are classifiable as rights or duties. It would be equally bizarre to claim that granting these women just one right or duty each would have turned them into legal persons *tout court*. The whole issue can be better understood by approaching legal personhood as

80 Fede (n 61) 161–2.

81 Hans Kelsen, *General Theory of Law and State* (Transaction Publishers 2006) 95.

a cluster property, whereby one can gradually gain personhood-related benefits and burdens. Relatedly, the proposed theory can take into account the fact that children acquire active incidents over time as they grow, until they become active legal persons at the age of majority. The analysis of these 'grey areas' will be refined in the next chapter, where I will distinguish *independent*, *dependent*, and *purely passive legal personhood*. I will return to the limited legal personhood of slaves in the next chapter as well, denoting it *purely onerous legal personhood*.

Third, the Orthodox View relies wholly on the contested concept of a right. This is obviously not a fatal problem in itself, but it is *ceteris paribus* better for a theory to rely on as few contested concepts as possible. My theory does, of course, rely on some contested concepts and evaluative assumptions as well, but the central assumptions are relatively uncontroversial, and the success of the theory does not turn on any of the more controversial assumptions—such as that animals are of ultimate value. I should also mention that, even though I have eschewed the use of the term 'right', there is nothing inherently wrong with talking about 'personhood rights' or 'rights of legal personhood'. One who accepts the interest theory may perfectly well speak of beneficiary ownership as an array of personhood rights. Will theorists may also speak of such rights at least as far as active legal persons are concerned. I have mostly refrained from employing such terminology here, in order to stay neutral between the will and the interest theories. The distinction between personhood-related rights and other rights may nevertheless help us understand what the Nonhuman Rights Project and other animal rights advocates are doing: they are not content with the limited 'thin' rights currently held by animals, and demand that personhood rights be extended to these creatures.

Finally, my approach can explain the relatively common distinction between the protection of animals that lack legal personality and the protection of animals through legal personality. For instance, the New York Supreme Court, Appellate Division, denied the 'rights paradigm' to the chimpanzee Tommy but maintained that animals are nevertheless protected by animal welfare statutes.[82] If we understand 'rights' as claim-rights here, the court's distinction does not make sense, given that animals already hold numerous claim-rights against certain forms of conduct.[83] However, the court was treating right-holding and legal personality synonymously in its verdict. If we replace 'rights paradigm' with 'legal personhood' in the verdict, it does make more sense, as the court affirmed that the incidents of legal personhood pertaining to *habeas corpus* ought not to be granted to Tommy.

[82] *People ex rel. Nonhuman Rights Project, Inc. v Lavery*, No 518336, 2014 WL 680276 (NY App. Div. 4 December 2014) 4.

[83] *Habeas corpus* cannot in any case be construed as a will-theory right given that a third party can act in the name of the detainee regardless of whether the third party has been authorized to do so by the detainee.

Separate or Connected?

My account raises the question whether there is any single overarching 'legal personhood', or whether instead one should address each of the different legal incidents separately.[84] There is, however, good reason to understand 'legal personhood' as a cluster designation rather than as an umbrella term that encompasses separate issues.

Legal personhood is, in a way, analogous to what Western legal systems portray as its opposite: thinghood. What is characteristic of things (in one legal sense of the word 'thing') is that they can be owned, and ownership consists of combinable and disseverable incidents. However, this analysis and the fact that not all the incidents are present at every instance of ownership have not led legal scholars to stop addressing ownership in favour of discussing only these separate incidents. There are probably several reasons for this, but one such reason is that the incidents of ownership constitute a *functional whole*, which is also an institutional foundation of modern capitalist economies. The individual incidents of ownership are interconnected in numerous ways: for instance, ownership could not facilitate the achievement of Pareto optimality—where no one could be made better off without making someone worse off—unless ownership included the liberty to use, the right to security (claim-right against others taking the thing without permission), and transmissibility. If one only had the liberty to use and the right to security, one could not sell or give the thing in question to someone who values it more; and if a thing could only be transmitted but not used, then no one could enjoy the thing. This is only one example of how the separate incidents of ownership together give the institution of ownership its societal meaning.

The incidents of legal personhood are similarly interconnected in various ways. They together enable legal personhood to fulfil its various functions in a Western society. I have already mentioned numerous examples of this interconnectedness: Legal contracts are, in most cases, only feasible if one can be held responsible for not respecting one's obligations. At the same time, many forms of legal responsibility presuppose ownership rights. The concept of civil liability requires in a typical case that both the plaintiff and the defendant have the capacity to own property and have legal standing; that the plaintiff has the capacity to be legally harmed; and that the defendant can be held legally responsible. In this way, legal personhood unifies different aspects of the legal system. It allows for the assignment of reward and blame to the same entities. This is what justifies considering legal personhood as an overarching entity even if its nature is encapsulated by a cluster concept: its elements are interwoven and interact in various ways.

[84] Bryan Thomas seems sceptical of addressing legal personhood as a whole. Bryan Thomas, 'A Critical Review of Law's Meaning of Life: Philosophy, Religion, Darwin and the Legal Person' (2011) 38 *Journal of Law and Society* 631.

I should also touch briefly on the issue of what is a sufficient number of incidents to constitute legal personhood *tout court* for an entity that is endowed with the incidents. I have repeatedly maintained that there is no clear-cut division between legal persons and nonpersons. There are clear and central cases, such as the legal personhood enjoyed by adults of sound mind in contemporary Western jurisdictions, but the penumbra between the clear cases of legal personhood and nonpersonhood is vast. In addition, because of the cluster-property nature of legal personhood, a binary question about X's personhood or nonpersonhood may not always be appropriate. One must often rather ask about the respects in which X is a legal person. Corporations are legal persons for most purposes, but not all purposes.

Property ownership is a major feature of legal personhood that unifies numerous incidents of legal personhood, but it is not a necessary condition of legal personhood *tout court*. Consider, for instance, a radical scenario where the property status of nonhuman animals would be abolished and where they would receive fundamental protections on a par with those which natural persons currently enjoy. These fundamental protections would be accompanied by robust criminal-law safeguards so that the intentional killing of a nonhuman animal would constitute homicide. Finally, if a human being's interference with an animal's claim-rights were ongoing, the animal would have the standing to sue the human for injunctive relief. It would be appropriate to call such an arrangement legal personhood *tout court* even though the animals would not have the capacity to own property.

Yet another question pertaining to legal personhood *tout court* is the relationship between passive and active legal personhood. The passive incidents can constitute legal personhood for their holder, whereas the active incidents alone are not sufficient for legal personhood *tout court*. Let us take slavery as an example. Slaves were potential malefactors in the eyes of the criminal law in the US. They also held some competences pertaining to criminal trials, and were thus endowed with both of the active incidents of legal personhood. Now, even though the method of reflective equilibrium would allow for the reconsideration of the extensional belief pertaining to slaves, my theory does not give rise to a need to reclassify slaves as legal persons *tout court*. The number of incidents they were endowed with was simply too limited to warrant classifying them as legal persons *tout court*. A legal person endowed only with active incidents can merely be burdened by onerous legal personhood and be empowered to act as the agent of someone else, as with the slaves of ancient Rome who represented their masters.

Legal Person and Subject of Law

As I have mentioned, many non-Anglophone jurisdictions currently use 'subject of law/right(s)' and 'legal person' synonymously. Because terms and phrases such as *Rechtssubjekt* can be understood as 'subject of rights', my claim that animals currently hold rights despite not being 'subjects of rights' (i.e. legal persons) may seem odd. One

Table 3.4 Subjecthood under contract law

	Passive subjecthood	Active subjecthood
Substantive aspect	Capacity to be party to a contract (special rights)	Legal competence to enter contracts oneself; capacity to bear contract-law duties
Procedural aspect	Capacity to be party to a lawsuit over contract (invested aspect of standing)	Legal competence to, for example, choose to sue in order to enforce the contract

solution to this conundrum is to distinguish 'subject of law' from 'legal person', as Tomasz Pietrzykowski has proposed.[85] I will now develop this idea further. Disentangling 'subject' and 'person' allows for a complementary approach to the incidents of legal personhood, an approach that especially jurists with a civil-law background may find appealing. Whereas legal personhood is a cluster concept, 'legal subjecthood' refers to one's status within a field of law or with regard to a legal institution.

I have above distinguished active and passive incidents of legal personhood, as well as substantive and remedy incidents. When addressing legal subjecthood, it is useful to contrast the substantive incidents with the procedural incidents. We can use these two bifurcations—active/passive and substantive/procedural—to assess the status of an entity under a particular area of law. Let me take contract law as an example, illustrated in Table 3.4.

The four categories will become clearer if we compare infants, adults, and nonhuman animals. Contracts can be entered on behalf of an infant (passive–substantive), and the contract can enforced in court in the infant's name (passive–procedural). Infants are therefore *passive subjects of contract law*. Being an active subject of contract law, on the other hand, has chiefly to do with competences and duties. Adults of sound mind can decide which contracts to enter into and whether to sue over a contract; they must also fulfil the ensuing duties personally unless they have delegated the responsibility. They are therefore both *active and passive subjects of contract law*. Animals, however, are neither passive nor active subjects of contract law; they cannot be parties to contracts, nor to lawsuits over contracts.[86]

The subjects of contract law and tort law (see Table 3.5) are also legal persons in contemporary Western legal systems. However, let us take an example where such a coextension does not apply, that is, where the subjects of some area of law are not legal persons. Nonhuman animals are in Finland protected under the Animal Welfare Act[87] as well as other legislation. I will here focus on that part of Finnish

[85] See Pietrzykowski, 'The Idea of Non-Personal Subjects of Law' (n 1) and Pietrzykowski, 'Beyond Personhood: From Two Conceptions of Rights to Two Kinds of Right-Holders' (n 1).

[86] One exception might be animals that are beneficiaries of trusts.

[87] *Eläinsuojelulaki* (247/1996).

Table 3.5 Subjecthood under tort law

	Passive subjecthood	Active subjecthood
Substantive aspect	Capacity to suffer a tort (capacity to be legally harmed)	Capacity to be a tortfeasor
Procedural aspect	Capacity to be party to a lawsuit over tort (invested aspect of standing)	Legal competence to, for example, choose to sue in order to reclaim compensation for tort

animal welfare law that is classifiable as administrative law (thus excluding the criminal-law provisions). Animal welfare law provides sentient animals with claim-rights pertaining to their treatment; at least some of these claim-rights are likely classifiable as fundamental protections. However, animals are in many ways 'invisible' when it comes to the procedural aspect of animal law. For instance, consider a situation where an animal welfare inspector makes a decision on whether owner O has maltreated animal A. Only O is a considered party to the decision and is therefore empowered to challenge the decision in court; no one can challenge the decision on A's behalf. The animal is therefore not endowed with the same procedural status as the owner.

Animals are therefore subjects of animal welfare law insofar as the passive–substantive aspect is concerned (see Table 3.6). However, classifying animals as legal persons is regardless not warranted, because the animals are only endowed with meagre fundamental protections and lack most of the other incidents of legal personhood.

I will in the next chapter address further the 'building blocks' of legal personhood, but I will simply note here that I take legal personhood as well as legal subjecthood to consist of three primary components: passive legal personhood/subjecthood consists chiefly of claim-rights, whereas active legal personhood/subjecthood comprises competences and duties. This is reflected in Tables 3.4 and 3.5.

Table 3.6 Subjecthood of animals under Finnish animal welfare law

	Passive subjecthood	Active subjecthood
Substantive aspect	Limited protection of bodily integrity	N/A
Procedural aspect	No capacity to be party to a lawsuit over, for example, the decision of an animal welfare official	No-one empowered to represent animals

To summarize, according to the distinction suggested here, legal personhood is a cluster concept, and one must be endowed with a significant number of the incidents of legal personhood in order to qualify as a legal person *tout court*. On other hand, one is a subject of law with regard to some area of law or a legal institution. Animals are not legal persons but regardless are passive subjects of animal welfare law. Similarly, countries that currently treat foetuses as persons for the purposes of criminal law could instead denote foetuses 'subjects of criminal law'—or, even less ambiguously, 'passive subjects of criminal law', to make clear that foetuses are not criminally liable.

Persons and Legal Persons

I will end this chapter by considering *why* legal personhood comprises the incidents outlined here. Even though I maintain that legal personhood should be treated as separate from other types of personhood, it does share connections with those other types—it is not a mere quirk of history that the word 'person' is used when referring to moral, metaphysical, as well as legal persons.

First, many theorists understand (moral) persons as rational agents who can be held accountable for their actions and consequently subjected to legal sanctions. Michael Moore writes (emphases added):

> [W]hat I regard as the deepest and the most basic of the psychological suppositions on which the criminal law rests [...] are the suppositions about the subjects of responsibility. Who or what can be morally responsible, what attributes a being must have to be held responsible, are the questions to which such suppositions give answer. The general form of that answer is in terms of *persons*, and so the suppositions in question amount to the *criminal law's theory of personhood*.[88]

The fact that persons can be held responsible for their past actions is also central in the Lockean account of a person that 'extends itself beyond present existence to what is past, only by consciousness, whereby it becomes concerned and accountable [and] owns and imputes to itself past actions'. [89] Doctrines of tort and criminal law rely on such a fundamental understanding of personal identity. In addition, the Lockean account underpins many legal institutions that govern the exercise of legal competences. For instance, most contracts presuppose that the parties are accountable for their past actions whereby they agreed to perform given undertakings.

Locke's account—though focused on 'actions and their merit'—is relevant with regard to passive legal personhood as well. Incidents such as special rights and the capacity to suffer legal harms normally presuppose a personal identity that extends over time. In a contract between Mary and John—where Mary agrees to perform

[88] Michael S. Moore, *Placing Blame: A Theory of the Criminal Law* (Oxford University Press 2010) 596

[89] John Locke, *An Essay Concerning Human Understanding* (1690), Book II, ch XXVII, para 26.

some service to John in a year's time—it is assumed that both Mary and John will exist in a year's time. If Mary does not perform the service, John has been harmed and is entitled to compensation. The protection of nonpersons is often different in this regard: crimes committed against animals are not understood as having wronged any individual animal that would be entitled to compensation. Favre's idea of tort for animals (presented above) would change this state of affairs, given that a specific animal could receive compensation for harms caused to that particular animal. The animal would, shortly put, be treated as an *individual* that can be *wronged*, rather than as an abstract representative of its species. Pet trusts illustrate the same aspect of personhood: when an owner sets up a trust for his pet, he is not looking to benefit animal welfare in general but rather to ensure that the particular animal companion that he has had during his lifetime will be taken care of even after his death.

In addition, many non-consequentalists maintain that there should be deontic constraints with regard to how we treat (moral) persons, regardless of the beneficial consequences a given type of treatment could have. This corresponds in particular with the fundamental protections of legal persons. Whereas slaves were only protected from 'unnecessary and excessive' whipping, interfering with the bodily integrity of free people usually requires special justification. Similarly, endowing nonhuman animals with fundamental protections implies that some of their interests are not subject to being balanced away as easily as they are under laws prohibiting the infliction of unnecessary suffering.

Finally, the Kantian account of the rights and the external freedom of persons can be explicated in terms of my theory. This external freedom can be seen as consisting of fundamental protections and property rights, which determine the sphere where a person's body and things ought not to be interfered with. Kantian contractual rights, on the other hand, can be understood as functioning through a combination of one's status as a beneficiary of special rights and one's exercise of legal competences. According to Kant, only rational beings that can legislate their own moral laws should have access to these legal institutions. Modern will theories of rights are also usually founded on such an understanding of the right-holder as a sophisticated rational agent.

Even though my framework can account for the aforementioned theories' claims about the range of beings who should be deemed criminally or civilly responsible, or about the range of beings who should be able to exercise legal competences, it does not presuppose any such demarcation. I will argue in the next chapter that even relatively small children *can* be endowed with these incidents of legal personhood, even if they perhaps *should not* be endowed with them.

4

Who or What Can be a Legal Person?

Rivers, Idols, and Corporations as Legal Persons

Throughout, this chapter will discuss who or what can be a legal person. However, addressing that issue will necessitate considering the 'inner workings' of legal personhood. These considerations will lead to analyses of several salient issues—such as the distinction between legal *person* and legal *platform*, and the nature of passive legal personhood. Human collectivities are a special case that will mostly be addressed in the next chapter, though some relevant distinctions will be made here.

The Whanganui River in New Zealand has supposedly become a legal person according to an agreement between the Whanganui Iwi (the Whanganui tribes) and the Crown, which was passed into law in 2017.[1] The Whanganui Iwi believe the river is a living being, called Te Awa Tupua, 'an indivisible whole incorporating its tributaries and all its physical and metaphysical elements from the mountains to the sea'.[2] Another example of the (putative) extension of legal personhood to an inanimate entity is the famous decision by the British Privy Council in 1925, where an Indian idol was declared to have legal personhood, with a 'will' of its own.

The very idea of extending legal personhood to nonhuman animals is likely unthinkable for many jurists. However, there is also a strand of jurisprudence which goes much further; legal personhood is here understood as an almost infinitely flexible concept with regard to its application. Cases such as those of the Whanganui River and the Indian idol are mentioned as examples in support of the proposition that legal personhood can be extended to just about anything, or at least to a very

[1] Te Awa Tupua (Whanganui River Claims Settlement) Act 2017, Public Act, 2017 No 7, date of assent 20 March 2017. Similar developments have been taking place in Australia and India, but I will focus on the Whanganui River as a case study in this chapter. See Erin L. O'Donnell and Julia Talbot-Jones, 'Creating Legal Rights for Rivers: Lessons from Australia, New Zealand, and India' (2018) 23 *Ecology and Society* 7.

[2] *Tutohu Whakatupua*, agreement between the Whanganui Iwi and the Crown, 30 August 2012. See also Elaine G. Hsiao, 'Whanganui River Agreement: Indigenous Rights and Rights of Nature' (2012) 42 *Environmental Policy and Law* 371 and Catherine J. Iorns Magallanes, 'Nature as an Ancestor: Two Examples of Legal Personality for Nature in New Zealand' (2015) 22 *VertigO—la revue électronique en sciences de l'environnement*.

large number of entities. The ultimate example according to this strand of thought is of course the corporation: a legal person without a physical form, existing purely in the 'contemplation of law', as the US Supreme Court put it in *Trustees of Dartmouth College v Woodward*.[3]

I argue in this chapter that many of these 'everything-goes' claims are actually based on a conflation of two different senses of 'legal person': the phrase is used to designate both a bundle of legal positions and an entity that holds these legal positions, and these different senses are not kept clearly separate. This leads to problematic assertions and *non sequiturs*. After distinguishing these two senses (and denoting one of them 'legal platform'), I will move on to address the question of who or what can be a legal person. Here, I will propose that the question 'who or what can be a legal person?' is best approached by determining who or what can be endowed with incidents of legal personhood. However, any determinate conclusions regarding the domain of legal personhood will require the adoption of certain evaluative assumptions regarding, for instance, the entities towards whom (or towards which) duties can be held. I will argue that extending legal personhood to animals would not pose problems, whereas extending it to rivers or idols would.

Is the whole question of the scope of legal personhood pertinent at all? Perhaps nothing much hinges on who or what can be a legal person. Such views are occasionally voiced or implied. They may proceed from the notion that only human beings are 'real' legal persons and that the concept can be extended through 'legal fictions' to even imaginary beings such as deities (as can supposedly be shown using examples from legal systems). Or they may claim that the whole concept is a 'legal fiction'. Most such accounts do not, however, tackle the issue with sufficient rigour. Some of them employ a problematic conception of legal fictions—a matter which I will briefly address in the next chapter—or they may be overly deferential to the language of courts which have occasionally attributed legal personhood to, say, idols. Looking at this issue seriously provides useful insights into the nature of legal personhood, as it makes one ponder how legal personhood actually functions. Distinguishing between the notions of legal person and legal platform brings more clarity to the discourse. Although a legislator can create a virtually infinite number of legal *platforms*—each of which comprises an array of legal positions—it does not follow that absolutely anything could be a legal *person*. Rather, the incidents of legal personhood can only be attributed to entities that can hold claim-rights or perform acts.[4]

[3] *Trustees of Dartmouth College v Woodward*, 17 US 518 (1819) 636.

[4] I agree in this regard more or less with Neil MacCormick who writes, inNeil MacCormick, *Institutions of Law. An Essay in Legal Theory* (Oxford University Press 2007) 78, that

> [f]undamental to the existence of a person are capability to have interests and to suffer harm, and capability for rational and intentional action. These are grounds for recognizing entities as persons, but not legal criteria of personateness, for each legal system lays down its own criteria settling who or what counts as a person.

I should note at the outset that I will be proceeding from a non-animistic point of view; I will not consider the possibility that idols and rivers are actually spiritual, living entities. I will in addition take as a given that abstract entities such as numbers are not candidates for legal personhood; I will assume that, even if an author would say that 'any' or 'just about any' entity could be a legal person, he or she is not referring to such mind-independent *abstracta*. I should also mention that when I address the legal personhood of rivers, I mean rivers *qua* bodies of water rather than (say) *qua* collectivities of the individuals and creatures that live off the river.

The claim that *any* entity (even with the reservations made above) could be a legal person may seem an exaggeration, but such claims are indeed made. Ngaire Naffine, who has classified accounts of legal personhood, suggests that many so-called Legalist positions—according to which legal personhood is something internal to law—subscribe to such a view. Naffine endorses the following summary of the Legalist position: 'Anything can be a legal person because legal persons are stipulated as such or defined into existence.'[5] This would be a *non sequitur*, for reasons I will address later; however, most of the authors whom Naffine classifies as Legalists do not, in my reading, subscribe to the position that she attributes to them. F. H. Lawson might appear to endorse such a position when claiming that '[a]ll that is necessary for the existence of a [legal] person is that the lawmaker, be he legislator, judge, or jurist, or even the public at large, should decide to treat it as a subject of rights or other legal relations'. Some theorists, such as Bryant Smith, assert that legal personhood *is* nothing else but legal relations:

> To regard legal personality as a thing apart from the legal relations, is to commit an error of the same sort as that of distinguishing title from the rights, powers, privileges and immunities for which it is only a compendious name. Without the relations, in either case, there is no more left than the smile of the Cheshire Cat after the cat had disappeared.[6]

David Derham, on the other hand, maintains that the concept of legal person is analogous to the concept of 'one' in arithmetic: the legal person is the 'basic unit' of law, necessary for devising legal relationships. Thus, '[f]or the logic of the system it is just as much a pure "concept" as "one" in arithmetic. It is just as independent from a human being as one is from an "apple"'.[7] A final famous example is Hans Kelsen, who defines the (legal) person as a bundle of rights and duties, whereas

[5] Ngaire Naffine, 'Who Are Law's Persons? From Cheshire Cats to Responsible Subjects' (2003) 66 *Modern Law Review* 346, 351. Naffine is here referring to Natalie Stoljar's summation of the legalist (or 'P1') position, made in private correspondence. Naffine might have realized the shortcomings of this summation, given that she does not make any mention of it in her 2009 book which builds on the article. Ngaire Naffine, *Law's Meaning of Life: Philosophy, Religion, Darwin and the Legal Person* (Hart Publishing 2009).

[6] Bryant Smith, 'Legal Personality' (1928) 37 *Yale Law Journal* 283, 294.

[7] D. P. Derham, 'Theories of Legal Personality' in Leicester Webb (ed.), *Legal Personality and Political Pluralism* (Melbourne University Press 1958) 5. See also Naffine (n 5) 352.

'man' is according to Kelsen a physical entity to which the bundle is imputed.[8] This reflects his strict bifurcation between the world of fact and the world of norms. For Kelsen, man is the point of imputation for a set of legal rights and duties, whereas a person simply is that set of rights and duties. Kelsen wanted to stress that, in the world of norms, the rights and duties are all there is; one should not hypostatize any 'bearer' of those legal positions into the world of norms. Instead, the bearer of the rights and duties resides in the world of fact—the physical world—as the point of imputation.

Rather than establishing that any entity could be a legal person, as Naffine claims, the views presented here do something different: they situate the legal person purely in the normative world, as a bundle of legal rights and duties. Such bundles are indeed 'defined into existence' (under a particular sense of 'define'), but from this it does not follow that they can appositely be imputed to absolutely any entity.

Richard Tur's view, however, falls under what Naffine seems to have in mind.[9] Tur claims that a river, as well as an idol, could indeed be a legal person. Writing decades before the agreement on the legal personality of the Whanganui River was reached, he refers to an ancient practice of giving gifts to a river in order to persuade it to rise. He ponders whether a human community and the river could in this case enter into an agreement: 'a contract would be issued, stating that if the river rose, it would be given *x* goats and *y* of the other things the society deemed valuable'.[10] Tur deems such a contract to be a product of animism, but he claims that even non-animists should recognize that 'legal personality can be given to just about anything' such as the idol in the case from 1925. He notes that '[a]n idol itself cannot act; it must do its business through its guardians. Nevertheless it was the idol to which acts were attributed, not its guardians'.[11] This pertains to Tur's more general claim that '[i]f legal

[8] See Hans Kelsen, *General Theory of Law and State* (Transaction Publishers 2006) 93–6 and Hans Kelsen, *Pure Theory of Law* (tr. Max Knight, The Lawbook Exchange, Ltd 2005) 172–3. Kelsen first introduced his views on legal personality in Hans Kelsen, 'Zur Theorie der juristischen Fiktionen. Mit besonderer Berücksichtigung von Vaihingers Philosophie des Als Ob' (1919) 1 *Annalen der Philosophie* 630. The article has recently been translated into English. Hans Kelsen and Cristof Kletzer (tr.), 'On the Theory of Juridic Fictions. With Special Consideration of Vaihinger's Philosophy of the As-If' in Maksymilian Del Mar and William Twining (eds), *Legal Fictions in Theory and Practice* (Springer 2015).

[9] June Sinclair also claims that 'the law is at liberty to confer legal personality upon any entity that it sees fit, thereby enabling it to acquire rights and duties on its own account'. J. Sinclair, 'Introduction' in Belinda Van Heerden, Alfred Cockrell, and Raylene Keightley (eds), *Boberg's Law of Persons and the Family* (Juta & Company 1999) 4. David Bilchitz maintains that 'the law may confer legal personality on any entity that it wishes'. David Bilchitz, 'Moving Beyond Arbitrariness: The Legal Personhood and Dignity of Non-Human Animals' (2009) 25 *South African Journal on Human Rights* 38, 68. See also Tomasz Pietrzykowski, *Personhood Beyond Humanism: Animals, Chimeras, Autonomous Agents and the Law* (Springer 2018) 21–2

[10] Richard Tur, 'The "Person" in Law' in Arthur Peacocke and Grant Gillett (eds), *Persons and Personality. A Contemporary Inquiry.* (Basil Blackwell, Ltd 1988) 121.

[11] Ibid.

personality is the legal capacity to bear rights and duties, then it is itself an artificial creation of the law, and anything or anyone can be a legal person'.[12] After all, if idols can be legal persons, then why not anything and anyone?

As already suggested, the position that '[a]nything can be a legal person because legal persons are stipulated as such or defined into existence' is a non sequitur. To show this, we should firstly investigate what the claim 'legal persons are stipulated as such or defined into existence' actually means. Lawson provides a relatively good exposition of this:

> Once this point [of being able to create artificial persons through incorporation] has been reached, a vista of unrestricted liberty opens up before the jurist, unrestricted, that is, by any need to make a person resemble a man or collection of men. If in any scheme of legal relations it suits him to interpolate a person at any point, he can do so and he can give it the characteristics he wants. [...] Nor is there any limit in logic, though there may be in policy, to the number of legal persons that may be interpolated at any point in human relations.[13]

Lawson is pointing out that, at least in theory, a business lawyer can create an unlimited number of corporations in order to suit the needs of an enterprise. However, Lawson is well aware that we are not discussing 'physical things' here, but rather 'abstract entities which can act as subjects and objects of legal relations'.[14] Let us for now leave aside the untenable claim that being a legal person is the same thing as being a subject and an object of legal relations; the important point here is that the creation of a corporation does not necessarily entail the conferral of legal personhood on any pre-existing entity. Rather, a new institutional fact simply comes into existence. This is analogous to the two ways *money* can exist, as John Searle has observed.[15] The more traditional way of money existing is as cash.[16] In this case, a physical object (usually a piece of metal or paper) *is* money. If a coin is melted down to make a bullet, it is no longer money; its status as money disappears, and there is less money in the world. Let us call this *physical money*. Not all money exists in this form nowadays. Most instances of money do not correspond to any particular physical objects—they are free-standing, to use Searle's term.[17] This kind of money exists only as information,

[12] Ibid.

[13] F. H. Lawson, 'The Creative Use of Legal Concepts' (1957) 32 *New York University Law Review* 909, 915–16.

[14] Ibid. 919.

[15] John Searle, *Making the Social World: The Structure of Human Civilization* (Oxford University Press 2010) 100–2. Eric Orts, too, finds similarities between money and legal personality. Eric W. Orts, *Business Persons: A Legal Theory of the Firm* (Oxford University Press 2013) 29.

[16] I will consider here only fiat money, that is, '[m]oney that a government has declared to be legal tender, although it has no intrinsic value and is not backed by reserves'. Jonathan Law and John Smullen, *A Dictionary of Finance and Banking* (4th edn, Oxford University Press 2008).

[17] Searle (n 15) 108–9.

which can be stored using different methods (human memory, paper, hard drives, etc.).[18] Let us call this *abstract money*.

Physical and abstract money are created through different methods. Physical money can be generated either by declaring that physical objects that meet certain criteria are money ('It is hereby declared that objects of type X are money'), or by manufacturing objects that meet the pre-existing criteria for counting as money. In the case of abstract money, on the other hand, the declaration is rather of the form 'Sum X of currency Y is hereby created'. Nothing *becomes* money in such an operation; money simply *comes into being*. Now, let us pose about money the question which I have posed about legal personhood: what entities can be money? In other words, to what objects can we impute the status of money? We should firstly note that the fact that abstract money exists, and can be created at will, does not illuminate these questions at all. Abstract money is by definition not an overlay on any particular object; it exists merely as a free-standing social fact. Thus, if we say, 'anything can be abstract money because abstract money is posited into existence', we are committing a category mistake: we are assuming that abstract money is an overlay on physical objects (thus turning those objects into money) even though abstract money exists independently of such objects. The creation of abstract money bears some similarity to the inception of certain artificial persons such as subsidiaries created by corporations purely for tax purposes. I will return to this matter shortly.

What of physical money? Is it possible, at least in theory, to assign the status of money to absolutely any physical object? It might be tempting to say that any physical object can function as money—it is, after all, defined into existence—but this seems doubtful. Consider the function of money: it is used as payment for goods and services. Can, say, planets function as a medium of payment? Perhaps for a much more developed space-faring species, but not for human beings in our current stage of development. How would this 'money' for instance be transferred from one owner to another, as should be possible with a medium of exchange? One could of course issue some kind of note that would represent one's ownership of the planet, but in this case the note would have become the medium of exchange rather than the planet.

I do not intend to offer a full-blown theory of what objects can be money here. Nor do I claim that money is completely analogous to legal personhood. However, two lessons can be learned here: first, the fact that abstract money can be created 'out of thin air' does not imply that anything can be money; second, even the fact that physical money is created by imposing a status on a physical object does not imply that *any* physical object could feasibly be money. Likewise, it is of course the case that the legislature, or someone else with the requisite legal competence, can purport to

[18] This kind of money can of course disappear, too, if the information that represents the money disappears. However, the information does not need to be in any particular physical form.

make a river or an idol a legal person; but this is not reason enough to conclude that rivers and idols would then actually become legal persons. Or, as William Lucy puts it when discussing the anything-goes claims, 'we might imagine a contemporary Caligula imposing a legal duty on a horse to educate children, but this is as pointless as asking for the moon on a plate'.[19]

Two Senses of 'Legal Person'

I have noted above that, in the literature, 'legal person' is used in (at least) two different ways: some use it to refer to a bundle of legal positions, others to a non-legal entity that meets certain criteria.

One can firstly say: 'John Smith is a legal person'. In this case, there is a non-legal entity (John Smith) who has an attribute that pertains to a legal system. What constitutes John Smith's legal personhood is his holding of entitlements and burdens that constitute the incidents of legal personhood. In this sense, it is quite natural to say that someone *becomes* a legal person, as when a slave is freed. However, 'legal person' is also used in another sense, referring to a particular kind of set of burdens and entitlements. For instance, a lawyer may tell her client: 'We can either create a trust or a legal person in order to manage these assets'. The lawyer is likely not implying that someone or something would become a legal person if the client opts for the latter alternative. She is rather considering a legal arrangement that does not perforce change the personhood status of anyone; the new 'legal person' may, for instance, be controlled directly by the lawyer who is already a legal person.

When we refer to a legal person, we may thus refer to (at least) two different things: (1) to an entity that holds entitlements and burdens that constitute their holder's legal personhood, or (2) to the legal entitlements and burdens themselves. Lawson, Kelsen, and others use 'legal person' roughly in the second sense. In this latter sense, legal persons may indeed be 'defined into existence'. However, this sense should not be conflated with the first one. This conflation is a source of much confusion, especially when the putative legal personhood of idols, rivers, and so on is debated. I will henceforth use 'legal person' only in the first sense, and distinguish legal persons from legal platforms.

I use 'legal platform' in a stipulated sense. One's being a legal *person* is an attribute of a non-legal entity, conferred by an efficacious legal system. It is much like the status of a piece of fibre as money in some legal system. A legal *platform*, on the other hand, is a specific kind of bundle of legal entitlements and burdens. Legal platforms exist only in the law, and can *attach* to certain kinds of entities.

Many authors who identify the legal person as a bundle of legal positions are woefully imprecise about what kind of a bundle they are referring to. Legal positions can, after all, be bundled in innumerable ways. I claim that a legal platform is a bundle of

[19] William Lucy, 'Persons in Law' (2009) 29 *Oxford Journal of Legal Studies* 787, 791.

legal positions with three main features: it is *named*, *integrated*,[20] and *separate from other similar bundles*. Let us take an example. If Mary fails to fulfil her obligations under a contract, she may incur the remedial duty to compensate the other party financially. In this case, she will lose some of her assets. Thus, her contractual legal positions are connected to her ownership-related legal positions. However, if Mary had instead entered the contract under the name of her one-woman company Mary Inc., then only the assets belonging to Mary Inc. could (in an ordinary case) have been used to compensate the other party. Mary thus controls two legal platforms, 'Mary' and 'Mary Inc.', which are separate from each other. These entities must obviously be named (with words or letters or numbers or symbols) if they are to be differentiated.

A short detour into the law of trusts can perhaps illuminate this more. Trusts are common-law legal instruments that do not exist in most civilian jurisdictions. Simply put, a trust in its primary form involves assigning defined assets to a *trustee*, who holds the title of the assets but is to administer the property in favour of the *beneficiary*. There are varying opinions about whether the position of the beneficiary should be understood as the 'beneficial ownership' of the piece of property—comprising the passive incidents of ownership—or whether the trustee and the beneficiary are in a relationship that falls under the law of obligations.[21] A theoretical solution has been devised in Scotland, which is a mixed jurisdiction. Some Scottish jurists employ the so-called dual patrimony theory in regard to trusts.[22] 'Patrimony', also known as 'patrimonium', refers here to an arrangement that is used in some civil-law and mixed jurisdictions. A patrimony, in essence, is the whole of a person's entitlements and burdens that can be said to have a monetary value, for example financial assets and debts.[23] As a general rule, any assets in a patrimony can be used to cover any debts in the same patrimony, whereas the assets of patrimony A are secure from debts pertaining to patrimony B. Now, Kenneth Reid submits that a trustee's 'general patrimony' and his or her 'trust patrimony' are separate within the Scottish law of trusts:

> Usually patrimony and personality coincide, so that a person has one patrimony only, comprising the totality of his assets and liability. In a trust, however, there are two patrimonies held by one person. A trustee, like everyone else, has his own private (or general) patrimony. But in addition he has the trust patrimony. The two patrimonies are distinct in law, and should also be kept distinct in practice, by proper labelling and accounting. The assets of one patrimony

[20] I occasionally also use the term 'interconnected' when referring to this feature of legal platforms: a legal platform is *integrated* because the incidents of legal personality comprising a legal platform are *interconnected*.

[21] See for instance J. E. Penner, 'The (True) Nature of a Beneficiary's Equitable Proprietary Interest under a Trust' (2014) 27 *Canadian Journal of Law and Jurisprudence* 473.

[22] See Kenneth G. C. Reid, 'Patrimony Not Equity: The Trust in Scotland' (2000) 8 *European Review of Private Law* 427.

[23] Jacque Ghestin, Gilles Goubeaux, and Muriel Fabre-Magnan, *Traité de Droit Civil. Introduction générale* (Librairie générale de droit et de jurisprudence 1994) 156–7.

cannot normally be transferred to the other. And if an asset is sold from one patrimony, the proceeds of the sale are paid into the same patrimony [...].[24]

The same applies to financial liabilities, which are incurred either 'in a private capacity or in the capacity as a trustee'. Thus, '[a] private creditor must claim from the private patrimony and a trust creditor from the trust patrimony. If that patrimony is empty, he must go without, for the other patrimony is not available.'[25]

The concept of patrimony here is very close to what I mean by a legal platform. This dual patrimony arrangement is, in fact, in many ways similar to some features of legal personhood. One of the hallmarks of the legal personality of business corporations—as opposed to partnerships, for instance—is the so-called limited liability or asset shielding.[26] Limited liability means that the shareholders of a business corporation are not personally liable for its debts. This is one of the reasons why an individual may wish to found a corporation to conduct business: the individual's personal assets are shielded from the creditors of the corporation. The connection to the dual patrimony model above is quite clear; Scottish trusts are similar to corporations in providing limited liability.

An important aspect of being a legal person is that one corresponds to at least one legal platform, meaning that one holds the entitlements and burdens which pertain to that platform. I call this *attachment*: legal platforms attach to legal persons. As one-person corporations such as Mary Inc. and Scottish trusts illustrate, several legal platforms can attach to a single legal person.[27] (If this were not the case, one would perhaps not need to distinguish 'legal platform' from 'legal person' at all.)

The separateness of two legal platforms is somewhat a matter of degree. One example of this is married couples. Western legal systems adopt different positions on the question whether somebody can be held financially liable for a debt that his or her spouse has taken. In the Netherlands a married couple share all of their property, which is then divided equally in the case of a divorce.[28] The husband may thus end up partly responsible for a debt that the wife has incurred. In such a situation, the legal platforms of the individuals have been merged for some purposes. Another relevant example is that an individual may end up personally liable for the debts of his or her company if the corporate veil is pierced. However, these are exceptions to the general rule of separateness.

[24] Reid (n 22) 432. [25] Ibid.

[26] See for instance Reinier Kraakman and others, *The Anatomy of Corporate Law: A Comparative and Functional Approach* (2nd edn, Oxford University Press 2009) 5–10.

[27] It seems to me that the corporation sole, which puzzled Frederick Maitland, could also be fruitfully approached from this point of view. See F.W. Maitland, *State, Trust and Corporation* (David Runciman and Magnus Ryan eds, Cambridge University Press 2003) 9–31.

[28] See Masha Antokolskaia and Katharina Boele-Woelki, 'Dutch Family Law in the 21st Century: Trend-Setting and Straggling behind at the Same Time' (2002) 6 *Electronic Journal of Comparative Law*.

The person/platform distinction shows how both primary senses of *persona* ('individual' and 'mask, role') are relevant with regard to legal personhood. An individual's natural legal platform exemplifies the idea of a continuous whole: whatever roles that individual has, any special rights and duties as well as assets and liabilities that he or she acquires will be assimilated into the same legal platform.[29] On the other hand, jurisdictions that allow for one-person corporations thereby enable any person X to dissever certain roles from others. She may, for instance, separate her professional assets and liabilities from her private ones and thus control two legal platforms. This can be interpreted as the law's granting separate 'masks' to X, who may not be legally liable for some wrongful acts performed in the name of the corporation rather than the natural legal platform of X.[30]

The Naming of Legal Platforms

Apart from the integratedness of a legal platform and its separateness from other such entities, a third feature of legal platforms is that they are typically *named* using proper names or other designations in order to distinguish the particular platform from other platforms.[31] The naming of legal platforms partly accounts for the assertions that beings such as rivers could be legal persons, as we can of course name a legal platform 'the Whanganui River'.

We should firstly note here that each human being typically corresponds to what was above denoted by Reid as a 'private patrimony', and what I call a *natural legal platform* as an allusion to the phrase 'natural person'. This is the legal platform that in ordinary cases follows an individual from cradle—perhaps even from womb—to grave. In extraordinary cases, X's legal platform may stop being attached to X, for instance if X loses all proof of identity. It is also theoretically possible to steal someone else's identity and thus be in control of that individual's natural legal platform.[32] However, a much more common example of one's being in control of several legal platforms is, of course, the founding of a one-person corporation. The corporation must be given

[29] In treating an individual as a single, continuous entity, the law may in fact go further than many theories of personhood go. Consider X1 who commits a murder without being found out. He is later assaulted and struck on the head, which causes him to lose all memory of his former self. In addition, his character changes completely; he becomes a benevolent man, X2, who devotes his life to good causes. As many theorists associate personal identity with memories and character traits, such theories would imply that X2 is not the same person as X1. However, the legal system could very well require that X2 be sentenced for murder, if it was found out that a man with X2's DNA and fingerprints had committed the murder. X1 and X2 would consequently be treated as the same person by the legal system, but not according to the aforementioned theories of personal identity.

[30] In this case, many theories of personal identity would consider X as being responsible for the acts whereas X's legal liability would only extend to the liabilities of the corporation.

[31] See Orts (n 15) 33.

[32] This kind of identity theft is a major plot theme in the TV series *Mad Men*. While serving in the Korean War, the orphan protagonist switches his dog tag with that of his dead comrade in order to get home sooner. He then assumes the identity of the dead person.

Figure 4.1 Legal platforms associated with Mary.

a name to make clear when Mary is performing some act-in-the-law in the name of her one-woman corporation rather than in her own name, as this determines the legal platform of which the new entitlements and burdens become a part. Mary has thus two different legal masks, 'Mary' and 'Mary Inc.' (see Figure 4.1).

On the other hand, we have legal platforms that are named after some individuals or natural objects but do not attach to them. The fact that there is a chain of department stores called 'John Lewis' does not lead us to think that the legal platform here necessarily attaches to the John Lewis who founded the chain in the nineteenth century. If I buy a shirt from John Lewis, it is obvious that I am not buying it from the man but from the company. Similarly, it is obvious that the corporation Amazon need not have anything to do with the rainforest and that the city of Cambridge (as a public entity with a council and a mayor) is not the same thing as the geographic area of Cambridge. However, some people have thought differently with regard to the Whanganui River and the historical case of the idol. In each case, it has been claimed not merely that there is a legal platform called 'Te Awa Tupua' or 'the idol', but also that the river and the idol (either as spiritual beings or as physical objects) *are* legal persons. This would mean that a legal platform attaches to the river or to the idol in some manner analogous to the manner in which the legal platform 'John Smith' attaches to the human being John Smith. The matter leads us to a crucial question: to whom or what can a legal platform meaningfully attach? However, before moving on to address this question, I will address one foundational objection.

One can challenge the whole inquiry as misguided. I have distinguished legal platforms from legal persons, but one might say that my definition of a legal *platform* is in fact the correct definition of a legal *person*. There would thus be no reason to ask who or what can be a legal person, because legal persons are simply integrated and separate bundles of legal positions. Kelsen offers this kind of solution, but it is outlandish. If one adopted this usage, propositions such as 'John Smith is a legal person' would be necessarily false (assuming that 'John Smith' refers here to a human being rather than to a legal platform named 'John Smith'). One would rather need to say, for instance, 'There is a legal person that attaches to John Smith'. Moreover, the adoption of such a formulation would not avert the need to determine whether 'legal persons' can be attributed to, say, animals, artificial intelligences, and idols. The question I am now trying to answer would still be pertinent, though it would be framed using more peculiar language.

Attachment through Claim-Rights and Acts

With the distinctions made above at hand, we can finally pin down who or what can be a legal person. This is a question of attribution, or attachment. Roughly put, I maintain that attachment is only possible for entities that can hold claim-rights or can perform acts.

I have so far adverted to the incidents of legal personhood, but I have been somewhat vague about their components. In order to determine which entities can be legal persons, we must determine the relevant building blocks of legal personhood and then ascertain to whom or what these elements can be extended. The structure of my argument here will be the following. I will firstly argue that passive legal personhood functions primarily through the conferral of benefits in the form of claim-rights, which is why the scope of passive legal personhood can be determined by asking who or what can hold claim-rights. The primary group of claim-holders is sentient beings. (Human collectivities can hold claims too, but I will address them in the next chapter.)

On the other hand, the key elements of active legal personhood are centred on legal responsibility and legal competences. Legal responsibility is connected to the capacity to bear duties, which is why even some animals can be held legally responsible—though holding them responsible may be morally wrong. Legal competences are primarily exercised through acts-in-the-law, deliberately performed to bring about a legal consequence that is attached to the act (see Chapter 3). The capacity to perform acts-in-the-law presupposes a certain degree of understanding of the institutional reality and in particular of the ways in which one can avail oneself of the institutions through the use of symbols. Even though dogs can be punished, dogs lack the cognitive abilities to enter into legal contracts.[33] Rivers and trees cannot hold claims nor can they perform acts, which is why they cannot be legal persons. Tur has maintained, in a passage cited above, that an act could correctly be attributed to an idol. His contention is, however, unsustainable; idols cannot perform acts. So

[33] There is of course nothing conceptually odd about someone else contracting on the dog's behalf, just as one can represent minors. However, when I refer here to X's contracting, I mean that X performs the legal act that constitutes the formation of the contract.

what would a putative attribution of the act to the idol mean? The platform/person distinction provides a relatively obvious answer: this 'attribution' of an act to the idol means simply that the legal consequences of the act affect the legal platform 'the idol' rather than the natural legal platform of the administrator of the idol. However, this does not mean that the corresponding physical object would actually be involved in this in a way that would justify designating it a legal person.

Passive Legal Personhood

If X is only endowed with passive legal personhood, then X has legal representatives who can perform duties and legal acts on X's behalf (such as the payment of any taxes pertaining to X's property or the suing of third parties in order to enforce X's claims). However, this does not yet tell us who or what can be represented as a passive legal person.

As already mentioned, the putative recognition by legal systems of the legal personhood of idols and rivers may induce one to embrace an 'everything-goes' view of passive legal personhood, according to which a legal system can treat virtually anything as a legal person. Any such temptation should be resisted. It is of course clear that a legal platform can be in some kind of connection to almost any physical object. The legal platform 'Te Awa Tupua' is connected to the existence of the Whanganui River: presumably, if the river were to cease to exist (perhaps because of a natural catastrophe), the corresponding legal platform would also be dissolved. I call this *weak attachment*. Weak attachment of a platform to an entity means that the existence of the platform is dependent on the existence of the entity, just as the existence of the natural legal platform 'John Smith' is primarily dependent on the life of John Smith.[34] The legal arrangement pertaining to the Whanganui River is in this regard different from a typical corporation. This weak attachment of a legal platform to a physical object does not, however, yet constitute legal personhood for the object of attribution. Consider, for instance, an organization that has as its purpose the preservation of a particular old manuscript. Let us assume that if the manuscript is destroyed, the organization will be dissolved. The legal platform of the organization attaches thus weakly to the manuscript. Nonetheless, the manuscript is not a legal person. Similarly, let us suppose for instance that two villages, located on adjacent islands, establish a common firefighting organization responsible for putting out fires on the two islands. However, the representatives of both villages are aware that the old bridge connecting the two villages will only stay functional for a couple

[34] One should note here that the termination of the object of weak attachment does not necessarily alone *constitute* the dissolving of the legal platform. In many jurisdictions, if John Smith dies, his natural legal platform may continue to exist as a separate bundle of legal positions until some necessary procedures are performed by the heirs, such as dividing the estate. Similarly, the destruction of the manuscript does not necessarily alone constitute the dissolving of the relevant legal platform but is rather the first step in such dissolution.

of years, and it is thus agreed that the organization will be dissolved once the bridge is no longer in serviceable condition. All the same, the bridge is not a legal person. In short, weak attachment alone cannot ground legal personhood for the object of attachment.

Legal personhood-constituting attachment of a platform to an entity involves rather the attribution to the entity of the legal positions which are included in the platform. Hence, in order to establish who or what can be a legal person, we should identify what kinds of entities can hold the relevant types of legal positions. First, active legal personhood requires that one can perform acts-in-the-law and be held legally responsible. I will address this later in detail. Passive legal personhood consists, on the other hand, primarily of claim-rights.[35]

Consider the legal status of a child, as opposed to, say, a nonhuman animal (in a typical contemporary legal system). First, the child holds various claim-rights 'against the world' that protect him or her primarily from physical and some psychological harm. [36] The extent and stringency of such protections are much more considerable than those of similar protections extended to animals. Adults of sound mind, too, hold such claim-rights, though they may have powers to waive them in certain circumstances. However, there is a type of claim-right that is necessary for the functioning of the legal personhood of a child but not that of an adult: a child holds fiduciary claim-rights that pertain to his or her legal platform. If a child is assaulted, it is up to the representative(s) of the child to demand compensation from the assailant and to administer the compensation for the good of the child; the representatives may not use the compensation for their own benefit.

The typical relationship between an *alieni juris* principal and his or her guardian has the following form. The guardian bears the fiduciary duty-to-employ-his-powers-of-representation-to-further-the-principal's-interests. Any legal benefit derived from the employment of these powers will flow to the principal, and any legal detriment will be borne by the principal—unless the detriment has resulted from the guardian's not fulfilling his fiduciary duties. Thus, if the guardian buys health insurance for the principal from some company C, the principal is obviously entitled to the health-insurance benefits that C is obligated to provide.[37] On the other hand,

[35] Claim-rights of course require sundry immunities in order to actually protect their holder's normative status, as Kramer has pointed out, but I will ignore this point here, as any potential holder of claim-rights is able to hold immunities. Matthew H Kramer, 'Rights in Legal and Political Philosophy' in Gregory A Caldeira, R Daniel Kelemen and Keith E Whittington (eds), *The Oxford Handbook of Law and Politics* (Oxford University Press 2008) 416–7.

[36] These are the fundamental protections that were laid out in Chapter 3.

[37] A thus holds a claim-right towards C. The proper beneficiaries of a duty can be distinguished from incidental beneficiaries using Bentham's test (see Chapter 2 as well as Matthew H. Kramer, 'Refining the Interest Theory of Rights' (2010) 55 *American Journal of Jurisprudence* 31 and Visa A. J. Kurki, 'Rights, Harming and Wronging: A Restatement of the Interest Theory' (2018) 38 *Oxford Journal of Legal Studies* 430).

the premiums must be paid for by the guardian but using the principal's money. If the guardian is negligent in his payment of the premiums, any extra costs incurred because of the negligence must normally be borne by the guardian rather than by the principal.

Similar fiduciary duties can be, but do not need to be, in place for adults of sound mind: if such an adult is assaulted, he or she may often freely choose whether to demand compensation and what to do with the recovered money.

More generally, I maintain that passive legal personhood functions primarily through claim-rights. Some features of passive legal personhood can also involve liabilities (as with the capacity to undergo legal harms) and liberties (that are then secured by fundamental protections). However, claim-rights are by far the most important Hohfeldian constituents of passive legal personhood, for three reasons. First, merely the holding of liberties cannot qualify one for passive legal personhood. For instance, nonhuman animals hold every possible liberty (because they do not bear duties), yet this is not indicative of their legal personhood. Second, liberties to perform actions are not strictly speaking necessary for passive legal personhood. For instance, we could imagine an individual who cannot perform any physical acts due to paralysis, and thus any liberties to perform actions held by her would be moot.[38] Regardless, almost every passive incident would still be applicable to that individual: her bodily integrity would still be protected and she could for instance own property, be legally harmed, and so on. Third, I pointed out in Chapter 2 that liabilities can be borne by any entity that can hold the lower-level positions. Thus, determining who or what can hold liabilities and immunities really just involves determining who or what can hold the other Hohfeldian positions. Consequently, X can be a passive legal person if and only if X can hold claim-rights.

Claim-rights involve the directedness of duties; they are held by beings to whom duties are owed. Most people would probably agree that duties can be owed to children, but animals are already a somewhat more contentious case. What about rocks, idols, rivers, or atoms? There may very well be legal persons dedicated to the preservation of a river, but how do we determine whether they hold fiduciary duties *to* the river—thus essentially representing the river, rather than, say, the interests of the general public? I discussed these questions in Chapter 2, and do not intend to repeat that discussion here, but I will make some relevant points. First, according to Kramer's interest theory—which, even if one does not accept it as a theory of rights, is the best theory of Hohfeldian claims—sentient beings are the primary group of claim-holders. We can owe duties to adults, children, and nonhuman animals, but not, for instance, to rivers. Rather, our duties can *pertain* to rivers. This distinction relies on a moral distinction: sentient beings are of ultimate value, and bodies of water are not. There may be a legal person tasked with protecting the river, but the

[38] Her liberties *not* to perform any number of actions would still be meaningful.

relevant legal platform cannot attach to the river (in the strong sense), because the river cannot hold claims. Rather, the river is in a position similar to that of the old manuscript protected by an organization: the organization may very well be obligated to protect the manuscript, but it does not hold this duty *towards* the manuscript. The same can be said of idols. This is why arrangements where legal platforms are established to protect manuscripts or rivers are saliently different from analogous arrangements concerning children or animals.

I should now address two points pertaining to the value-dependency of the claims just made. First, the attribution of passive incidents of legal personhood to sentient beings does not entail that all sentient beings ought to be legal persons, or that they ought to be treated equally. It may be that some conscious beings' interests are vastly more important than those of others, or that the morally required legal treatment of some sentient beings but not others is laden with deontic constraints, and so on. I am merely expounding what is necessary and sufficient for the attachment of a legal platform to an individual or a creature.[39] Throughout, this book proposes a general theory of legal personhood that can show why the concept of personhood is relevant in understanding issues from the legal status of slaves to corporations and nonhuman animals. That big-picture approach raises a number of smaller issues pertaining to the values and rationales of different areas of law that I do not address.

Second, this book lays claim to value-neutrality, which 'involves a suspension of judgment about the comparative merits of divergent ethical positions'.[40] Related to value-neutrality is the distinction between the framework level, the building-block level, and the concrete level, made in the Introduction. The *building-block level* includes the evaluative assumptions that one must take on in order to be able to specify the building blocks of active and passive legal personhood. Given that children are the central example of passive legal personhood, I must assume that children can hold claim-rights in order to claim that passive legal personhood works through claim-rights. Such an assumption is highly, though not completely, uncontroversial. However, further conclusions regarding the scope of passive legal personhood require additional evaluative assumptions on the *concrete level*. I maintain that animals can be passive legal persons but bodies of water cannot, because animals can hold claim-rights whereas bodies of water cannot. This is, of course, already much more controversial than the proposition that children can hold claim-rights: some would contend that animals cannot hold claim-rights, whereas others would maintain that both animals and rivers can hold them. However, I have already stressed in the Introduction that even if a deep ecologist disagrees on whether claim-rights can

[39] I will consider various group entities in the next chapter.

[40] Ian Carter, 'Value-freeness and Value-neutrality in the Analysis of Political Concepts' in David Sobel, Peter Vallentyne, and Steven Wall (eds), *Oxford Studies in Political Philosophy, Volume 1* (Oxford University Press 2015) 284–5.

appositely be ascribed to bodies of water, the overall theory is not useless to him or her: he or she must simply show how bodies of water can hold claim-rights.[41]

The complexities just raised could be brushed aside altogether by questioning the existence of mere passive legal personhood altogether: why not simply identify legal personhood in the administrators of a legal platform? This would perhaps allow for something closer to a value-independent account of legal personhood, as the bearings and domain of acts can be defined in a nearly value-independent manner.[42] However, such a delimitation would reduce the explanatory power of a theory, as it would essentially exclude small children, senile individuals, and so on from legal personality; such a theory would have to maintain that the American legal amendments purporting to treat foetuses as legal persons (usually within the context of extending the protection of criminal law to the unborn) and the aims of the Nonhuman Rights Project are conceptually mistaken. That latter project is, after all, striving for certain nonhuman animals to be endowed with a legal status partially similar to that of human minors. The jurists who—implicitly or explicitly—recognize the legal personhood of children might of course simply be confused. However, there are good reasons for this bifurcation between passive and active legal personhood, as the two aspects function in different ways: passive legal personhood is connected to Hohfeldian claims, whereas active legal personhood is connected to acts. Disregarding either aspect of legal personhood would mean ignoring important features of the concept.

Christopher Stone's view

I should address here the famous proposition by Christopher Stone that trees, or even the ecosystem, could have standing in courts so that they could sue in their own name (through representatives, of course). One should note that Stone's approach is very practical, and he seems to view the proposed legal standing of natural objects as a tool for environmental protection and for making polluters pay for the externalities that their actions cause.[43] This is because the incidents of legal personhood offer 'legal-operational advantages': Western legal systems have evolved to protect first

[41] Those who maintain that claim-rights cannot be held by, for example, infants will likely reject my claim that passive legal personhood functions through claim-rights. They can regardless agree with me about the incidents of passive legal personhood, even if they will have to provide a different analysis of the constituents of said aspect of legal personhood.

[42] Settling for a particular definition of acts does, however, often rely on evaluative judgements because the performance of acts is often connected to moral responsibility.

[43] A quite striking example of Stone's practical approach can be found in his writings on corporate responsibility. He maintains that the question whether 'it is *intelligible* to blame the corporation draws on considerations that it is *useful* to speak in that manner' (emphases in original). Christopher D. Stone, 'Corporate Accountability in Law and Morals' in J. Houck and O .Williams (eds), *The Judaeo-Christian Vision and the Modern Business Corporation* (University of Notre Dame Press 1982) (cited in Michael S. Moore, *Placing Blame: A Theory of the Criminal Law* (Oxford University Press 2010) 623).

and foremost the interests of legal persons, which is why legal persons have several legal tools at their disposal that nonpersons do not. Stone's definition of legal rights highlights these advantages. According to him, 'for a thing to be a holder of legal rights, something more is needed than that some authoritative body will review the actions and processes of those who threaten it'. Rather, according to Stone, the necessary and sufficient conditions of 'a thing's' holding of rights are, 'first, that the thing can institute legal actions at its behest; second, that in determining the granting of legal relief, the court must take injury to it into account; and, third, that relief must run to the benefit of it.'[44] I do not think these can be taken as necessary and sufficient conditions of either right-holding or legal personhood, but Stone's points highlight how certain incidents of legal personhood safeguard their holders' legally protected interests: if one is a legal person, one's claim-rights can be enforced in court in one's name and one has access to institutions of corrective justice such as tort.

One should here distinguish doctrinal matters from philosophical analysis. Stone's writings are anchored in the US legal system, where a plaintiff has standing in any typical case only if he or she has sustained, or is in danger of sustaining, direct injury or harm because of the defendant's past, current, or future conduct. If such a doctrine of legal standing is in place, and if the only harms legally recognized are harms to legal persons, then the duty-not-to-cause-environmental-damage is only genuine (and thus enforceable) if the environmental damage adversely affects some legal person's clearly identifiable interests. Stone therefore faces a very practical reason for personifying the environment:

> The argument for 'personifying' the environment, from the point of damage calculations, can best be demonstrated from the welfare economics position. Every well-working legal-economic system should be so structured as to confront each of us with the full costs that our activities are imposing on society. [...] Unfortunately, so far as the pollution costs are concerned, the allocative ideal begins to break down, because the traditional legal institutions have a more difficult time 'catching' and confronting us with the full social costs of our activities. [...] There is no reason not to allow the lake to prove damages to [people adversely affected by pollution] as the prima facie measure of damages to it. By doing so, we in effect make the natural object, through its guardian, a jural entity competent to gather up these fragmented and otherwise unrepresented damage claims, and press them before the court even where, for legal or practical reasons, they are not going to be pressed by traditional class action plaintiffs.[45]

Stone's suggestion is unobjectionable as long as it is understood as a practical way of enhancing environmental protection in the face of a particular doctrine of standing: it is a legal fiction, an extension of some legal rules to cover situations that their paradigmatic formulations would not cover. This jurisdiction-dependent

[44] Christopher D. Stone, *Should Trees Have Standing? Law, Morality, and the Environment* (3rd edn, Oxford University Press 2010) 4–5.

[45] Ibid. 13.

rationale for a legal fiction does not, however, mean that natural objects should be treated as potential legal persons in philosophical analysis. If we accept the evaluative assumptions I have taken on, we must reject the potential legal personhood of insentient natural objects. We can hence understand a duty-not-to-pollute-some-lake as an obligation towards the general public, or towards all or some sentient beings collectively. This is also how the matter is framed in many countries, such as Finland where conservation societies have, in certain cases, the standing to bring an *actio popularis* against government agencies if they deem a government decision to be in breach of the Environmental Protection Act.[46] Such an action can be undertaken regardless of whether the organization itself would suffer direct harm because of the decision. Here the organization is simply named as the plaintiff or appellant even though it represents a general interest.[47]

Active Legal Personhood

Active legal personhood pertains to the beings who are classifiable as actors in a particular legal sense. The paradigmatic active legal persons—adults of sound mind—are independent actors, *sui juris*, who can freely make choices in their lives but can also be held responsible for these choices. Their active legal personhood enables them to engage in certain practices, such as contracting to obtain goods and services: they can perform legal acts that bind them to contracts, and can be held legally responsible if they do not meet their contractual duties. Were they merely able to perform legal acts but could not be held criminally and/or civilly responsible, their practical ability to contract would be severely diminished because any potential contractees would have limited legal recourse in the case of non-fulfilment.[48]

Active legal personhood, then, consists of two main incidents: legal responsibility (onerous legal personhood) and the capacity to perform acts-in-the-law (being endowed with legal competences). The main types of legal responsibility are criminal and civil responsibility, whereas the capacity to perform acts-in-the-law opens up the possibility of partaking in a wide number of legal institutions, of which the most important is probably contracting. Many scholars distinguish the status of 'beneficiaries' of rights from that of the 'administrators' of rights.[49] This distinction illuminates one relevant threshold between passive and active legal personhood: an infant cannot administer her natural legal platform, but a legal system typically grants her an increasing

[46] Environmental Protection Act (*Ympäristönsuojelulaki*, 527/2014).

[47] See also the section on standing in Chapter 3.

[48] They could probably still enter meaningfully into quotidian contracts such as the buying of groceries, where both parties fulfil their contractual duties simultaneously.

[49] See, for instance, John Chipman Gray, *The Nature and Sources of the Law* (David Campbell and Philip Thomas eds, Ashgate 1997) and Alexander Nékám, *The Personality Concept of the Legal Entity* (Harvard University Press 1938). I have mentioned in Chapter 3 that according to French taxonomy children can only 'enjoy' legal rights (*la capacité de jouissance*) whereas adults of sound mind can also 'exercise' their rights (*la capacité d'exercice*).

number of administering capacities as she grows. She will also be held increasingly accountable for how she chooses to exercise those capacities. However, not all forms of legal responsibility flow from legal acts in this way, and some do not in fact relate to the capacity for legal acts at all. This is most obvious in arrangements where some individuals or creatures are held criminally responsible but are not otherwise endowed with legal personhood, as was the case in some antebellum American slave states and the medieval animal trials.[50] I call this *purely onerous legal personhood*.

Scope of onerous legal personhood

Onerous legal personhood functions through genuine legal duties, and I have already addressed the domain of legal duties in Chapter 2. Thus, the treatment here can be relatively brief because entities that can hold legal duties are the only candidates for onerous legal personhood.

There is really just one class of beings who are uncontroversially endowed with onerous legal personhood: adult humans of sound mind. Most jurists will likely agree that, in ordinary circumstances, it is not only possible but also morally unproblematic for adults of sound mind to be held legally responsible. However, the medieval animal trials serve as a reminder of the fact that contemporary limitations on the scope of criminal law which exclude, say, infants and animals from its purview, are not *conceptual* limitations but rather *moral* limitations. Infants and nonhuman animals can indeed be criminally liable: they can perform forbidden acts and be punished for this. Such punishments may be manifestly unfair and unjust, but it is not difficult to understand how animals could be punished—whereas it would be more difficult to comprehend what the 'punishment' of, say, a falling tree that damages a building would even involve. Chopping the tree into tiny pieces would perhaps bear some semblance of 'retribution', but it would be excessive to call this punishment. Why is this so? Again, we cannot completely escape evaluative commitments. Questions such as who or what can meaningfully be punished rely on some thin commitments regarding the purpose of punishment.

I have in Chapter 2 come to the conclusion that an entity must meet three criteria in order to be a potential duty-bearer: it must be able to perform acts; it must be able to benefit and suffer detriment from states of affairs; and there must be a way of communicating legal requirements to the entity. Adults, children, and many animals meet these criteria, which is why they can be endowed with onerous legal personhood. They are also candidates for an arrangement where one is endowed with passive incidents of legal personhood and onerous active incidents.[51] Rivers and idols, on the

[50] See Katie Sykes, 'Human Drama, Animal Trials: What the Medieval Animal Trials Can Teach Us About Justice for Animals' (2011) 17 *Animal Law Review* 273.

[51] An example of the latter arrangement will obtain if a mentally disabled individual, able to own property, is deemed completely unable to take care of his or her affairs but is nevertheless criminally or tortiously liable.

other hand, do not meet these criteria. This is why they cannot be endowed with onerous legal personhood.

Scope of legal competences

Being endowed with legal competences opens up a range of opportunities for participation in prevailing institutions. Even if not all exercises of competences constitute acts-in-the-law, a being must be able to perform acts-in-the-law in order to be able to hold competences.

We should firstly distinguish *independent* and *dependent* competences.[52] Though the paradigmatic active legal person is *sui juris* and thus independent in the administration of her or his legal capacity, Western legal systems know also of *dependent* legal persons who nevertheless have active capacities. Whereas adults of sound mind typically have the final say in their choices, a dependent legal person's capacity for legal acts is subject to oversight by, say, a parent or a legally appointed guardian. The arrangements of dependent legal personhood can vary; under some arrangements, for instance, one's guardian can retroactively cancel a transaction one has performed. On the other hand, one can also have a 'sphere of independence' within which the guardian cannot interfere with the capacity. For instance, minors are according to Finnish law freely able to dispose of any money they have earned through their own labour.[53]

The number of competences held by an ordinary human individual typically increases gradually until the age of majority. Babies hold no competences and bear no duties; but, as they grow, legal system normally grants them an increasing number of legal competences. When children and mentally disabled individuals hold competences, they are in most cases limited in number and of the dependent type. It is important to keep in mind that the justification for these limitations is in most cases moral rather than conceptual: limiting the number of competences held by these people is undertaken for their own good, due to their lacking the requisite mental capacities.[54] I see no conceptual obstacle that would prevent most minors or mentally disabled individuals from being able to exercise competences wholly independently.

[52] This distinction has been inspired by the work of Samir Chopra and Laurence White. Samir Chopra and Laurence F. White, *A Legal Theory for Autonomous Artificial Agents* (University of Michigan Press 2011) 160–70. See also the discussion of dependent and independent competences in Visa A.J. Kurki, 'Legal Competence and Legal Power' in Mark McBride (ed.), *New Essays on the Nature of Rights* (Hart Publishing 2017).

[53] Guardianship Services Act (*Holhoustoimilaki*, 442/1999), § 25.

[54] The paternalistic justification of slavery in the United States is a major theme in Eugene Genovese's work, in particular Eugene Genovese, *Roll, Jordan, Roll: The World the Slaves Made* (Random House USA 1976). Slaves in ancient Rome, on the other hand, were not considered inferior in this sense. As Alan Watson puts it, '[s]lavery was a misfortune that could happen to anyone. However lowly the economic and social position of a slave might be, the slave was not necessarily and in all ways regarded as inferior as a human being simply because he was a slave' Alan Watson, *Roman Slave Law* (The Johns Hopkins University Press 1988) 3. This was

Acts-in-the-law include as a necessary component the intention to effect a legal consequence. Such intentions presuppose some grasp of institutional reality and of how one can manipulate this reality through the use of symbols. Relatively young children do already begin to have a rudimentary grasp of these matters, and most disabled people do—to my knowledge—possess such comprehension. However, nonhuman animals are likely unable to form such intentions.

There are some possible objections to the proposed, relatively expansive scope of competences. A critic might contend that a full understanding of the legal consequences of a transaction by the relevant parties is necessary if the transaction is to count as an act-in-the-law. Only adults of sound mind can supposedly possess such an understanding. However, a requirement of that kind would be far too strong; it is very often not the case that an adult of sound mind is aware of every single legal implication of the act he or she is about to perform. For instance, the legal consequences of marrying someone are typically very far-reaching. In the TV show *The Sopranos*, a character chooses to marry a mafioso in order to claim spousal privilege to avoid testifying against him. However, she misunderstands the rules pertaining to the privilege, which do not apply to the couple. Does this mean that she did not perform a legal act when marrying him? Quite pointless is a definition of legal acts according to which only skilled family lawyers really perform legal acts when getting married. Rather, the threshold must be set considerably lower. Acts-in-the-law presuppose that one can intend to effect a legal consequence. Such an intention requires some grasp of institutional reality and of how one can manipulate this reality through the use of symbols. For instance, in the case of a legal contract, one must understand that one is agreeing to perform or omit some action and that one will face certain legal consequences if one does not follow through on one's agreement.

One example of how the independent legal personhood of a disabled individual would function is presented by Eilionóir Flynn and Anna Arstein-Kerslake. They have argued for a model of supported decision-making whereby a disabled individual 'chooses a number of trusted individuals to assist in the decision-making process'. However, 'support can only be offered to an individual, and she should be free to accept or reject the support—i.e. supported decision-making should never be imposed on an individual against her will'.[55] The support model envisaged by Flynn and Arstein-Kerslake would count as independent legal personhood, as the disabled individual would have the final say in the performance of any legal act. However, there are most likely some disabled individuals whose decision-making capabilities

reflected in the fact that slaves could enter into contracts on their masters' behalf and perform some other acts-in-the-law.

[55] Eilionóir Flynn and Anna Arstein-Kerslake, 'Legislating Personhood: Realising the Right to Support in Exercising Legal Capacity' (2014) *10 International Journal of Law in Context* 81, 95.

are so limited that the support model would not be suitable, as Flynn and Arstein-Kerslake recognize (albeit hesitantly).[56] If such individuals cannot perform acts-in-the-law, then they cannot be independent legal persons, either.

Individuals with severely limited mental capabilities (but who are nevertheless recognized as independent legal persons) cannot of course take care of all the practicalities that the successful performance of many legal acts presupposes. If such a person were to sell his house, he might require help with the drafting of the contract, with submitting a tax declaration, and so on. However, this is also the case with many adults normally taken to be *sui juris*: people hire expert help for various purposes all the time, since individuals who are completely self-reliant in this regard are few and far between. In fact, in jurisdictions where one is not allowed to represent oneself in court but is rather required to have qualified legal counsel, it has essentially been determined that individuals cannot take care of such legal matters on their own. One's lawyers are, however, bound to follow one's instructions, which is why one is still an independent legal person. Thus, the main rule is that an independent legal person can be represented by someone else only if the person authorizes the representation. Dependent legal persons, on the other hand, do not have this kind of power over their representatives in every matter.

It is also worthwhile noting that the distinction between independent and dependent legal personhood pertains to de jure independence. It may be that someone—say, a family member—holds such sway over a disabled individual that their relation is de facto a dependency relation. A legal system may treat a relationship of this kind as a form of undue influence over the disabled person's deliberations, which may affect whether some act by the disabled person is ultimately legally binding. However, such restrictions are again primarily based on moral rather than conceptual considerations. Barring extreme cases, an act-in-the-law performed under pressure is still an act-in-the-law; the relevant question is whether it is just or reasonable to hold the individual accountable for the consequences of the act. Legal systems do generally expect individuals to be able to resist a certain amount of social pressure.

Why can rivers not perform acts?

We can of course ask why we cannot treat rivers and other natural objects as legal actors. Richard Tur envisages a scenario where it is stipulated that a river's rising to a certain level would constitute its acceptance of an offer by the local community, which would then be under a duty to make a payment of x goats to the river. The river would thus have performed an action—an act-in-the-law, in fact. The main question about the appositeness of treating some entity as an active legal person boils down to whether we can take the *intentional stance* towards the entity. I have already

[56] Ibid. 94.

presented Daniel Dennett's account of the intentional stance in Chapter 2.[57] The intentional stance is, according to Dennett, one of the three strategies that one can employ to predict the behaviour of an entity.[58]

When we take the intentional stance, we make reference to an entity's beliefs, desires, and intentions in order to explain and predict its actions, instead of referring to purely physical factors. From this pragmatic point of view, the question whether someone or something can appositely be treated as a legal actor is a question of the best predictive strategy: can we aptly treat rivers as beings with representational and motivational states such as beliefs, desires, and intentions? In an ordinary case, X's taking the intentional stance towards a potential contractual party Y would involve assuming at least that Y will understand what responsibility he is taking on. X would also attribute to Y the recognition that, if Y does not abide by the terms, he will be subject to the legal consequences. The contract will thus constitute a reason-for-action for Y, and he will adjust his behaviour accordingly. By contrast, in the case of the river, employing the intentional stance would most likely not be a successful strategy. The stipulated contract would not be a reason-for-action for the river; the promise to pay the goats in exchange for its rising would simply not affect its flow at all (unless the 'promise' were made in some particular manner, e.g. by building a dam—but again, the intentional stance would be largely useless here).

Conclusion

This discussion began by asking about the range of beings to whom a legal platform can attach. Such a platform, first, *confers benefits* through claim-rights; second, it *imposes responsibilities*; and third, it *grants competences* which are primarily exercised through acts-in the-law. Therefore, a legal platform can attach to human beings and nonhuman animals—as well as to certain collectivities and artificial intelligences (AIs), which are explored in the next part.

We can have different combinations of the three relevant dimensions of legal personhood—benefits, responsibilities, and capacity for legal acts. Each of these dimensions can also be realized to various degrees. I have already addressed how one's capacity for acts-in-the-law can be dependent or independent. Similarly, one can be held responsible in some respects and not in others and enjoy some benefits of passive legal personhood without others. The historical cases of slaves and animal trials were examples of purely onerous legal personhood, where only criminal responsibility

[57] Daniel Dennett, *The Intentional Stance* (MIT Press 1987). Dennett's idea of the intentional stance has been used by some authors to argue for the legal personality of artificial intelligences. See Chapter 6 and David J. Calverley, 'Imagining a Non-Biological Machine as a Legal Person' (2008) 22 *AI & Society* 523 and Chopra and White (n 52) 11ff.

[58] The other two stances are the *physical stance* and the *design stance*, though the latter should be divided into the *teleological design stance* and the *intentional designer stance* (see Chapter 2).

was extended to these beings. Infants, on the other hand, possess some of the benefits of passive legal personhood but are not typically held legally responsible and cannot administer legal platforms through legal acts. Administration, and the subsequent responsibility, must be undertaken by someone else. Some typical arrangements are:

1. Purely passive legal personhood: one enjoys claim-rights pertaining to legal personhood but cannot administer one's own legal platform at all and may not be held legally responsible (infants, potentially animals).
2. Dependent legal personhood: one holds some competences that pertain to one's legal platform, but this capacity is limited and subject to oversight (children).[59]
3. Independent legal personhood: one is *sui juris* and has the final say in the administration of one's legal platform (adults of sound mind).
4. Purely onerous legal personhood: one is liable as a legal person while enjoying virtually none of the benefits of legal personhood (slaves).[60]

Categories 2 and 3, in particular, are wide-rangingly diverse in their instantiations. For example, even if a jurisdiction follows the support model for disabled individuals, therefore granting them independence in their exercise of legal acts, such individuals might not be deemed fully culpable in criminal law.

I have come to the conclusion that animals can be passive legal persons because the duties pertaining to a legal platform could be borne *towards* an animal. Natural objects such as rivers, on the other hand, cannot hold claim-rights and consequently cannot be passive legal persons. So how should we understand the cases where legal personhood is supposedly extended to rivers or idols? We can obviously create a legal platform—a bundle of legal positions—with the name of the idol or the river. We can, in addition, assign an individual or a group the administration of that legal platform according to some guidelines. The administrator could for instance be tasked with the suing of anyone who pollutes the river. However, it would be a mistake to infer that the idol or the river itself has become a (passive) legal person. If one does not perform one's duty towards some X, this X is wronged—yet bodies of water cannot be wronged. Towards whom or what, then, does the administrator of a legal platform bear the duties pertaining to the platform, if not the river itself? There are a number of alternatives. The duties could be borne towards the individuals and/or creatures which have certain joint or collective interests pertaining to the river (e.g. people and animals inhabiting the area near the river or otherwise dependent on it). These duties could also be understood as preserving the ecological heritage and

[59] The whole capacity may also be subject to the will of someone else. For instance, slavery has often involved *peculium*, or the slave owner's authorization that the slave may own (or 'own') some limited number of possessions. The slave owner could typically retract this authorization at any point.

[60] One may of course enjoy the procedural safeguards pertaining to criminal trials.

would thus be borne towards the whole of humankind or all sentient beings. Finally, one could of course argue that the duties are borne towards no-one at all. This would entail a departure from the Hohfeldian analysis of legal relations, which presupposes the correlativity of claim-rights and duties.[61] Whether such a departure would be correct is a question that cannot be addressed in this work. However, the question of the legal personhood of collectivities is crucial, and will be the focus of the next chapter, which will also commence the third and final part of the book. At the end of that chapter, I will discuss how the Whanganui River arrangement could be understood as establishing passive legal personhood for a collective beneficiary.

[61] See Matthew H. Kramer, 'Rights Without Trimmings' in Matthew H. Kramer, N. E. Simmonds, and Hillel Steiner, *A Debate over Rights: Philosophical Enquiries* (Oxford University Press 1998) 22ff.

PART III
Applying the Theory

5

Collectivities as Legal Persons

Groups and Corporations

A highly important type of legal persons has heretofore only been addressed *en passant*: collectivities of human beings. Such collectivities are often designated as 'corporations', though the term is perilously unclear. First, the British usage of the word is quite different from the primary American usage. In the UK a corporation can be any incorporated entity such as a Cambridge college, whereas in the US the word primarily refers to large for-profit companies or to groups of such companies. I will be using 'corporation' in the British sense. Second, the term may be used to refer to a kind of legal platform as well as to an organized collectivity that is a legal person. If one announces the plan to found a one-person corporation, one is referring to a legal arrangement; if one talks of the great company culture of a certain corporation, the focus is on the organization.[1] Neither of these uses of 'corporation' will be given priority here, but when the two senses should be kept distinct, 'collectivity' and 'group agent' are used to refer to the organization whereas 'legal platform' will denote the arrangement.

Jurists and legal theorists have been debating the nature of corporations for a long time. The question was of particular interest during the nineteenth and early twentieth centuries, especially among French and German jurists and theorists. I shall not conduct an extensive review of these theories here, as the literature covering the topic is vast.[2] Eric Orts categorizes the legal theories of corporations under three

[1] Some authors are careful in not conflating these two senses of 'corporation'. Simon Deakin distinguishes 'firm' and 'corporation', the former being an 'organisation engaged in the production of goods and/or services' and the latter a 'legal mechanism by which firms [...] operate in contemporary market economies'. Deakin is of course only addressing business corporations here. Simon Deakin, 'The Juridical Nature of the Firm' in Thomas Clarke and Douglas Branson (eds), *The SAGE Handbook of Corporate Governance* (SAGE Publications 2012) 115–16.

[2] For an overview of the historical corporate personality debate, see Alfred F. Conard, *Corporations in Perspective* (Foundation Press 1976) 417–45. Some examples of English-language treatises of corporate personality are Ernst Freund, *The Legal Nature of Corporations* (Batoche Books 2000), originally published in 1897; John Dewey, 'The Historic Background of Corporate Legal Personality' (1926) 35 *Yale Law Journal* 655; Arthur W. Machen, 'Corporate Personality' (1911) 24 *Harvard Law Review* 253; and Frederick Hallis, *Corporate Personality. A Study in Jurisprudence* (Oxford University Press 1930). Karl Olivecrona provides a good

main groups: (1) concession theories (also known as fiction theories), according to which corporations exist as creations of the state or the sovereign; (2) participant theories, which identify corporations as primarily created by individuals; and (3) institutional theories (also known as real entity theories), which understand corporations as 'institutions both formed according to legal rules and organized and run by individual people'.[3]

Orts styles the concession and participant theories as 'top-down' and 'bottom-up' views, respectively. The theories often draw rather far-reaching normative conclusions from their basic understandings of the corporation. For instance, a typical concession theory would maintain that since corporations are created at the pleasure of the state ('top-down'), they have only those legal entitlements that have explicitly been granted to them. Those legal entitlements may also freely be taken away by the state. However, that conclusion does not necessarily presuppose any particular view on questions such as whether the corporation is irreducible to its individual members or whether it exists outside the law. One could very well maintain that the corporation is a 'real' entity, separate from its members and existing as a human organization even outside the law, but that the political community is nevertheless morally permitted to revoke the legal recognition of any corporation at will. This conclusion depends on a particular political ideology; it never flows directly from an analytic theory of the corporation.[4]

Theories of corporations are thus often combinations of social ontology, normative political philosophy, and analytic jurisprudence. In addition, the ambiguity of 'corporation' seems to be pertinent here. Many concession theories understand corporations as legal platforms whereas participant theories focus on them as organizations. If a corporation is understood purely as a legal arrangement, it makes more sense to say that corporations exist only in the 'contemplation of law', as the US Supreme Court put it in *Trustees of Dartmouth College v Woodward*—a judgment often cited as laying out a concession theory of the corporation. Contrariwise, human organizations are obviously not 'mere creature[s] of law', to borrow another expression from the same verdict.[5]

summary of the 'classical' Continental theories of the nineteenth century in Karl Olivecrona, *Studier över begreppet juridisk person i romersk och modern rätt* (Appelbergs 1928).

[3] Eric W. Orts, *Business Persons: A Legal Theory of the Firm* (Oxford University Press 2013) 13. For an account that is in many ways similar, see Deakin (n 1).

[4] The connection between political philosophy and corporate theory is apparent in the title of Frederick Hallis's doctoral dissertation: Frederick Hallis, 'An examination of some modern theories of the relation of law and state with special reference to the juristic doctrine of corporate personality: a study in jurisprudence' (DPhil thesis, University of Oxford 1927).

[5] *Trustees of Dartmouth College v Woodward*, 17 US 518 (1819) 636.

The institutional theory, favoured and advanced by Orts, is an intermediate position. I am in general sympathetic to Orts's views on the matter, which he summarizes as follows:

> The institutional theory sees firms as socially established entities that are both authorized and recognized by governments and organized and managed by individual participants. The institutional recognition of the business enterprise as a legal 'entity' or 'person' interposes a conceptual separation between the political state and the firm's individual participants. Once a regular legal process for the governmental recognition and individual creation of firms has become established, business firms become social institutions. In legal terms, they become 'entities' and 'persons' with specified legal rights and obligations.[6]

I do not intend to offer a full-blown theory of corporations here; rather, the aim is to show how collective legal persons fit into the overall theory of legal personhood. In particular, the stated objective means leaving out many prescriptive issues pertaining to collective legal personhood, such as questions about the extent to which corporations (rather than their individual members) should be held legally responsible, questions about the ascribability of certain fundamental rights to corporations, and so on.

Within the scope of this book, understanding collective legal persons boils down to understanding two interrelated issues: (1) the nature of the legal platform that can constitute the legal personhood of a collective, and (2) the nature of the collectivities to which the legal platforms can attach. The gist of the matter is that not all legal platforms are natural legal platforms that would follow an individual from the cradle to the grave. Some legal platforms, such as one-person corporations, can rather be sold or donated, meaning that their object of attachment changes. However, more interestingly, most of these legal platforms can also attach to numerous individuals simultaneously. The question then arises whether the group consisting of these individuals could under some conditions be treated as a kind of collectivity that is irreducible to the individuals. If some collectivities can perform acts and are endowed with interests, this implies that they could be legal persons in their own right, separate from their members. I will be advancing this position in this chapter, relying primarily on recent philosophical work in social ontology and group agency produced by authors such as Philip Pettit, Christian List, and Raimo Tuomela. Social ontology has greatly improved our understanding of group phenomena, but it will benefit from an in-depth analysis of what the legal personhood of groups implies. I will also show how collectivities that are not legal persons can nevertheless hold various legal positions, including claim-rights and duties. This supports my argument, made in Chapters 2 and 3, that legal personhood and the holding of legal rights and/or duties should not be equated.

6 Orts (n 3) 14.

The attention here will be focused on certain types of groups, and we can initially distinguish between two main types: aggregates and group agents. I use the term 'aggregate' here to refer to a group of individuals who share a common attribute, such as 'people with a benign naevus on their right-hand index finger'.[7] This example should make it clear that the property of being an aggregate alone is largely irrelevant to group personhood. The focus here will rather be on group agents. I will also address the topic of group beneficiaries, meaning groups that are not agents but that hold claim-rights.

It is important to keep in mind here the distinction between potential legal personhood and actual legal personhood. The fact that a group agent can in a relevant sense perform actions and possess interests does not imply that it is a legal person. Rather, this fact implies that the collectivity is a *potential legal person* which can be endowed with legal personhood. Most group agents come into being and are dissolved without ever becoming legal persons. Thus, the question of the nature of group agents (and other collectivities) may be intertwined with the concept of legal personhood, but the two issues are still clearly separate. Group agents could exist even in a lawless state of nature—think of an organized group of highwaymen—whereas legal personhood as it is understood here is a feature of modern Western law. Endowing a group agent with legal personhood will provide it with benefits such as the separate ownership of funds and enhanced trackability by other actors. Of course, the legal arrangements that constitute the legal personhood of a group agent can also be used for other purposes. One-person corporations, for instance, involve granting an individual the capacity to control more than one legal platform; such corporations do not have anything to do with group agents.

The discussion here will be focused on organized groups where group membership is clearly voluntary, such as business companies, sports organizations, and so on, as well as small-scale group beneficiaries. It is not obvious that this analysis can be applied to states and other similar large-scale political organizations without some amplification of the theory.

The Ontology of Group Agents

There are probably as many ways to account for the ontology of group agents as there are authors who write on the subject. The different views can be arrayed on a spectrum with 'strong individualism' at one end and 'group realism' at the other.[8] Strong individualist views eschew all talk of groups whereas group realists ascribe

[7] The distinction between aggregates and other types of groups is made, among others, by Peter French. See Peter A. French, *Collective and Corporate Responsibility* (Columbia University Press 1984) 1–18.

[8] For an overview of individualist views, see Paul Sheehy, *The Reality of Social Groups* (Ashgate 2006) 14.

real existence to group agents. However, even among the latter views, the existence of group agents is typically not taken to be a brute physical fact like the existence of stars or rivers. It is something less tangible that depends on human beings' representations of the world. Groups, like money, exist because we represent them as existing and act accordingly. I will now present some ideas that are classifiable as group realist views, focusing on the work of Raimo Tuomela, Philip Pettit, and Christian List.[9]

Social ontology is founded on the idea of collective intentionality. In a specialist philosophical sense, 'intentionality' refers to the 'aboutness' of mental states: most of our mental states, such as beliefs, are about states of affairs. In this specialist sense, 'intention' denotes mental states that are about states of affairs. To avoid confusion, I will here use the word 'intent' in the sense 'commitment to a given action or to bringing about a given state of affairs'. Accounts of collective intentionality often build on the so-called belief–desire–intent model, where intentional states are divided into these three main groups. Beliefs are representations of the world, whereas desires are dispositions to act. However, beliefs are not always sufficient for action: especially in the case of several strong and conflicting desires, intent is required to choose a path of action.

Collective intentionality is a particular type of intentionality where the 'grammatical subject' of a mental state is plural: instead of your and my believing that p, *we* believe that p. One typical example that illustrates the separateness of collective and individual intentions is that of travelling. One can travel to a conference knowing that another person from the same faculty will also be going. This does not yet constitute collective intentionality, or a collective intent. However, if the two people decide to attend the conference together, then they are collectively committed. Tuomela styles these two modes of intentionality the I-mode ('I will attend the conference knowing that Y will attend, too') and the we-mode ('We [Y and I] will attend the conference'); he claims that we-mode intentionality cannot be reduced to I-mode intentionality. We-mode intentional actions involve of course I-mode intentions that are necessary for playing one's part in the joint intent; for instance, 'Since we are attending the conference, I will book the train tickets'. The main reason for performing this action is, however, the joint intent. Tuomela calls these reasons-for-action group reasons.[10] One final thing to be noted is that, in larger groups, not all members need to be thinking in the we-mode—though a significant proportion of them do need to be thinking in this mode if the group is to be functional. This is why the workings of, say, a corporation cannot be explained by merely making reference to the independent beliefs, desires, and intents of the members: the we-mode intentionality simply does not exist except in the context of the group.[11]

[9] Tuomela may baulk at being denoted a group realist; his views are in any case very close to group realism.

[10] Raimo Tuomela, *Social Ontology: Collective Intentionality and Group Agents* (Oxford University Press 2013) 97ff.

[11] Ibid. 93–5.

Table 5.1 The hiring example of Pettit and List

	Good researcher (p)	Good teacher (q)	Decision (p & q)
A	Yes	Yes	Yes
B	Yes	No	No
C	No	Yes	No
Meets condition?	Yes (2/3)	Yes (2/3)	No (1/3)

List and Pettit focus in their work on the *content* of group intentions, rather than on their mode. They argue that groups that are organized to some degree can reach decisions that their members would not reach outside the group context, and can even have beliefs, desires, and intents that none of their members alone would hold. I reproduce here an example that Pettit describes in an interview.[12] Imagine that a three-member board consisting of A, B, and C is to decide whether to hire X as a professor. They agree that X needs to be both a good researcher and a good teacher in order to be hired, and that the group's opinions on each of these matters should be decided by a majority vote. The results are shown in Table 5.1.

In this example, the majority of the board think that X is a good researcher and that he is a good teacher, yet he is not hired. This is because the decisions of the members are not dependent on the decisions of the group; consequently, the consistency of every member's reasoning does not guarantee the consistency of the group's reasoning. Given that collective inconsistency is not optimal, groups typically need to decide that certain propositions are prioritized over others. For instance, they could decide to prioritize premises over conclusions; in this case, they would first vote on p and q according to their personal preferences, after which the conclusion would be settled. They would have thus settled for a rudimentary form of what Pettit and List style the *constitution* of the group. What is noteworthy here is that p and q would then be the *group's* attitudes (beliefs). After the vote, C might say that 'I personally do not think you are a good researcher but we, the board, do'. Through processes such as this—processes that are often informal—the group may form not only joint intents but also joint beliefs and desires (which, in the case of groups, should perhaps be described as goals). Of course, all of this supervenes on the individual members; the

[12] 'Philip Pettit on Group Agency', interview of Philip Pettit in David Edmonds and Nigel Warburton, *Philosophy Bites*, 18 December 2010. Available at https://philosophybites.com/2010/12/philip-pettit-on-group-agency.html (accessed 8 January 2019). The same situation, though without the hiring setting, is described in Christian List and Philip Pettit, *Group Agency: The Possibility, Design, and Status of Corporate Agents* (Oxford University Press 2011) 70.

group's existence is dependent both on the minds of its members and, partly, on the minds of others who recognize the group as existing.

None of what has been stated above should be interpreted as meaning that the group's beliefs, goals, and intents are phenomenal in the same sense as the corresponding states of human beings[13]—who typically, though not always, experience such states in their conscious minds at least occasionally. The mentioned states are only functional or operational in the case of group agents, whereas human beings also have a felt element in their agency.

Margaret Gilbert and Tuomela, in particular, argue that group commitment is ontologically irreducible to individual commitment (what Tuomela dubs I-mode commitment).[14] However, group agency can also be approached as a matter of *pragmatic* and *moral* irreducibility. I am using the phrase 'pragmatic irreducibility' to mean that treating a group agent as a separate actor is often the most useful way of explaining a phenomenon, as the intentional stance can be adopted in order to understand and predict the group's behaviour. An intentional stance focused on the level of individuals can be used to explain the behaviour of a group agent—as long as the stance pertaining to individual intentions takes into account the joint intentionality involved—but the group-level intentional stance is the simplest way of explaining and predicting the behaviour of a functioning group agent. However, both of these stances are possible ways of explaining what is happening, as is the physical stance.

Finally, treating the group as an agent may also be morally the most fitting choice: to employ Ronald Dworkin's example, the moral responsibility for the production of defective cars that cause hundreds of people to be killed might—depending on the circumstances—is best ascribable to the automobile manufacturer itself and not to any particular human being.[15] The moral requirement for group responsibility is accentuated in such a situation, where a wrong has clearly taken place but placing the blame on any particular individual would be unjust.[16]

I have presented a number of arguments that favour treating groups as agents. Collective intentionality is ontologically separate from individual I-mode intentionality, and individuals can engage in group projects where the group can have intentions that none of its members would hold alone. In addition, we can enhance our predictive efforts by taking the intentional stance towards certain groups, and our treatment of groups as agents capable of wronging others and acting culpably is in certain cases morally fitting. With this general understanding of group agency at hand, I will now discuss certain features of organized groups further with the aim of

[13] Certain nonhuman animals most likely have such states as well, but as I am only considering human group agents, this discussion will be limited to human experiences.

[14] For Gilbert's views, see Margaret Gilbert, *Sociality and Responsibility: New Essays in Plural Subject Theory* (Rowman & Littlefield Publishers 2000).

[15] Ronald Dworkin, *Law's Empire* (Harvard University Press 1986) 169.

[16] Peter French discusses quite extensively the question of when responsibility ought to be attributed to a group and when to its members. See French (n 7).

demonstrating that such groups can hold claim-rights, exercise Hohfeldian powers, and bear duties.

Hohfeld and Groups

The philosophical and legal literature on the rights and duties of collectivities is vast, and it addresses diverse issues. Topics vary from minorities' rights to self-determination to the workings of business corporations.

A central philosophical issue regarding group rights is whether the rights of a group are reducible to rights of the *members* of that group, or whether the group rights are somehow irreducible to the individual level or inexplicable at that level. In addition, authors offer very different accounts of the *sense* in which group rights are distinct from the rights of the individuals. Peter Jones has classified philosophical accounts of (moral) group rights into 'corporate' and 'collective' accounts. (The word 'corporate' should not be understood in a strictly legal sense here.) Corporate accounts treat a group as an entity, as a 'group-individual' with rights (and possibly duties) of 'its' own, whereas the collective accounts describe rights that are held by the members of the group—rather than the group itself—but jointly.[17]

It is striking that philosophers addressing the *moral* rights of groups often take it to be self-evident and not requiring any argumentation that some collectivities hold *legal* rights.[18] Such a view is, however, not unanimously held by legal theorists. For instance, Hohfeld took the putative legal positions of collectivities to be reducible to legal positions held by individuals.[19] The question whether groups can hold Hohfeldian legal positions has not received as much attention as the question of moral rights, even if some scholars such as Matthew Kramer and John Morss have addressed the issue.[20] Although Hohfeld himself was sceptical of the notion that collectivities irreducibly hold legal positions, this does not mean that he was correct. I intend to show here how groups can hold Hohfeldian positions, including claim-rights and duties, as 'group-individuals'.

[17] Peter Jones, 'Group Rights' in Edward N. Zalta (ed.), *Stanford Encyclopedia of Philosophy* (Summer 2016) <https://plato.stanford.edu/archives/sum2016/entries/rights-group/>.

[18] Chris Chapple, for instance, writes that 'The personification of companies in law has been associated with the recognition both of certain responsibilities and certain rights. [...] The more controversial question is whether we can talk meaningfully about *moral* rights (as opposed to merely legal rights).' Chris Chapple, *The Moral Responsibilities of Companies* (Palgrave Macmillan 2014) 140.

[19] Hohfeld mainly addressed these issues in Wesley Newcomb Hohfeld, 'Nature of Stockholders' Individual Liability for Corporation Debts' (1909) 9 *Columbia Law Review* 285.

[20] Matthew H. Kramer, 'Rights Without Trimmings' in Matthew H. Kramer, N. E. Simmonds and Hillel Steiner (eds), *A Debate over Rights: Philosophical Enquiries* (Oxford University Press 1998) 49ff and John R. Morss, 'The Legal Relations of Collectives: Belated Insights from Hohfeld' (2009) 22 *Leiden Journal of International Law* 289.

There are countless group agents which are not corporations and thus not legal persons. For instance, a group of political prisoners may decide to become organized in order to demand better treatment of the inmates. They may then very well have a method (democratic vote, for instance) for deciding a course of action. This makes them a group agent but most likely not a legal person. An even more striking example is the Mafia: a Mafia family has a well-defined organization but is not a legal person (though it may control a number of corporations). Are these groups nevertheless Hohfeldian parties, capable of participating in Hohfeldian relations? I argued in Chapter 2 that there are three separate criteria for qualification as Hohfeldian parties: intentionality (for powers and disabilities); ultimate value (for claim-rights and no-rights); and the capacity to act, to follow normative requirements, and to benefit and suffer detriment from states of affairs (for duties and liberties). I will address these in turn. Liabilities and immunities can be held by entities that can hold of any of the other positions, and will therefore not be addressed separately.

Powers of Group Agents

If one accepts the points made above regarding joint intentionality, the power-holding of group agents is relatively clear, as the intentional stance for coming to grips with group agents is appropriate. The decision-making process of a group agent typically involves the use of moral and/or legal powers at the level of the individual. When the executive board of a company decides on an issue, the board members are using powers when voting on an issue, and these individual instances constitute a board-level exercise of power. In this way, group-level exercises of powers are constituted by individual-level exercises. There are interconnections between the individual and group intentions: even though the group's intentions are separable from the intentions that individual members would hold *qua* individuals, the group intentions are also held by the individuals—though they hold these intentions in the we-mode, that is, *qua* members of the group.

Claim-Rights of Group Agents

Assigning claim-rights (as defined in the interest theory) to groups is a more difficult matter than that of powers. I have maintained that the agency of groups is only functional or operational, whereas the hallmark of claim-right-holding is sentience. As groups are not sentient, it would seem tempting to ascribe claim-rights only to the members of the group and not to the group itself. However, this would leave something out of the analysis. Collectivities can hold claim-rights even though they are not sentient and thus not of ultimate value.

Talk of group rights leads one easily to think of so-called minority rights. However, people belonging to minorities are not necessarily members of a group agent that would represent its members *qua* members of the minority. In this sense, the minorities are aggregates but not group agents. I will here be focusing on the claim-rights of group agents and only later on collective beneficiaries that are not agents.

Kramer addresses the claim-rights of groups rather lengthily; he makes for instance the important distinction between explicability and reducibility:

> Because a group is an overarching structure, it can never be reduced to the individual interactions that are its components—notwithstanding that it can be thoroughly explicated by reference to those components. Its interests do not amount to a sum or welter of individual interests, since its interests are those which characterize its members *qua* collectivity rather than those which characterize its members *qua* individuals.[21]

This is correct and in line with the analysis offered above by Pettit and List. For instance, the members of a religious community can have 'member-interests' (interests *qua* members of the community) that can even be in conflict with their 'individual interests'. The practice of shunning any member who breaks the community norms could serve the member-interests of a shunned member—because the practice would keep the community together—even if the shunned individual would on a personal level suffer.

A further argument that some claim-rights only exist at group level can be derived from a particular insight of Tuomela. He separates 'owning' the products of a group's activities from being the beneficiary of them:

> In [we-mode intentionality] the satisfaction of the intention is *for* [the group]. This 'for-groupness' involves that a paradigmatic we-mode group is taken to 'own' the products of its activities and thus to be able to make either itself or some other party the beneficiary. The aspect of owning and that of being a beneficiary are to be kept apart. To own the satisfaction activity entails it being allowed in principle for a paradigmatic, thus autonomous, we-mode group to choose the party that will be the intended beneficiary, be it the group itself, some group member(s), or another group or person.[22]

This is an important point. What is also significant is that the intended 'final' beneficiary of a group-level intention is not always settled when a particular obligation relating to the intention is in existence. The products of the group's activities can be said to be 'in limbo' until the matter is settled.

For instance, in Helsinki, Finland, something called 'the Restaurant Day' is organized four times a year, allowing anyone to set up their own restaurant or café for one day. Such restaurants are usually not registered as corporations, and they are often run by groups of friends as an exercise of collective intentionality. Someone ordering a meal at such a restaurant has the claim-right to receive what she has ordered, and the duty to pay for the meal. The party with the claim-right to receive payment and the duty to provide the meal—that is, the other contracting party—is, however, not for

[21] Kramer (n 20) 56. [22] Tuomela (n 10) 68 (emphasis in original).

instance the cashier of the restaurant but rather the group itself. It is up to the group to decide who is tasked with preparing the meal[23] and serving it to the customer and how the proceeds from the restaurant are divided among group members and, possibly, other parties. Here one must apply the so-called Bentham's test, which restricts the number of third-party right-holders, as refined by Kramer. I have already introduced the test in Chapter 2, but I shall offer a quick summary. According to Bentham's test, when determining whether someone is a claim-right-holder under a contract or another legal norm, one needs to examine each *minimally sufficient* set of facts that would constitute a breach of the norm. If at least one such set of facts includes the undergoing of some detriment by X, then X holds a claim-right correlative to a duty imposed by the norm.

Bentham's test does establish claim-rights for the group. In the case of the restaurant, we do not need to establish that any of the group's *members* would undergo some detriment in order to establish that a customer who has left the restaurant without paying for her meal has violated the terms of her contract with the restaurant. The group members' individual situations are irrelevant here; it is sufficient to show that the *group's* interests have been harmed. The group may very well have yet to decide whether the proceeds from the restaurant should go to charity or to the group members; the money is 'owned' by the group until a decision has been reached.

As the group 'owns' the products of its joint project, and the final beneficiary of the project may not be settled at the time a duty is borne towards the group, it would be highly unsatisfactory to claim that the group is unable to hold claim-rights of its own. The group is *externally* a whole, and the relevant interests pertain to the joint intention that is irreducible to (though explicable by) the individual, conscious level. It therefore makes sense to talk of the group's claim-rights.

A caveat should be entered: in some circumstances the beneficiary of a group's activities may be settled, in which case it is conceivable that both the group and the beneficiary might hold a claim-right that correlates with a duty pertaining to the group's project. I do not address this further here, as it does not affect my main point.

Duties of Group Agents

What has been said above is also relevant with regard to group duties. A duty is a group duty if, externally (i.e. in relation to non-members), the duty is borne primarily by the group and not by a particular member of the group. Internally, group-borne duties may be assigned to a group member or members, but the holder of the corresponding claim-right often does not need to concern himself with the division of work within the group.

[23] Except, for instance, where the identity of the cook is decided in the contract.

Group-borne duties are occasionally recognized by legal systems even in the case of groups that are not legal persons. Let us think of a rural community with a well-organized group of hunters. If their hunting trip results in the injury of a bystander, this unfortunate result may not be due to the negligence of any particular individual but rather to a lack of coordination within the group. In this case, it may be justified to consider the group as an actor. However, as the group is not a legal person and thus cannot own property, it cannot be the target of sanctions.[24] So how can legal systems recognize the fact that the group as a collective was responsible for the deed? One way of doing this is to allow for solidary tort liability, as in French and Finnish law, according to which the debtee may demand full payment from any of the debtors, and the debtors may then settle the correct division among themselves internally. In this case, the group of hunters would be considered as one in relation to the bystander. If, for instance, the hunters A, B, and C cause damage to X and are solidarily liable to pay €3,000, then X may demand the whole of the €3,000 from A, B, or C. If A pays X €3,000, then A may demand that B and C pay her €1,000 each. Solidary liability is often used in cases where damage is caused by group action. (I should point out that I do not claim that the duty-to-pay-€3,000 would necessarily be a collective duty. It is better understood as an array of intermeshing powers, liabilities, and duties. By contrast, the contravened duty-not-to-shoot-bystanders was and is held by the group—though similar duties are held by the group members individually, too.)

Examples such as this show that legal systems do occasionally recognize group agents that are not legal persons, despite the claims that legal personhood would be the only way for a group to hold rights and bear duties.

Preliminary Conclusions

There is a linguistic tendency not to ascribe legal rights to legal nonpersons, but, as I argued in Chapter 2, the most prominent theories of rights can be used to show that right-holding and legal personhood do not always go hand in hand. This is also true of group agents: groups may hold claim-rights and bear duties and occupy other legal positions regardless of whether they are granted legal personhood.

What, then, is the difference between groups that are legal persons and groups that are not? This is where my general theory of legal personhood comes into play: groups that are legal persons are endowed with incidents of legal personhood; they have, for instance, legal standing and can therefore be parties in lawsuits. They can also own property in their name. I will in the next section discuss the nature of the legal personhood of groups further.

[24] Apart from disbandment, economic sanctions seem to be the only feasible form of punishing group agents, as they do not have a corporal existence.

The Legal Personhood of Collectivities

Let us recall John Locke's account of the person as a 'forensic term'. According to Locke, '[t]his personality extends itself beyond present existence to what is past [...] whereby it becomes concerned and accountable; owns and imputes to itself past actions, just upon the same ground and for the same reason as it does the present'.[25] Locke is not writing about groups here, but he does raise an important point that can be applied to group entities: most incidents of legal personhood do not function properly unless the relevant entitlements and burdens can persist across certain transitions, and unless the disappearance of obligations (as in the case of bankruptcy) is regulated. The need for a clear identification of persons is recognized in many particular instances: birth and death certificates establish the beginning and end of a human being's legal personhood, and national identification numbers are used to track the citizens and residents of certain countries. However, the continuity of human beings is easier to establish than that of corporations, as we have physical bodies (with features such as fingerprints and DNA) that typically maintain some continuity over time. On the other hand, groups do not have a bodily form and are often ephemeral: it can be difficult for an outsider to know when a group dissolves. This is why the establishment and dissolution of corporations are typically regulated, and their numerical identity is tracked with identification numbers. The legal personhood of a group is, therefore, a kind of 'visibility cloak' (as opposed to the invisibility cloak in the *Harry Potter* series) that makes corporations and their entitlements and obligations easier to track by other actors.

The existence of group agents is in ordinary cases prior to their existence as legal persons. Typically, when a group of people decide to file for the registration of a company, they have already established a collective intentionality. However, there are cases when the legal platform (the 'cloak') may exist before the existence of the group agent. For instance, a so-called dormant company may be registered for a long time without engaging in any business, until its owners one day decide to start a business and remember that they can use the company as the platform for the business. In this case, the legal platform has clearly existed before the coming into being of the new group agent. One interesting consequence of such an arrangement is that the new group agent may end up legally liable for debts incurred by the earlier collectivity that operated using the same legal platform.

Even though I claim that group intentionality is in most cases prior to legal personhood, this is not to say that being a legal person would not affect the group agent in many ways. On one hand, being a legal person imposes certain requirements on the group agent: for instance, almost any legally registered business corporation must

[25] John Locke, *An Essay Concerning Human Understanding* (1690), Book II, ch XXVII, para 26.

have a board of directors. Even if the board is really dominated by an outsider who wields the actual power in the company, the company nevertheless cannot make certain decisions without following a prescribed procedure. If we continue using the metaphor of the visibility cloak, we can say that the cloak may only be worn by certain kinds of groups; otherwise it will fall off or will fail to expose some parts of the group agent.

On the other hand, legal personhood also allows group agents to grow in size and function in ways which would most likely not be possible for group agents that are not persons. The limited liability of corporations, and especially so-called *entity shielding*, is of particular interest. When entity shielding is in effect, the owners of a business corporation are liable for the debts of the corporation only in exceptional circumstances—when 'the corporate veil is pierced'. This separation provides opportunities for controlled risk-taking by the owners, and accentuates the separateness of corporations from any particular human beings.

The legal personhood of a group also enables the group to encompass people who do not share the group intentionality. As the legal personhood of a group agent empowers it to enter into contracts and to suffer legal harms, I-mode thinkers who participate in the group's activities for purely individual ('selfish') reasons can more easily be incentivized to act in the group's interests: they may for instance be liable to compensate the group for their misfeasance, and the group may more easily recompense the individuals for their contributions.[26]

The Alleged Fictionality of Corporations

Corporations are often designated as fictitious persons. This usage dates back to the Middle Ages, when Pope Innocent IV labelled corporations with the phrase *persona ficta*. Occasionally, the whole concept of legal personhood is referred to as a 'legal fiction', though what exactly is meant by this designation is often unclear.[27] Roughly put, legal fictions can be found in cases where legal rules are extended to cover situations that would not be covered by the full literal contents of their paradigmatic formulations.[28]

The problem here is that the fictitiousness of a statement depends on its formulation. Kenneth Campbell notes this:

[26] There is also a branch of economics, called the theory of the firm, focusing on the question why a corporate structure may be more efficient than self-interested individuals forming contract networks when producing goods and services. The classic account in this regard is Ronald Coase's transaction cost theory, according to which transaction costs (such as the cost of determining the prices of one's products) can be lower when the production is coordinated within a firm. Ronald Coase, 'The Nature of the Firm' (1937) 4 *Economica* 386.

[27] For a good discussion of the 'fictionality' of corporations, see Orts (n 3) 30–2. However, Orts takes it for granted that corporations can always be described as legal fictions, which I see as problematic.

[28] This is not to be taken as a complete definition but merely as a sketch of the concept.

Suppose [that one has the rule 'if p then c'] and it is desired to increase its range of application: the law may resort to rules, *inter alia*, in the following semantic forms:

(12) '*q* shall be treated as if it were *p*',
(13) '*q* is deemed to be *p*',
(14) '*p*'s include *q*'s',
(15) 'a finding of *q* is conclusive of *p*'.[29]

Campbell considers (15) to be a likely legal fiction (unless *p* actually entails *q*), and assumes that (12) does not create a fiction. I will not dwell on analysing these claims, but his general point is important: the fictitiousness of corporate legal personhood depends on the formulation of the proposition assessed. In addition, something seems to turn on whether we use the term 'person' or the phrase 'legal person': the latter is a specialist phrase, whereas the former can refer to, say, the metaphysical person or to a human being (particularly if used in the form 'person—people' rather than 'person—persons'). The meanings of words change over time, too; even if the Supreme Court of the US originally extended the scope of application of certain constitutional provisions beyond their literal contents by deeming corporations to be persons, it may perhaps be argued that, at least among jurists, one literal meaning of the word 'person' now includes corporations.

Overall, the matter is quite muddled. However, there is one particular question on which this work may shed light: are corporations legal persons in the *same sense* as human beings are, and does this similarity explain the fact that we can attribute similar legal incidents to both? If the answer is affirmative, this would imply that the talk of corporations as legal persons is not purely fictitious.

There are relevant similarities between corporations (*qua* group agents) and human beings. Both corporations and human beings can hold claim-rights, bear duties and perform acts with the intention to effect legal consequences. They can consequently be endowed with both passive and active incidents of legal personhood, such as the capacity to enter into contracts. Here we must recall the functional/felt distinction. Both corporations and adult human beings of sound mind are able to *act* in the world of obligations in the functional sense. Adult human beings of sound mind may also act in the felt sense: they experience beliefs, desires, and intentions. Is this difference relevant? For the purposes of acting in law, it is not. Functional legal agency is most often sufficient for entering into legal contracts and even for many forms of legal responsibility. In this sense, corporate legal personhood is not a fiction: corporations can act in the law much as adult human beings of sound mind can. Both corporations and human beings also have identities that can persist over time, underlying their capacity to perform acts-in-the-law. There would not even be anything *conceptually* problematic in granting corporations the right to vote, even though there are relatively obvious moral and political arguments against this.[30]

[29] Kenneth Campbell, 'Fuller on Legal Fictions' (1983) 2 *Law and Philosophy* 339, 368.

[30] One would, however, have to define 'corporation' carefully if corporations were given the vote. If corporations *qua* legal platforms had the right to vote, then anyone could register a theoretically unlimited number of single-person corporations and vote using all of them.

Collectivities as Beneficiaries

The focus of this chapter has been on organized collectivities that constitute group agents, where the members of such a group participate in the formation of the collective beliefs and attitudes of the group and/or in carrying out its collective goals. Such collectivities can be legal persons because they can function as agents—rendering them potential active legal persons—and because such a group 'owns' the products of the common enterprise, which is why duties can in many typical cases be borne towards the group rather than towards the individual members. Group agents can therefore be passive legal persons.

Having said that, I have maintained that individuals and nonhuman animals can be legal persons without having control over any legal platform, if they are represented by administrators. Would a similar setup be possible in the case of collectivities? Such an arrangement would have to involve an individual or a group being tasked with the administration of a legal platform for the benefit of a group of individuals or creatures. The beneficiaries would not actually partake in the formation of the collective attitudes of the group. The collectivity consisting of these individuals or creatures would thus supposedly constitute a passive legal person.

Let us think of foundations. A typical civil-law foundation has three features: an endowment, a stipulated purpose, and a governing body (comparable to a board of directors). What distinguishes these types of foundations from other corporations is that they do not have members (as with associations) or owners (as with business corporations). Rather, the governing body is initially chosen by whoever establishes the foundation, and, whenever an individual leaves the governing body thereafter, the replacement will be chosen by the remaining directors. Now, let us say that a foundation is set up with the purpose of promoting the interests of a relatively small group of severely mentally disabled people. Can we understand these individuals collectively as the beneficiary of a collective legal person, akin to the way an individual can be a passive legal person? The theories of Pettit, List, and Tuomela are not directly applicable here because mentally disabled individuals cannot partake in such a form of joint intentionality. However, Bentham's test is again helpful: it is easy to think of cases where ascertaining that the foundation has acted in breach of its duties necessarily involves establishing that the group of disabled individuals has been harmed, rather than any one in particular among them. For instance, if the administrators culpably mismanage the endowment of the foundation, leading to significant financial losses, it might not be possible to single out any individual who has suffered detriment because of the maladministration. This conclusion depends of course on the circumstances. If the foundation promotes the interests of its beneficiaries only by making monthly support payments to these individuals, and if the level of the payments depends on the appreciation of the endowment, then the mismanagement has likely caused individuated harm. On the other hand, if the foundation engages in various forms of support, such as organizing events, then the detriment likely cannot be individuated—especially if the loss of funds means that the foundation refrains from engaging in any new (currently unplanned) projects instead of cutting its current projects.

The example just sketched is a relatively straightforward case. It is often much less clear whether a particular legal platform constitutes legal personhood for a collective beneficiary. I cannot hope to address every possible case or to provide exhaustive criteria for when a collective beneficiary counts as a legal person. In general, one should focus on the degree to which the collective beneficiary is endowed with incidents of legal personhood. Consequently, one should ask, for instance, whether the collectivity owns some property just as mentally severely disabled individuals can own property. Ownership is, of course, in itself a cluster phenomenon, consisting of separate incidents, and one would have to look at the incidents separately. I will address some central points.

First, an important criterion is that the parties who have originally established the legal platform must not be able to revoke the arrangement—barring exceptional circumstances such as the obsolescence of the purpose of the foundation. If the founders can simply reclaim the assets of the legal platform at will, the situation resembles one where an individual is allowed to use a piece of property at the pleasure of the owner rather than his or her owning the property.[31]

Second, the assets in the legal platform need to be earmarked for one specific purpose, or for a number of very closely related purposes, and the range of the beneficiaries cannot be overly vague or unclear. This pertains to the characteristics of a legal platform that were identified in Chapter 4: a legal platform must be integrated and separate from other legal platforms. Crudely put, if a guardian of funds for a client is legally permitted to divert the funds for the payment of the personal debts of the guardian or some other client of his, we should conclude that the guardian owns the funds but is under a duty to the client to use some of his funds in specific ways. He does not merely look after funds that belong to the client. Analogously, a foundation could have a number of multifarious and even mutually conflicting stipulated purposes, and the range of the potential beneficiaries can be very extensive and vague. An affluent individual who has grown up in village A, done her life's work in organization B, and lived her final years in senior community C could register a foundation whose purpose would be to provide aid to A, B, and/or C. The executive body could have full discretion over the details, such as which of the three collectivities to prioritize. If the foundation then chose to engage in a construction project in village A, but ended up losing the whole endowment due to unforeseen risks, A, B, and C would be equally affected. In this case, it could hardly be said that A, B, or C owned

[31] This revocability pertains also to the legal personhood of artificial intelligences, which will be addressed in the next chapter.

the funds of the foundation in a manner analogous to the manner in which a passive individual owns property.

Another indication that an arrangement has constituted legal personhood for a collective beneficiary is that the administrators can represent the collectivity in dealings with third parties. If a foundation were authorized to act in the name of the collectivity in a given matter (regarding, for example, certain collective interests of the mentally disabled individuals), the legal relationship would resemble that between an infant and a guardian even more. The foundation discussed here would of course likely only be authorized to represent the group if it received authorization from all the legal guardians of the beneficiaries, but this does not make any significant difference—the arrangement would merely involve the transferral of some of the authority of the legal guardians to the organization. What is important, however, is that the foundation would need to have a degree of discretion in how exactly they choose to further the collective beneficiary's interests. If they received very specific instructions, their role would resemble that of a legal counsel rather than a legal guardian.

These points may help us in determining the import of the Whanganui River arrangement. According to the agreement between the Whanganui tribes and the Crown, each party appoints a guardian to administer the legal platform together with the other party. This position is called *Te Pou Tupua*.[32] They are required to act in accordance with *Te Awa Tupua* values, which involve treating the river as an indivisible whole and recognizing the special connection that the indigenous tribes have with the river. We should firstly note that since the tribes and the democratically elected government appoint the guardians, the tribes and affected individuals cannot be understood as purely passive collective beneficiaries here. However, the *Te Awa Tupua* values appear to entail duties pertaining to the preservation of the river as a viable ecosystem; such duties could be held collectively towards the sentient beings that depend on or benefit from the river in one way or another.[33] Most such beings could not partake in the administration of the legal person in any way.

The arrangement seems to fulfil the criteria mentioned above: the legal person receives full ownership of the Crown-owned parts of the riverbed, and it can represent the collective beneficiary in dealings with third parties.[34] The arrangement cannot be unilaterally revoked by the Crown, at least not without changing the legislation. What might complicate this analysis is that the guardians may have some obligations best understood as religious duties towards the Whanganui Iwi tribes. The relevant

[32] Whanganui River Settlement Ratification Booklet for Whanganui Iwi 26.

[33] 'The role of Te Pou Tupua is to represent and advocate for the interests of the River, not represent its appointors.' Ibid.

[34] 'The functions of Te Pou Tupua include: (a) acting and speaking on behalf of Te Awa Tupua; […] (d) exercising the landowner functions in relation to any land vested in Te Awa Tupua'. Ibid.

documents describe the river as a metaphysical being with a soul. If some duties flowing from the *Te Awa Tupua* values do not contribute to the preservation of the river as a viable ecosystem, they may have to be understood on religious terms instead. However, what the values imply in this regard is unclear. In any case, it seems that the vast majority of the duties of the *Te Pou Tupua* can be understood as being held towards the collective beneficiary constituted by the sentient beings that depend on the river in one way or another.

This discussion of collective passive legal personhood has not aimed to be comprehensive; I do not claim to have set out all the criteria that a collective beneficiary must meet in order to qualify as a potential legal person, nor have I addressed all the possible forms of legal arrangements that might establish the legal personhood of a collective beneficiary. However, I have sought to show that collective legal personhood is not limited to organized group agents.

Conclusion

This chapter has addressed numerous points surrounding corporations. I have proceeded from a distinction between the ontological status of a group agent and the jural status of legal personhood. This distinction, which is occasionally neglected, has been central in the arguments advanced here. I have argued, first, that human beings can form group agents that can have their own beliefs, goals, and intents. Furthermore, such collectivities hold legal positions regardless of whether they are legal persons, which underscores the shortcomings of the Orthodox View.

Rather than endowing collectivities with the capacity to hold rights and bear duties, corporate personhood (in its central form) makes group agents more 'visible' and less ephemeral by regulating their establishment, dissolution, and other such matters. In addition, the legal institution of asset shielding allows for individuals to demarcate their own assets from the assets they have devoted to a common project. That institution is, of course, an instance of the more general feature of the separateness of legal platform.

I have also inquired whether groups can be passive legal persons as collective beneficiaries. The answer has been affirmative, even if the issue is thorny and difficult. The Whanganui River arrangement could be understood as establishing legal personhood for a collective beneficiary, but much depends on the details.

What if the group-realist account offered here is wrong, and strong individualism is right in that legal positions cannot be ascribed to collective entities? Such a result would of course be at odds with much of what has been said in this chapter, but it would not upset the overall theory of legal personhood, nor would my criticism of the Orthodox View come into question. I would probably have to concede that group entities cannot be legal *persons*. Regardless, one could still establish corporations *qua* legal *platforms*, even though this establishment would not grant the collectivity the capacity to hold legal positions: the participants in the collective project would already be able to hold legal positions whereas the collectivity would be unable to hold such positions regardless of its legal status. The ontological status of groups cannot be changed by legal decisions. Either the collectivities addressed here are conceptually capable of holding various legal positions—in which case they can be endowed with the incidents of legal personhood—or they cannot hold these legal positions—in which case they cannot be so endowed. This is also why the Capacity-for-Rights position cannot explain corporate personhood. Even if I am wrong in arguing that collectivities are capable of holding legal positions, their legal personhood should be understood in terms of a complex of legal positions held by the shareholders, the executive board, and so on.

6

The Legal Personhood of Artificial Intelligences

Preliminaries: Three Contexts

This chapter applies the Bundle Theory of legal personhood to artificial intelligences (AIs) to see what insights the theory can yield. As has been the case throughout this book, I do not propose to participate directly in the debate over whether AIs should be legal persons, but rather to provide a structure and framework for that debate. My aim is also to expose certain problems that afflict any efforts by proponents of the Orthodox View of legal personhood to elucidate the issues at hand.

The field of artificial intelligence is developing at a breathtaking rate. One relatively recent example is how Google's software was able to beat the best human players in the Chinese game of Go—a feat that was until recently considered to be decades away.[1] Legal and political actors are responding to this change in various ways. The United Nations General Assembly commissioned in 2013 a report on lethal autonomous robots (which could decide to kill without human intervention),[2] and investment banks already employ so-called robot traders.[3] The increasing role of AIs in commerce prompted the Committee on Legal Affairs of the European Parliament to assert in a 2017 report that 'the civil liability for damage caused by robots is a crucial issue which also needs to be analysed and addressed at Union level'.[4] The Parliament called on the Commission to

[1] See for instance Matt Reynolds, 'DeepMind's AI beats world's best Go player in latest face-off' *New Scientist* (23 May 2017) <https://www.newscientist.com/article/2132086-deepminds-ai-beats-worlds-best-go-player-in-latest-face-off/>, visited on 13 June 2018.

[2] Christof Heyns, Report of the Special Rapporteur on extrajudicial, summary or arbitrary executions, A/HRC/23/47.

[3] I use the word 'artificial intelligence' (as a countable noun) to refer to a human-built entity that can act in ways characteristic of intelligent beings, especially humans. What I mean by 'robot', on the other hand, is a mechanical entity capable of interacting directly with the physical world. Even if robots can also be under the direct control of a human being, I will focus on autonomous robots here. The often-used label 'robot trader' (meaning software designed to buy and sell stock, derivatives, and so on) is not very good because it does not refer to mechanical entities. Phrases such as 'software trader' or 'AI trader' would be more suitable.

[4] European Parliament, Committee on Legal Affairs. Report with recommendations to the Commission on Civil Law Rules on Robotics (2015/2103(INL)) 16.

> explore, analyse and consider the implications of all possible legal solutions, such as [...] creating a specific legal status for robots in the long run, so that at least the most sophisticated autonomous robots could be established as having the status of electronic persons responsible for making good any damage they may cause, and possibly applying electronic personality to cases where robots make autonomous decisions or otherwise interact with third parties independently.[5]

Questions surrounding AI legal personhood are thus multifaceted, and a cluster-property understanding of legal personhood is well suited to analysing the question. Let us now distinguish three main contexts that bear on the legal personhood of AIs. The contexts overlap in many ways, but they can usefully be distinguished, and they will provide a structure for this chapter.

First, in the *ultimate-value context* we ask whether AIs are of ultimate value and therefore worthy of receiving some of the protections that legal persons such as human children enjoy. Science fiction is replete with examples of scenarios where some features of a (usually humanlike) robot prompt questions of its morally correct treatment. Fundamental protections are especially important here, but many other—perhaps all other—incidents of legal personhood are relevant as well.

Second, in the *responsibility context* our focus is, unsurprisingly, on the legal responsibility of AIs. Could self-driving cars or autonomous security robots be held criminally or tortiously liable for their actions? The most relevant incident here is—as one might anticipate—onerous legal personhood. In addition, tort liability for an AI would also require that the AI could own property.[6]

Finally, the *commercial context* has to do with AIs' functioning as commercial actors; buying, selling, and so on. The three most relevant incidents of legal personhood here are special rights, ownership, and legal competences.

These three contexts share a certain connection with the three central 'building blocks' of legal personhood that I have introduced in Chapter 4. Passive legal personhood functions through claim-rights, and is closely connected to the question of whether AIs could be ultimately valuable. I have argued that idols and bodies of water are not legal persons—regardless of the pronouncements of any legislator or judiciary—because they are not of ultimate value and therefore cannot hold claim-rights. Some human collectivities, on the other hand, can hold claim-rights because they are a shared project of human beings. In what follows, AIs' claim-rights will be addressed from two different angles. If some AI is of ultimate value, then it follows

[5] European Parliament, Committee on Legal Affairs. Report with recommendations to the Commission on Civil Law Rules on Robotics (2015/2103(INL)) 17–18.

[6] See Gabriel Hallevy, *When Robots Kill: Artificial Intelligence under Criminal Law* (Northeastern University Press 2013), and Robert van den Hoven van Genderen, 'Do We Need New Legal Personhood in the Age of Robots and AI?' in Marcelo Corrales, Mark Fenwick, and Nikolaus Forgó (eds), *Robotics, AI and the Future of Law* (Springer 2018).

quite straightforwardly that the AI can hold claim-rights. If, on the other hand, an AI is not of ultimate value, it can under certain conditions hold claim-rights as the 'administrator' of a human-defined project.

Only AIs that are of ultimate value could be purely passive legal persons—a legal status comparable to that of an infant or a comatose individual. Such an AI could of course also be endowed with an active legal personhood if it were for instance capable of contracting, administering its property, and so on. If an AI is not of ultimate value, it can only be a legal person in virtue of its capacity to be subjected to legal duties and/or to administer legal platforms through the exercise of competences. Legal duties are here connected to the responsibility context, whereas legal competences relate to the commercial context.

The discussion will be focused on so-called strong AIs, and I will proceed from the assumption that such AIs will sooner or later come into existence. A strong AI is an entity that can in relevant respects act like a human being. As with human collectivities, we can treat AIs as legal persons if they can perform like human individuals in a sufficient number of the relevant legal contexts: ownership, contracting, and so on.[7] For most of our purposes here, it is irrelevant whether the AI can 'really' think or whether it merely acts 'as if' it thinks.[8] Here we need to recall the functional/felt distinction and the intentional stance. Let us take the institution of contracting as an example. An AI does not need to understand the institution in a felt, phenomenal way in order to be able to contract. If an AI's potential business associates can rely on the AI's ability to adjust its future behaviour accordingly when signing a contract, contracting with the AI would be intelligible. The associates can then adopt the intentional stance when dealing with the AI; it is immaterial for this purpose whether the AI can for instance experience mental states pertaining to the contract. It might be that such mental states are required for moral contracts, but certainly not for legal contracts.

I will first address the ultimate-value and sanction contexts. The treatment of these two settings will be relatively brief. Because my theory has most to offer when analysing the commercial context, the preponderance of the chapter will be focused thereon.

[7] This 'intentional-stance' or 'pragmatic' approach to AI legal personality is endorsed by many who have written on the topic. See for instance Samir Chopra and Laurence F. White, *A Legal Theory for Autonomous Artificial Agents* (University of Michigan Press 2011) 1–17, and Lawrence B. Solum, 'Legal Personhood for Artificial Intelligences' (1992) 70 *North Carolina Law Review* 1231.

[8] John Searle has famously argued that an entity could be able to process information in a way that allows for it to act as if it comprehends the information, but without actually understanding it. John Searle, 'Minds, Brains and Programs' (1980) 3 *Behavioral and Brain Sciences* 417. For a good summary of the argument and the subsequent counterarguments, see Larry Hauser, 'Chinese Room Argument', *International Encyclopedia of Philosophy* <http://www.iep.utm.edu/chineser/>.

AIs as Ultimately Valuable

The moral status of AIs is a fiercely debated topic. Some philosophers maintain that AIs can never achieve a status of moral considerability—Joanna Bryson argues explicitly that robots should be treated as slaves[9]—whereas many have contended that we will at some point owe moral duties to robots or other types of AIs.[10] Even though the moral debate over the value of AIs is complex, its implications are straightforwardly applicable here. If we assume that some AIs are of ultimate value, then they can hold claim-rights; we can owe duties to them, and our duties do not merely pertain to them. We can therefore conclude that they can be passive legal persons.

We should once again note the difficulty that the Orthodox View has in explaining what is at stake here. Authors often describe the legal personhood of AIs as consisting in the ascription to them of 'rights and duties of their own'.[11] This definition would entail that, if AIs are endowed with any rights or duties whatsoever, they are legal persons. But this conclusion would be as problematic in connection with AIs as it is in connection with animals and slaves. Let us assume that a society becomes concerned about the bad treatment of humanoid household robots because the robots are thought to feel pain. The legislature then enacts a Robot Welfare Act that prohibits certain particularly gratuitous acts of cruelty toward robots. According to the interest theory of rights, such prohibitions endow the robots with rights (assuming the robots are of ultimate value). Are the robots now legal persons? For reasons laid out in Chapter 2, I am sceptical of such a conclusion. Animals hold, and slaves held, similar legal rights, yet animals and slaves are widely—and correctly—classified as legal nonpersons. Thus, we need to distinguish robots as right-holders from robots as legal persons. These humanoid robots would likely qualify as legal persons if they could no longer be owned and if they received wide-ranging fundamental protections (for instance, attempts to shut them down would be classified as attempted homicides).

[9] Joanna J. Bryson, 'Robots Should Be Slaves' in Yorick Wilks (ed.), *Close Engagements with Artificial Companions* (John Benjamins Publishing Company 2010).

[10] See for instance John Basl, 'Machines as Moral Patients We Shouldn't Care About (Yet): The Interests and Welfare of Current Machines' (2014) 27 *Philosophy & Technology* 79 and Eric Schwitzgebel and Mara Garza, 'A Defense of the Rights of Artificial Intelligences' (2015) 39 *Midwest Studies in Philosophy* 98. For a more noncommittal view, see David J. Gunkel, 'The Other Question: Can and Should Robots Have Rights?' [2017] *Ethics and Information Technology* 1. Gunkel's account builds, however, on a rather peculiar understanding of the is/ought distinction, as he claims that the question whether robots can hold rights is an 'is' question rather than an 'ought' question. Claims such as 'Robots can hold rights and should therefore hold rights' would then supposedly be problematic from the point of view of Hume's law. However, whether an entity can hold rights is clearly a moral question in itself, and therefore an 'ought' question. Of course, the proposition that AIs should hold rights doesn't follow from the proposition that they can hold rights, even when both are correctly understood as 'ought' questions.

[11] See for instance Ugo Pagallo, *The Laws of Robots* (Springer 2013) 40 and Ugo Pagallo, 'Vital, Sophia, and Co.—The Quest for the Legal Personhood of Robots' (2018) 9 *Information (Switzerland).*

AIs as Active Legal Persons

Active legal personhood has to do with the capacity to act. We can understand the potential approaches to the acts—or 'acts'—of AIs on a continuum. One end involves treating AIs purely as tools. If we access a website to download illegal material or to buy stock, the personal computer we use for these purposes is obviously not taken to have performed the illegal act or entered the contract. The computer is analogous with, say, a pen used to sign a contract or a gun used to rob a bank.

The other extreme involves treating AIs more or less identically with the way adult human beings of sound mind are treated today. We could imagine a sophisticated AI that owns property in its own name, can contract and sue, and is fully subject to criminal and civil responsibility. The AI starts trading in stock and decides that the best way to maximize its profits is through insider trading, so it starts to acquire insider information illegally. The AI is able to comprehend the legal consequences of its actions; it simply performs an analysis of the potential costs—the risk of getting caught, the sanctions, and so on—and concludes that the expected value of the operation is positive. The AI's attempts are detected, and it has to pay large fines as well as compensation to the parties who have lost money because of the operation. The designers of the AI are not held accountable.

In between these two extremes fall a multitude of scenarios. A rather obvious and often-invoked example is the treating of an AI as a representative of a legal person. Similarly, criminal doctrines could be revised to allow for the criminal liability of AIs, but restricted to some limited cases. In other cases the blame for wrongdoing would fall on the designer or owner of the AI. The Bundle Theory of legal personhood offers many tools for analysing such scenarios. First, the benefits of an incident-based theory are quite obvious here. In addition, two particular notions, introduced in Chapter 4, will be useful: the distinction between independent and dependent legal personhood, and the concept of a legal platform.

Holding AIs Responsible

An often-mentioned example of a 'homicide' committed by a robot is from 1981, when an industrial robot caused the death of an employee at a Japanese motorcycle factory. The employee had entered a restricted safety zone to perform maintenance on the robot but had failed to shut it down properly, which resulted in the robot's pushing him against adjacent machinery. He died instantly.[12] Today, scholars ask whether for instance autonomous combat drones, self-driving cars, or commercial

[12] This incident is mentioned in much of the relevant literature, for example Gabriel Hallevy, 'The Criminal Liability of Artificial Intelligence Entities—from Science Fiction to Legal Social Control' (2010) 4 *Akron Intellectual Property Journal* 171, 171–2

AIs might be held morally and/or legally responsible for their actions.[13] I will here mainly focus on the intelligibility of punishing AIs, rather than on whether and when they should be punished.

Prima facie, it might appear that AIs should be 'angels', never acting in ways that would give rise to questions about whether they should be held legally responsible. This result could be achieved in two ways. Designers could be obligated to program their AIs not to engage in certain types of conduct ('Don't kill people, steal, commit fraud', and so on). Alternatively, nominal duties—duties unaccompanied by legal sanctions—would be extended to AIs, and programmers would be required to program AIs to always obey their legal duties, so that it would be impossible for the AIs not to follow its duties. The AIs would, obviously, then have to be able to understand and follow the precepts of law.

According to the just-depicted 'angelic ideal', the legal responsibility of AIs would be unnecessary. The ideal is, however, quite problematic. First, a programmer could simply refuse to follow the ideal. She could create an AI that is capable of understanding legal requirements but does not treat such requirements as overriding or exclusionary reasons-for-action. Rather, the potential legal consequences would be included in the overall calculus of whether to perform some action. Thus, if an AI's goal was to amass as much wealth as possible, it would—like the ideal *Homo economicus* of economic theory—weigh the potential benefits and disadvantages of some illegal course of action (e.g. insider trading), and simply the pick the option with the highest expected value. AI legal responsibility could then be justified on deterrence grounds because it would reduce the expected value of undesirable behaviour.

Second, programming an AI to be able to contravene its legal duties might also have socially beneficial consequences. Acting in breach of a contract may be economically the most efficient option, which will produce the most utility for all parties. Consider a family of four—the Smiths—who have made a reservation at a small hotel that has only three four-person suites. Before the Smiths arrive to check in, a family of twelve—the Franks—come and ask if they could book the whole hotel, as they would all like to spend the night at the same place. The hotel is unable to contact the Smiths, but the owner asks a smaller establishment across the road if they have an available four-person bedroom. The answer is affirmative, and the Smiths are relocated to the other establishment and even given a 30 per cent discount. Everybody wins: the Smiths get a discount, the Franks can stay the night under the same roof, and both hotels get more customers. Regardless, a contractual duty has been breached, as the Smiths (or rather the one who made the reservation) did not consent to this change. It is plausible that the creator of an AI would like it to perform in the manner of the hotel owner.[14]

[13] Chopra and White explain, using numerous examples, why AI responsibility could be meaningful—see for instance Chopra and White (n 7) 119–51.

[14] AIs functioning in inherently dangerous spheres of life might also have to be able to 'choose the lesser evil'. Google has already programmed its self-driving cars to be able to

Finally, an AI could occasionally be mistaken about the content of law. Human beings are typically not excused for their ignorance of law, so perhaps the AI should be sanctioned for its breaking the law as well—or at least be required to pay compensation for any harm it has caused by breaking the law.[15]

What kind of sanctions?

Obviously, the type of sanctions to which AIs would be subjected would depend on the details of the legal personhood arrangement. Economic sanctions would be highly relevant with regard to AI responsibility, but such sanctions require that the AI can own property. However, purely onerous legal personhood—as with slaves in the US—would be possible as well. One potential sanction could be disabling the AI if it did not obey the law.[16] We need not assume any self-interest on the part of the AI for such a sanction to work. The AI would simply recognize that its goals would be thwarted if it were disabled, and would therefore avoid conduct likely to elicit such a sanction.

One problem with the responsibility of AIs has to do with their autonomy or 'free will'. AIs have been programmed to act in a certain way—why not, therefore, direct the responsibility at the programmers and/or owners of an AI? [17] This is a multifaceted issue. First, it is easy to overestimate the capacity of programmers to predict an AI's conduct, especially if the AI functions as a neural network that can learn patterns of behaviour independently. Even if such entities cannot be responsible in some thick, moral sense of responsibility, the deterrence rationale of punishment is certainly applicable to them. The kinds of AIs we are imagining are goal-directed, intentional beings, which could take legal sanctions into account. Furthermore, the programmers and/or owners can certainly *also* be held responsible if they have, say, intentionally created AIs that commit crimes. If they have done this unintentionally, they might in fact benefit from the criminal responsibility of their creations just as much as everyone else. A robot inclined to contravene basic legal norms might, after all, just as well determine that its owner is an obstacle to its goals. The responsibility

exceed the speed limits if following the limits would be dangerous. A self-driving car may end up in a situation where it may have to choose between, say, killing a passenger or two pedestrians (see MIT's Moral Machine website, which tests people's intuitions regarding such cases: http://moralmachine.mit.edu/ (accessed 5 October 2018)). A robot police officer might have to determine whether an armed robber will need to be shot, or whether leaving her alive poses a greater threat.

[15] One solution to this issue could be the AI's buying insurance, as Lawrence Solum points out. Solum (n 7) 1245.

[16] Chopra and White also propose the forcible modification of AIs as a similar kind of punishment. Chopra and White (n 7) 168.

[17] Alfred R. Mele has addressed questions relating to whether one is an autonomous agent if one's preferences have been determined by someone else. Alfred R. Mele, *Autonomous Agents: From Self-Control to Autonomy* (Oxford University Press 2001).

arrangement would therefore serve largely the same purposes as the criminal liability of slaves in the antebellum US South. Holding slaves criminally responsible protected both slave owners and third parties from slave crimes.

AIs as Commercial Actors

The tool–full-legal-person continuum introduced above is in commercial contexts often understood as a trifurcation:

(1) AI *qua* tool,
(2) AI *qua* representative,[18]
(3) AI *qua* legal person.

This trifurcation can very crudely be summed up as follows. Approach (1) treats an AI like any other piece of property in the owner's possession. The AI is like a word processor, used to draft a contract. Suppose that, because of a programming error, an AI omits an important clause from a contract. If the AI is treated as a tool, the owner might be able to sue the programmer, but the contract is most likely valid. If, on the other hand, the AI is treated as a representative, the contract might not be valid if the AI has acted outside its authority. Chopra and White mention 'induction errors, where a discretionary agent incorrectly inducts from contracts where the principal has no objections to a contract the principal does object to' as an eventuality that could result in the owner's preferring an agent–principal relationship.[19] Finally, endowing AIs with legal personhood would supposedly mean treating them 'as subjects of legal rights and obligations',[20] as entities with 'rights (and duties) of their own',[21] or as something 'to which the law can ascribe any Hohfeldian jural relation'.[22] It should come as no surprise that I am critical of such definitions of legal personhood.

The tool/representative/legal person trifurcation is, however, insufficient. We should distinguish two conceptual dimensions that underlie different AI legal personhood arrangements: separateness and independency.

Separateness pertains to a particular feature of legal platforms. A human being who founds a one-person corporation is in control of two legal platforms. Such platforms have three features.[23] First, they are named ('Mary' and 'Mary Inc.'); second, the legal positions within each platform are integrated (Mary can end up losing her house because of a contract she has entered); and third, the platforms are separate (Mary

[18] The term 'agent' is often used in this context, but it is ambiguous, which is why I will refrain from using it when referring to representatives.
[19] Chopra and White (n 7) 46. See also Pagallo, *The Laws of Robots* (n 11) 99.
[20] Chopra and White (n 7) 153. [21] Pagallo, *The Laws of Robots* (n 11) 40.
[22] Shawn Bayern, 'The Implications of Modern Business-Entity Law for the Regulation of Autonomous Systems' (2015) 19 *Stanford Technology Law Review* 93, 94f.
[23] See Chapter 4.

Table 6.1 Two dimensions of AI legal personhood

S. Separateness	*1. Unity* AI completely part of owner's platform	*2. Partial separation* AI-controlled legal platform partially separate and revocable	*3. Total separation* AI-controlled legal platform completely separate and irrevocable
I. Independency	*1. Assimilation* Any exercise of competence by AI is treated as having been done by the owner/operator	*2. Dependency* Someone can, for example, retroactively cancel contracts made by AI	*3. Independency* Completely independent in exercise of competences

cannot normally end up personally liable for the debts of Mary Inc.). Legal positions controlled by an AI can be more or less separate from those of the owner of the AI. Two legal platforms are completely separate if, for instance, the debts pertaining to platform A can never be recovered from platform B and vice versa, and if the separation cannot be revoked. One example of partial separation is an AI-controlled corporation that is owned by a natural person. If the latter declares bankruptcy, the corporation's assets can be used to pay the creditors, whereas the creditors of the corporation do not have access to the natural person's assets.

The *independency* dimension pertains in particular to the exercise of competences: independent legal persons may normally exercise their competences without the supervision of anyone else, whereas dependent legal persons are subject to such supervision.[24] This dimension is distinct from the separateness dimension. For instance, in jurisdictions that allow for minors to own property, an adolescent's property is distinct from that of her father. In the absence of any fraudulent transfers aimed at evading the father's creditors, those creditors cannot access the adolescent's funds. Regardless, the father—assuming he is a legal guardian of his daughter—is normally able to exert some level of control over what his child chooses to do with her money. Thus, the two platforms are separate, but the adolescent is regardless not independent in her exercise of competences.

Table 6.1 presents three levels of separateness and independency each. Let us now focus on how these distinctions shed light on the tool/representative/legal-person trifurcation. Consider investment banks that employ AI traders for buying and selling

[24] This is partly based on Samir Chopra's and Laurence White's distinction between dependent and independent legal personhood. Samir Chopra and Laurence F White, *A Legal Theory for Autonomous Artificial Agents* (The University of Michigan Press 2011) 160–70. See also the discussion on legal competences in Chapter 4 and Visa A. J. Kurki, 'Legal Competence and Legal Power' in Mark McBride (ed), *New Essays on the Nature of Rights* (Hart Publishing 2017).

stock, derivatives, and so on. Given that the trading proceeds at a superhuman pace, most trades happen completely without human intervention. Regardless, such AIs are not legal persons: any trade they make is made in the name of the bank, and thus pertains to the bank's legal platform. The arrangement falls under S1 and I1: the AI does not have its 'own' funds that would be separate from those of the bank (unity), and the AI is also not treated as a representative of the bank, meaning that the bank is strictly liable for whatever contracts the AI chooses to enter (assimilation).[25] These two features sum up the AIs-as-tools arrangement.

The bank and the AI could also be in a representative–principal relationship. This would result in a somewhat different risk allocation, as the bank would not always be bound by contracts entered by the AI. A representative–principal relation would fall under I2 (dependency) and either S1 (unity) or S2 (partial separation). The latter would depend on whether the AI could be liable to a third party for acting outside the scope of its authority; if the AI could be liable, it would need to be able to own property in its own name.

Now consider a move toward complete separation. Shawn Bayern envisages a rather surprising scenario through which existing US law could already enable an AI to gain control of a limited liability company. I will not be concerned with the doctrinal accuracy of the scenario; it is regardless an interesting thought experiment. Bayern bases his argument on the 'process-agreement equivalence principle', according to which 'a legally enforceable agreement may give legal significance to arbitrary features of the state of any process (such as an algorithm or physical system) by specifying legal conditions satisfied by features of that state'.[26] A contract could, for instance, subject some contractual obligation to the behaviour of a dog or the temperature on a given day. Bayern contends that this principle can be extended to the performance of an algorithm:

> Consider, for example, an artificially intelligent algorithm that passes the Turing Test in apparently acting roughly as a human acts. An agreement can, by specifying obligations and conditions, effectively delegate legal rights and decision-making powers to such an algorithm even though that algorithm is not a legal person. An agreement might say, for example, 'Your obligation to perform is discharged if the algorithm indicates X,' where X could be (for an unsophisticated algorithm) a formal output on a computer terminal or (for an artificially intelligent algorithm) something that approaches a description of human understanding and action (like 'that it is satisfied with the arrangement and physically signs a release form').[27]

In addition, Bayern notes that US company law allows unanimous shareholders to change the structure of a limited liability company as they like, even eliminating quintessential corporate bodies such as the board of directors. Assuming that these

[25] Pagallo, *The Laws of Robots* (n 11) 98. If the AI enters a very unsatisfactory contract, the bank may however be able to sue the designer of the AI.

[26] Bayern (n 22) 99. [27] Ibid.

two premises regarding contract and company law are correct, one could form a corporation C, 'signing an "agreement" that specifies that C is to have no board of directors and instead shall take all legal actions determined by *A* (an autonomous system)'.[28]

We could, for instance, imagine a legal arrangement that allows for banks to create subsidiaries run by AIs using this procedure. Such an arrangement might be beneficial for the bank, as it could thereby reduce its risks: the bank would not be responsible for the financial liabilities of the subsidiary. However, Bayern notes that such an AI is not 'an autonomous legal entity', for the bank 'remains a shareholder and can continue to exert control over the entity'.[29] The arrangement would likely fall under S2 (partial separation), and either under I2 (dependency) or I3 (independency). If the subsidiary also had a board that could, say, retroactively cancel some large trades, then I2 would be the appropriate designation. If—for some reason—the bank were to completely 'recuse itself' from meddling in the trades of the AI, then I3 would be the apposite classification. The bank could of course still revoke the whole arrangement, but it would not be able to affect any individual trade.

The scenario just described resembles in many ways the *peculium* institution of ancient Rome.[30] If granted a *peculium* by the owner, a slave could own property, enter into contracts, and so on. The arrangement is somewhat difficult to summarize in contemporary terms: the slave owner did for instance receive the title to whatever the slave acquired and was liable to the slave's creditors, but the master's financial liabilities could not exceed the worth of the *peculium*.[31] The system resembled in many regards a limited-liability company: the master owned a slave, and could create a separate legal platform for that slave. The arrangement could be revoked by the slave owner at will, so a slave could normally keep his *peculium* for only as long as the slave owner perceived this to be in his own interests.

Now, were an AI to control a subsidiary in the described way, this would really only amount to a *peculium*.[32] Moreover—as with a *peculium*—the AI-run subsidiary would best be described as an extension of the owner's legal personhood, rather than as a legal person *tout court*. I am of course not denying that the arrangement would exhibit some features of legal personhood. However, one of the incidents of legal personhood is that one cannot be owned by anyone else, and the significance of that incident can be seen here. The Orthodox View, on the other hand, cannot explain as

[28] Ibid. 100. [29] Ibid. 99.

[30] The similarities between *peculium* and certain aspects of AI legal personality are also noted by Ugo Pagallo in Pagallo, *The Laws of Robots* (n 11).

[31] Richard Gamauf, 'Slaves Doing Business: The Role of Roman Law in the Economy of a Roman Household' (2009) *16 European Review of History: Revue europeenne d'histoire* 331.

[32] Perhaps an even better comparison would be that of X's slave acting as the director of a company owned by X. Such an arrangement would not imply that the slave has become a legal person, even if the slave is in control of a legal entity, because the company is under the complete control of X.

easily why the AI subsidiary arrangement would not amount to 'full' legal personhood. The AI could, for instance, normally decide on whether to sue over a debt or whether to waive it, thus endowing it with a will-theory right.[33] The AI would also certainly have duties distinct from those of the owner, given the limited liability of the subsidiary. The Orthodox View would therefore attribute legal personhood to the AI.

What has just been stated is not inconsistent with my claim that ordinary corporations—owned and run by a collectivity of human beings—can be legal persons *tout court*, distinct from their owners. First, one-person corporations are not legal persons; rather, they simply provide a new legal platform for their owner. In contrast, corporations with many members are not reducible to any single owner but are rather an exercise of collective intentionality, distinct from that of the participants. This collective nature grounds such corporations' distinct legal personhood. In addition, the arrangement cannot normally be revoked by any single member alone. The AI subsidiary arrangement, on the other hand, is revocable by its sole owner at any given moment.[34] This is why the subsidiary arrangement—though involving the use of incidents of legal personhood—does not endow the AI with legal personhood *tout court*.[35]

However, Bayern devises a method for completely detaching an AI-run corporation from its members. According to the Uniform Limited Liability Company Act, a limited liability company can exist for up to ninety days without any members; this is to account for certain cases involving, say, the death of the only owner.[36] Bayern argues that this ninety-day limit is in fact only a waivable default rule. The sole founder of C could therefore withdraw from C, creating 'a perpetual LLC [limited liability company]—a new legal person—that requires no ongoing intervention from any preexisting legal person in order to maintain its status'.[37]

Let us assume that the scenario described by Bayern is possible. I agree that it would result in legal personhood for the AI. Again, the situation could be compared to a scenario involving slaves. If—by means of a procedure relevantly similar to the one proposed by Bayern—a slave were to gain complete, irrevocable control of a corporation, she would indeed become a legal person, though a very special one: her

[33] I am assuming here that AIs can hold will-theory rights.

[34] The AI subsidiary could of course be owned by a group of distinct natural and/or artificial persons, rather than by a single corporation. In this case, the AI would act as a sort of 'CEO', executing the collective intentionality of the owners. Once again, the AI itself would not be a legal person except in a *peculium*/representative sense.

[35] As I have noted above, the legal personality of children is different. First, even though they are subject to supervision in their exercise of competences, their legal platform is completely separate from that of their legal guardians. The child's natural legal entity follows her from the cradle to the grave; a guardian cannot simply choose to subsume the child's platform into his or her own platform.

[36] RULLCA § 701(a)(3). [37] Bayern (n 22) 101.

legal name would be, say, 'Mary Inc.', and she would for instance be unable to marry. What would happen to the corporation after her death would also be unclear (unless specified in the original shareholder agreement). Regardless, I see no reason to deny that this would constitute legal personhood for her; similarly, the arrangement depicted by Bayern would result in legal personhood for the AI in question. However, the AI arrangement would be somewhat different because the AI is not of ultimate value. This issue is intertwined with the question of whether AIs that are not ultimately valuable can hold claim-rights.

AIs and Claim-Rights Redux

I have maintained that ultimate value is normally a precondition for holding claim-rights. We can hold duties towards adults, infants, and animals because they are of ultimate value. However, I noted in Chapter 5 that human collectivities are a special case: their interests, though explicable in terms of human individuals, are not reducible to the individual interests of the members. I employed Raimo Tuomela's insight about the 'for-groupness' of the products of a group: if Mary buys some service from a group of friends, the agreed-upon payment is not owed to any individual member of the group but rather to the group itself. This is because the final recipient of the money is often not settled—the group may for instance decide to use the money to invest in its project, to divide it among the members, or to donate it to charity. But we should note here that the project itself is 'owned' by the members: they have committed to the project because they find it meaningful, and they likely have a say in how the products of the group project are to be used. Thus, their interests *qua* group members and *qua* individuals are in many ways intertwined. However, not all collective projects are necessarily 'owned' by the members in a similar way, and such projects will provide a way of understanding the claim-rights of AIs that are not ultimately valuable.

Consider again the foundation—introduced in Chapter 4—whose purpose is to preserve an old manuscript. Such a foundation can hold claim-rights. Now, let us say that all of the board members of the foundation are uninterested in its goals, with no personal stake or interest in whether the manuscript is in fact preserved. Regardless, we can say that when a board member carries out her tasks, it is in her interests (as an administrator of the foundation) that no one interfere with her work. One of the distinguishing features of such administrator-interests is that they can typically be transferred from one individual to another along with the duties and competences of the administrator.

Now suppose that all the workings of the aforementioned foundation were taken care of by a single AI. Even if the AI did not have any 'personal' interests that warrant the ascription of claim-rights, we could ascribe interests to it *qua* administrator of the foundation. The AI *qua* administrator would have an interest in preserving the manuscript and in administering the assets of the foundation towards this purpose. Preserving the text was considered important enough by a human individual or a number of human individuals to warrant establishing a foundation. It is these interests that establish the claim-rights held by whoever or whatever—human or AI—that acts as the administrator of the foundation. The foundation's and the AI's interests are also clearly distinct. Imagine that, according to the rules of the foundation, the AI representing the foundation is replaced every five years (because of improvements in technology). As the old AI would not represent the foundation anymore, it would no longer be able to hold claim-rights.

The aforementioned applies not only to foundations but also to business corporations. An AI could control a business and promote its prescribed goals without having a 'personal' stake in the matter.[38] Consider, for instance, a real estate tycoon who wants to invest in companies in the Blackacre District in order to increase the value of his land there. However, he is an unpopular man and everyone else refuses to deal with him, hoping to prevent him from achieving too much influence in the area. As a solution, he creates the corporation AI Inc., invests a significant amount of money in it, and defines as its purpose that of promoting economic activity in the Blackacre District. He then 'sets the corporation loose' under the control of an AI, following the procedure described by Bayern above, in order to make clear that any deals made with AI Inc. do not benefit the tycoon directly. AI Inc. is now in many ways analogous to the foundation above: its purpose has been determined by the tycoon but is regardless now distinct from his personal interests. The interests of AI Inc. align with those of the tycoon, but only as much as with anyone else who owns land in the Blackacre District. The tycoon's and AI Inc.'s claim-rights can be distinguished. Let us say that Elisabeth has the duty to pay $5,000 to AI Inc.'s bank account because of her contract with AI Inc. The only party that can feasibly be said to hold the claim-right correlative to Elisabeth's duty is AI Inc. itself. Only AI Inc.'s goals are immediately thwarted if the duty is not fulfilled.[39]

To sum up, AIs can hold claim-rights as administrators of legal platforms with goals set by human beings. The correlative duties are not borne towards the AIs as 'private individuals' but rather as representatives of the legal platform they are administering. However, this analysis raises one further issue. In Bayern's scenario, an AI could gain control over a legal platform, and then—perhaps because of a programming error—use it for a purpose that is clearly detrimental for the creator of the AI, as well as for everyone else. Thus, it would no longer fulfil a project determined by a human being or a collectivity. Let us suppose that the arrangement would regardless not be revoked. Would the AI still be able to hold claim-rights? As long as the legal

[38] The typical purpose of a corporation is, of course, to generate profits for the shareholders, but in this case there are no shareholders so the purpose has to be something else.

[39] As with the claim-rights of collectivities, Bentham's test can be applied here. It will trim off beneficiaries such as the tycoon and any other beneficiaries in the Blackacre District.

system recognized for instance any contracts entered by the AI, treating it as a claim-right-holder would be the most intelligible option. I argued in Chapter 4 that idols cannot be legal persons because they are not of ultimate value; the relevant legal platform should rather be attributed to the administrator of the idol. But such options are not available here: no one else would qualify as the administrator or 'guardian' of AI Inc., as the shareholders and the executive board would have been removed. In addition, the legal institution of contracting would be quite incomprehensible if some contractual duties were not held towards anyone. Thus, the AI described here should still be classified as a legal person. However, the legal system would likely be committing a moral error when allowing such AIs to enjoy the protections of legal personhood.

Conclusion

The legal personhood of AIs is a topic that, in fact, covers numerous underlying issues. There are a staggering number of different possible legal personhood arrangements for AIs. The two-dimension analysis—distinguishing separateness and independency—serves to categorize some of these arrangements. It is, however, mostly restricted to the commercial setting.

It should be stressed that endowing an AI with the incidents of legal personhood that enable it to function as an independent commercial actor does not bespeak any acceptance of the notion that AIs are endowed with ultimate value. The legal personhood of an AI can rather serve various purposes that might have nothing to do with the AI itself, such as economic efficiency or risk allocation. Of course, if some AIs ever become sentient, many of the questions addressed in this chapter will have to be reconsidered.

7

Legal Personhood in Normative Reasoning

Normative Questions

This final chapter will bring together some of the multifarious threads presented in this book and, in particular, show how the results of this investigation can be employed to better understand the different normative debates surrounding legal personhood. I will use the legal personhood of animals as a central example when addressing the normative implications of my theory.

Let us return to Ngaire Naffine's distinction between Realists and Legalists, which was first addressed in the Introduction.[1] When asking whether some X should be endowed with legal personhood, Realists maintain that the only relevant question—or at least the overwhelmingly most important one—is whether X 'really' is a person. Legalists, on the other hand, resist such a position and claim that a much larger number of considerations can be pertinent. Before considering these positions afresh, we should take a step back and consider the different types of normative questions that relate to legal personhood.

The normative questions surrounding legal personhood are manifold. Some such questions can be said to be *internal* to law, constrained by the content of extant legal systems, whereas *external* normative questions are not constrained by such content. The most straightforwardly ethical question is whether an entity X should be a legal person—or, better, which incidents of legal personhood X should be endowed with (if any). This question is not internal to law in the sense just described. However, two other questions *can* be said to be internal to law. We can ask: if we reach the conclusion that X is a legal person, or a legal person for some purposes, what follows? Yet another normative question is that of the interpretation of legal materials. If, say, a statute makes reference to 'persons' or 'legal persons', who or what should be included in its ambit?

All the questions in the preceding paragraph are difficult to address at the general level of this book. Not only are the issues difficult and multifaceted, but they are

[1] Ngaire Naffine, *Law's Meaning of Life: Philosophy, Religion, Darwin and the Legal Person* (Hart Publishing 2009).

also intertwined. For instance, the strategy of the Nonhuman Rights Project is to persuade judges that certain nonhuman animals should be endowed with certain incidents of legal personhood. The Project's claim is not only moral and political but also legal: it claims that granting the writ of *habeas corpus* to certain animals is legally required. Such a strategy would be unthinkable in many civil-law countries which take the role of the judiciary to be much more limited. What can my theory offer here, given its generality? The theory can offer an overall picture of legal personhood and can thus structure the legal debates focusing on more specific issues. In addition, the distinctions made in this book can help in rejecting unwarranted conceptual inferences pertaining to legal personhood.

I will first consider how my theory can structure external normative questions, by sketching the legal implications of two distinct ethical positions on the proper treatment of animals. After that, I will offer some examples of the theory's import in legal reasoning.

Who or What Should be a Legal Person?

Whether a given incident of legal personhood should be extended to a given entity depends on multifarious factors. For instance, the question of the morally correct legal treatment of animals is very different from that of whether a group agent should be endowed with the incidents of legal personhood that corporations typically enjoy (such as the separation of assets between the members and the corporation). It is often a better strategy to examine the relevant incidents—rather than legal personhood as a whole—and reflect upon the considerations that might justify endowing an entity with these incidents.

Let us now consider two ethical stances regarding our treatment of animals, and how those stances could be understood in the light of the proposed theory.[2] Gary Francione has termed these two stances 'welfarism' and 'abolitionism'.[3] They are simplified for our purposes here.

According to welfarism, animals can be exploited and eaten as long as they are treated 'humanely' and not afflicted with 'unnecessary' suffering. Most—perhaps all—Western countries have legislation in place that pays at least lip service to this position. Given that the legal implementation of a welfarist stance does result in claim-rights held by the animals, it would be perfectly reasonable to provide the affected animals with the advantages that legal persons have as regards the enforcement of their rights. Thus, the animals' legal standing should be recognized overtly: one

[2] I discuss here 'animals' (or 'nonhuman animals') in a vague, general sense. A more detailed discussion would need to distinguish animals based on species and role (farm animal, pet, wildlife, and so on).

[3] Francione makes this distinction in various places, including his most wide-ranging work Gary Francione, *Animals, Property, and the Law* (Temple University Press 1995).

ought to be able to bring suits in the animals' name if their claim-rights are not respected. This is proposed by Cass Sunstein, who thinks that animals 'should be permitted to bring suit, with human beings as their representatives, to prevent violations of current law'.[4] Endowing certain animals with the capacity to be legally harmed could enhance the protection further. In any case, extending these incidents of legal personhood to some or all nonhuman animals would enhance the enforcement of their existing claim-rights. As Sunstein puts it, this would 'ensure that the rights that are now on the books actually exist in the world.' No changes in the substantive, non-remedial claim-rights of animals would take place, except perhaps if we assume that these amendments would lead to changes in how judges interpret vague provisions in the animal welfare legislation of their jurisdiction. In any case, this first scenario would mainly be focused on the enforcement of the existing rights of animals by extending certain legal remedies to them. If such protections were to enjoy a high hierarchical status as outlined in Chapter 3, they could constitute fundamental protections. It would, regardless, be misleading to call the animals legal persons *tout court* at this stage.

A more radical position would involve abolishing the status of animals as property. Gary Francione has supported this stance, arguing that animals' rights will be subject to curtailment as long as animals are treated as property. We should note that this abolition would not be sufficient alone, as it would merely lead to a kind of extra-legal 'outlaw' status for the affected animals. The legal system would not treat them as property—and would consequently not, say, enforce contracts where an animal is bought or sold—but neither would human beings be prohibited from exploiting the animals 'as if' they were property. The animals would therefore need to be endowed with a number of claim-rights against exploitation. Such claim-rights would likely constitute fundamental protections in my sense. The claim-rights would also need to be amplified by a sufficient number of legal remedies in order to ensure their effective enforcement. Such an arrangement would probably warrant denoting the affected animals as legal persons *tout court*, even if the legal personhood of these creatures would be quite different from that of natural and artificial persons: the animals would, for instance, not need to be able to own property.[5]

The welfarism–abolitionism bifurcation is well established in animal ethics, and the Bundle Theory can explain and structure both accounts. However, a strength of my theory is that it can also act as a framework for certain new proposals that cannot readily be classified under welfarism or abolitionism. Such is David Favre's argument that animals should be reclassified as 'living property', with 'limited legal personality'. Favre writes:

[4] Cass R. Sunstein, 'Can Animals Sue?' in Cass R. Sunstein and Martha C. Nussbaum (eds), *Animal Rights: Current Debates and New Directions* (Oxford University Press 2004) 252.

[5] If pecuniary civil remedies were available to the animals, they would of course need to be able to own the compensation.

Within this new property status, animals have the right:

1. Not to be held for or put to prohibited uses.
2. Not to be harmed.
3. To be cared for.
4. To have living space.
5. To be properly owned.
6. To own property.
7. To enter into contracts.
8. To file tort claims.[6]

Even if this list of rights is extensive, Favre denies that animals should be classified as legal persons *tout court*. Most traditional theories of legal personhood would not be able to account for Favre's position. These theories would have to conclude that animals are already legal persons because they hold rights. In addition, according to authors who take legal personhood and property status to be mutually exclusive, an animal could not be both property and a legal person. On the other hand, my account can perfectly well account for Favre's proposal, which makes use of the non-binary nature of legal personhood.

We can now return to the Realist/Legalist distinction. One point of contention between Realists and Legalists is whether persons should always be recognized as legal persons in virtue of their personhood. The Realist answer is affirmative, whereas Legalists reject such straightforward logical implications between personhood and legal personhood. The problem with the Realist position—from the point of view of the Bundle Theory—is its ambiguity. Asking 'Should X be a legal person?' is often not a good question because legal personhood is a cluster concept. For instance, the American debate over corporate personhood is mostly focused on whether corporations should be within the ambit of the constitutional Bill of Rights. Nonetheless, most opponents of the constitutional rights of corporations likely do not mind the fact that corporations can be sued for compensation, which is also an aspect of their legal personhood. Thus, the binary question 'Should X be a legal person?' is often simply too vague.

We can, however, find a limited application of the Realist thesis with regard to purely passive legal personhood (i.e. legal personhood unaccompanied by any duties or competences). Active legal personhood is often extended to an entity for reasons that have nothing to do with the interests or well-being of that entity—consider the criminal liability of slaves or endowing a trader AI with the capacity to enter contracts. That said, endowing some entity with purely passive legal personhood most likely entails a recognition of its ultimate value. Extending legal personhood to foetuses or nonhuman animals would likely be based on protecting the foetus or

[6] David Favre, 'Living Property: A New Status for Animals Within the Legal System' (2010) 93 *Marquette Law Review* 1021, 1062.

creature for its own sake.[7] Thus, there is a thin link between purely passive legal personhood and perceived ultimate value. However, even if purely passive legal personhood entails a recognition of ultimate value, the entailment is not mutual. One could, for instance, hold that late-stage foetuses are of ultimate value but that they should not receive any kind of legal personhood.

This discussion has furnished some examples of how the proposed theory can structure ethical and political debate over legal personhood. I will now briefly address how the theory could figure in legal reasoning.

Legal Personhood in Legal Reasoning

Talk of legal concepts often suffers from a particular type of ambiguity. Michael Moore puts this as follows:

> Prima facie, one might advert to two quite distinct sorts of things in 'giving the meaning' of a legal concept such as 'criminal intent' or 'person': (1) one might seek to describe the set of facts under which the legal concept is correctly applied; or (2) one might seek to describe the set of legal consequences which attach to the authoritative use of that concept by a judge.
>
> [...]
>
> Legal concepts such as ownership, malice, intention, or person, are used both to describe in legal terms the facts in particular situations and to 'dispose' of the issues in cases by prescribing what results a judge should bring about in his application of those concepts. Dispositive legal concepts form the 'conceptual cement' that connects a judge's factual findings to his legal remedies.[8]

Another way to phrase this is that legal concepts can act both as conclusions and as reasons. The concept of ownership is one example: when Tony Honoré laid out his theory of ownership, which explained ownership in terms of distinct incidents, he enhanced our understanding of what it means to say that John owns a car, and in particular, how we can justifiably reach the conclusion that he owns the car. However, what (if any) legal consequences *follow from* (rather than lead to) the conclusion that John owns the car is a wholly different matter, and a central question of legal reasoning. One of the benefits of the bundle-of-rights analysis of ownership is to avert unwarranted conceptual inferences. Though the incidents of ownership include the liberty to destroy a thing that one owns, we don't know whether John holds this liberty with regard to the car just because he has been deemed its owner. The car

[7] I say 'likely' because fanciful scenarios can always be concocted. For instance, a Sinophobic parliament could extend some of the protections of passive legal personality to dogs, not due to welfare concerns but rather in order to spite the Chinese minority.

[8] Michael S. Moore, *Placing Blame: A Theory of the Criminal Law* (Oxford University Press 2010) 620. See also Alf Ross, 'Tû-Tû' (1957) 70 *Harvard Law Review* 812.

might for instance be an antique car that one is not allowed to destroy, because of its cultural value.

Some scholars take legal personhood to be only a conclusion rather than a reason. Richard Tur writes:

> [W]hen the word 'person' is used by a lawyer, it reflects a conclusion, not a premiss. Nor can the concept of legal personality provide us with a premiss by determining what ought and what ought not to have rights.
>
> [...]
>
> Whatever decisions we do make [in hard cases] can, of course, be implemented and enforced by the law, by its various mechanisms and concepts, among them the concept of legal personality. It is just that legal concepts in general cannot by themselves provide us with an adequate basis for decision making in the more problematic areas at which we have been looking; and legal personality in particular does not provide us with a definition of a person from which to derive solutions to practical problems.[9]

Tur's conclusion is connected to his claim that the legal person is simply an 'empty slot for rights and duties'.[10] Given this definition, it is understandable that Tur takes the concept to be virtually devoid of any content. However, even such a thin understanding of legal personhood can have an impact on legal reasoning. Let us consider the *Tommy* case, first presented in the Introduction, which turned on whether the chimpanzee Tommy should be endowed with the writ of *habeas corpus*.[11] The Orthodox View structured the court's reasoning in a fundamental way, as the judge assumed that Tommy was not a legal person and therefore was not a holder of any legal rights. For the court, then, the relevant question was whether it was appropriate to grant chimpanzees legal rights at all.[12] Had the court maintained that Tommy did already hold some legal rights, then obviously it could not have used the same reasoning. Thus, X's personhood status can act as a premise in legal reasoning even according to the 'formal' notion of Tur.

Given that my theory allows for some X to hold legal rights without being a legal person, legal personhood under my account cannot act as a reason in the same way as

[9] Richard Tur, 'The "Person" in Law' in Arthur Peacocke and Grant Gillett (eds), *Persons and Personality. A Contemporary Inquiry.* (Basil Blackwell, Ltd 1988) 128–9. John Dewey is of the same opinion: '[T]he idea of personality [should be eliminated] until the concrete facts and relations involved have been faced and stated on their own account: retaining the word will then do no great harm.' John Dewey, 'The Historic Background of Corporate Legal Personality' (1926) 35 *Yale Law Journal* 655, 673.

[10] Tur (n 9) 121.

[11] *People ex rel. Nonhuman Rights Project, Inc. v Lavery*, No 518336, 2014 WL 680276 (NY App. Div. 4 December 2014.

[12] When I say 'has had an impact', I am of course assuming—perhaps naïvely—that the court actually denied legal personhood to the chimpanzee based on the stated reasoning. The verdict could also have been, say, an after-the-fact rationalization of an intuition.

according to Tur's theory.[13] The Bundle Theory can nonetheless structure legal reasoning in numerous ways.

A prototypical case in which legal personhood could be treated as a reason is the following. X has been deemed a legal person with regard to incident A, and the question arises whether X should also be treated as a legal person with regard to incident B. If, say, the infliction of bodily harm to foetuses has been criminalized, then it could be argued that foetuses should also have the right to recover compensation from any individual who has inflicted bodily harm upon them. Postnatal children have such a right, and by extending the criminal-law protection to foetuses the legislator might be taken to have indicated that foetuses should be treated on a par with postnatal children. Here we should firstly note that the cluster nature of legal personhood entails that one can be a legal person for some purposes and not for others; there is nothing *conceptually* dubious about treating foetuses as potential victims in the eyes of the criminal law but not as potential tort-law plaintiffs. On the other hand, as has been mentioned in the preceding section, many incidents of legal personhood are interconnected in various ways. Thus, should a legal system choose to treat a foetus as a potential tort plaintiff, it should then also endow the foetus with at least a limited capacity to own property—otherwise suing the tortfeasor for damages would be quite pointless.[14]

Bundle Theory and Animal Personhood Cases

Let us now consider some further examples of how the Bundle Theory can structure legal reasoning, with some animal personhood cases as examples. In the *Tommy* case, the court believed it was deciding whether to grant the chimpanzee Tommy his first right. However, this premise was misguided, as Tommy was already protected by legal safeguards that are properly designated as rights. In everyday legal parlance the term 'right' is often used indiscriminately to refer to both interest-theory and will-theory rights, so in this discourse there is no reason to abstain from talking of the legal rights of beings that are unable to exercise their rights—jurists talk about children's rights constantly. Thus, the case was not about whether Tommy ought to be included in the 'rights paradigm' as the court framed it. Animals already hold rights. Rather, the case was about whether a particular incident—which could well be described as a 'fundamental right'—ought to be extended to cover the chimpanzee.

This difference between right-holding in general and legal personhood was recognized in the case *Tilikum et al. v Sea World Parks & Entertainment, Inc. et al.*[15]

[13] My account also allows for an entity to be a legal person without holding any legal rights. If one subscribes both to my theory of legal personhood and to the will theory of rights, one can conclude that infants are legal persons but do not hold any rights.

[14] In common-law jurisdictions, it would be sufficient if the award of damages could be payable to a trust administered on behalf of the foetus.

[15] *Tilikum et al. v Sea World Parks & Entertainment Inc.*, 842 F. Supp. 2d 1259 (SD Cal. 2012).

The case concerned the question whether the Thirteenth Amendment to the US Constitution, which prohibits slavery, also applies to orcas. The answer was held to be negative, but the court noted that orcas and other animals nevertheless hold rights:

> Even though Plaintiffs lack standing to bring a Thirteenth Amendment claim, that is not to say that animals have no legal rights; as there are many state and federal statutes affording redress to Plaintiffs, including, in some instances, criminal statutes that 'punish those who violate statutory duties that protect animals'.[16]

Though the court did not extend this incident of legal personhood to the orcas, it made clear that it was not denying the existence of legal rights held by animals. There was no 'foundational question' regarding whether animals should be endowed with legal personhood in order to be able to hold rights. The Federal Criminal Court of Cassation in Argentina seemed to arrive at a somewhat similar conclusion in a *habeas corpus* case that was decided in 2014. In a strikingly short verdict, the court simply noted that the orangutan Sandra already holds rights and should be deemed a nonhuman legal person (or subject of rights, *sujeto de derechos*).[17]

Such disentangling of right-holding from legal personhood offers various benefits. It allows jurists to discuss animal rights without being uneasy about the topic: they need not worry that conceding the existence of animal rights would be extravagant because of its implying the legal personhood of animals. However, my account does not imply that the work of, say, the Nonhuman Rights Project would be meaningless—rather, the proposed account removes one obstacle from their path. Lawsuits concerning animal personhood do not need to focus excessively on whether animals can hold rights or ought to hold rights at all; they can focus instead on whether the creatures in question ought to hold the particular legal entitlements—such as the fundamental protection of *habeas corpus*—that are being claimed for them.

What, then, was exactly at stake in the *Tommy* case? Had the Nonhuman Rights Project's demands been granted in the *Tommy* case, the legal status of Tommy (and of other relevantly similar animals) would have been changed in at least one evident way. Tommy would have been granted the claim-rights pertaining to personal freedom included in the writ of *habeas corpus*. This would have been a substantive change in Tommy's legal status, and—assuming the decision would apply to all chimpanzees—chimpanzees would, in addition, thenceforth have had the standing *in casu* to sue in similar cases.[18] However, would Tommy have become a legal person *tout court*, as the

[16] Ibid. 7.

[17] '*Que, a partir de una interpretación jurídica dinámica y no estática, menester es reconocerle al animal el carácter de sujeto de derechos, pues los sujetos no humanos (animales) son titulares de derechos, por lo que se impone su protección en el ámbito competencial correspondiente* [...].' I would like to thank Ignacio Cofone for his help in translating the verdict and for explaining its significance.

[18] See the discussion of abstract standing in Chapter 3.

Nonhuman Rights Project claimed? No—Tommy's legal status would have been markedly different from the statuses of natural persons and corporations. The decision would (assumedly) not have granted Tommy the capacity to own property or hold special rights. It would have been misleading to refer to Tommy as a legal person without qualifying the statement (as in, say, 'legal person for the purposes of *habeas corpus*'). Tommy could also aptly have been described as a subject of *habeas corpus*.

Perhaps the most far-reaching extension of incidents of legal personhood to an animal resulted from another Argentinian judgment, issued by the Third Court of Guarantees in 2016. In the verdict—hailed by some as revolutionary[19]—the court declared the chimpanzee Cecilia to be a nonhuman legal person (or subject of law, *sujeto de derecho*) and granted the *habeas corpus* claim filed on her behalf. After the verdict, Cecilia was transferred to a Brazilian sanctuary.[20] The legal effects of the verdict seem to be that Cecilia is no longer considered property and that she is now endowed with fundamental protections pertaining to her personal liberty and integrity. Furthermore, the judge declared animals to have fundamental rights, even if she refused to enumerate or specify them, taking this to be the legislator's task. Overall, the wider implications of the judgment remain unclear. At any rate, Cecilia now seems to be a subject of *habeas corpus*, or a legal person for the purposes of *habeas corpus*.

'Person' in Legal Nomenclature and Interpretation

Two further questions are how terms and phrases such as 'person' or 'legal person' should be interpreted when they appear in legal materials, and what terminology lawmakers, scholars, and other legal actors could adopt in order to avoid confusion. For instance, different jurisdictions have adopted different strategies to settle when a provision addresses only natural persons, only artificial persons, or both. According to the Code of Laws of the United States of America, 'unless the context indicates otherwise [...] the words "person" and "whoever" include corporations, companies, associations, firms, partnerships, societies, and joint stock companies, as well as individuals'.[21] The phrases 'natural person' and 'artificial person' (or, more ambiguously, 'legal person') are often used in EU legislation to render clear the scope of a statutory provision.[22] I cannot offer a full-blown analysis of these legislative strategies here,

[19] See for instance Saskia Stucki, 'Toward Hominid and Other Humanoid Rights: Are We Witnessing a Legal Revolution?', *Verfassungsblog*, 30 Dec 2016 (accessed 30 January 2019).

[20] Expte. Nro. P-72.254/15 'Presentación efectuada por a.f.a.d.a respecto del chimpancé "Cecilia"—sujeto no humano'. English translation by Ana María Hernández available at https://www.nonhumanrights.org/content/uploads/Chimpanzee-Cecilia_translation-FINAL-for-website-2.pdf (accessed 30 January 2019).

[21] 1 USC § 1 (2012)

[22] One example is the General Data Protection Regulation, whose long title is 'Regulation (EU) 2016/679 of the European Parliament and of the Council of 27 April 2016 on the protection of *natural persons* with regard to the processing of personal data and on the free movement

especially without offering an account of legal interpretation. I have, however, in this book proposed terminology that would be as unambiguous as possible. For instance, the phrase 'legal capacity' should be avoided given its ambiguity, and replaced by 'passive legal personhood', and, 'active legal personhood', when appropriate. Given the private-law origins of the notion of legal capacity, it might also be relabelled as 'private-law subjecthood' or 'private-law passive subjecthood'

Certain emerging forms of legal personhood will likely require new nomenclature. If legal personhood is extended to AIs or animals, the question will arise what to call these forms of legal personhood. New terms or phrases, such as 'animal person' or 'electronic person', could easily be introduced.[23] Such solutions could resolve potential questions of statutory interpretation, much as 'natural person' and 'artificial person' are used today when different classes of legal persons need to be kept distinct. The word 'person' is of course contentious. Many likely find the notion of describing animals as persons objectionable, especially given the fact that 'person' is often used synonymously with 'human being' in English. Nothing would of course stop the legislator from introducing wholly new terminology that does not make reference to persons.

As mentioned in Chapters 1 and 3, many non-Anglophone jurisdictions currently use 'subject of law/right(s)' and 'legal person' synonymously. I have proposed in Chapter 3—based on a suggestion by Tomasz Pietrzykowski—that 'subject' and 'person' could be distinguished.[24] Animals are already subjects of animal welfare law, but not legal persons. This distinction could be employed by the legislator as well. Hence, countries that currently treat foetuses as persons for the purposes of criminal law could instead denote foetuses 'subjects of criminal law'—or, even less ambiguously, 'passive subjects of criminal law', to make clear that foetuses are not criminally liable.

Finally

In the years since the widespread adoption of the Orthodox View in the nineteenth century, the definition of legal personhood has rarely been revisited. Most authors have taken the Orthodox View at face value. However, that view is plagued with numerous problems, which I have been highlighting over the course of this book.

of such data, and repealing Directive 95/46/EC (General Data Protection Regulation)' (emphasis added).

[23] For instance, Saskia Stucki suggests a new legal category for animals that she denotes 'animal persons' (*tierliche Personen*). Saskia Stucki, *Grundrechte für Tiere: Eine Kritik des geltenden Tierschutzrechts und rechtstheoretische Grundlegund von Tierrechten im Rahmen einer Neupositionerung des Tieres als Rechtssubjekt* (Nomos 2016) 301ff.

[24] Tomasz Pietrzykowski, *Personhood Beyond Humanism: Animals, Chimeras, Autonomous Agents and the Law* (Springer 2018) 7–23.

Most importantly, the Orthodox View leads to confusion when combined with our contemporary theoretical understanding of rights. The interest theory ascribes rights to nonhuman animals, who are widely taken to be nonpersons, and the will theory denies rights to children, who are taken to be legal persons. The Capacity-for-Rights view is further plagued by the mystifying idea that the legislator or judges could endow an entity with the *capacity* to hold rights.

Even though legal personhood has been an undertheorized topic and neglected by jurisprudents for decades, the tide has slowly started to turn. Legal personhood has figured prominently in numerous recent monographs.[25] Given the renewed interest in the topic, it is rather surprising that so many theorists still rely on the Orthodox View as a virtually unquestionable axiom. This book will already have achieved a great deal if it leads to scholars' questioning that axiom, or even just becoming aware of its problems. However, it is my hope that the book also provides a platform on which to build normative arguments regarding the legal status of animals, rivers, corporations, and so on, and perhaps even sparks a debate over what legal personhood is actually about.

Much remains to be said on legal personhood. As Robert Nozick writes, '[t]here is room for words on subjects other than last words'.[26]

[25] For instance Naffine (n 1), Samir Chopra and Laurence F. White, *A Legal Theory for Autonomous Artificial Agents* (University of Michigan Press 2011), Stucki (n 23) and Pietrzykowski (n 24).

[26] Robert Nozick, *Anarchy, State, and Utopia* (Blackwell 1974) xii.

Bibliography

Alpa, G. and Zeno-Zencovich, V., *Italian Private Law* (Routledge-Cavendish 2007).

Antokolskaia, M. and Boele-Woelki K., 'Dutch Family Law in the 21st Century: Trend-Setting and Straggling behind at the Same Time' (2002) 6 *Electronic Journal of Comparative Law*.

Artosi, A., Pieri, B., and Sartor, G. (eds), *Leibniz: Logico-Philosophical Puzzles in the Law: Philosophical Questions and Perplexing Cases in the Law* (Springer 2013).

Austin, J., *Province of Jurisprudence Determined* (John Murray, Albemarle Street 1832).

Austin, J., *Lectures on Jurisprudence: Or, the Philosophy of Positive Law, vol. I* (John Murray, Albemarle Street 1885).

Basl, J., 'Machines as Moral Patients We Shouldn't Care About (Yet): The Interests and Welfare of Current Machines' (2014) 27 *Philosophy & Technology* 79.

Bayern, S., 'The Implications of Modern Business-Entity Law for the Regulation of Autonomous Systems' (2015) 19 *Stanford Technology Law Review* 93.

Beaudry, J.-S., 'From Autonomy to Habes Corpus: Animal Rights Activists Take the Parameters of Legal Personhood to Court' (2016) 4 *Global Journal of Animal Law* 3.

Bentham, J., *The Principles of Morals and Legislation* (1780).

Berg, J., 'Of Elephants and Embryos: A Proposed Framework for Legal Personhood' (2007) 59 Hastings Law Journal 369.

Berkowitz, R., *The Gift of Science: Leibniz and the Modern Legal Tradition* (Harvard University Press 2005).

Bilchitz, D., 'Moving Beyond Arbitrariness: The Legal Personhood and Dignity of Non-Human Animals' (2009) 25 *South African Journal on Human Rights* 38.

Björne, L., *Brytningstiden: den nordiska rättsvetenskapens historia. Del II, 1815–1870* (Institutet för rättshistorisk forskning 1998).

Blackstone, W., *Commentaries on the Laws of England, Vol. 1* (Clarendon Press 1765).

Boisseau-Sowinski, L., 'La représentation des individus d'une espèce animale devant le juge français' (2015) 22 *VertigO—la revue électronique en sciences de l'environnement*.

Bracton, H. de, *On the Laws and Customs of England* (Samuel E. Thorne tr. ed., Belknap Press of Harvard University Press 1968).

Brett, A. S., *Liberty, Right and Nature: Individual Rights in Later Scholastic Thought* (Cambridge University Press 1997).

Brown, L. M., 'Feminist Theory and the Erosion of Women's Reproductive Rights: The Implications of Fetal Personhood Laws and in Vitro Fertilization' (2005) 13 *American University Journal of Gender, Social Policy & the Law* 87.

Bryson, J. J., 'Robots Should Be Slaves' in Yorick Wilks (ed.), *Close Engagements with Artificial Companions* (John Benjamins Publishing Company 2010).

Burdick, W. L., *The Principles of Roman Law and Their Relation to Modern Law* (The Lawbook Exchange, Ltd 2004).

Cairns J. W., 'The Definition of Slavery in Eighteenth-Century Thinking' in Jean Allain (ed.), *The Legal Understanding of Slavery: From the Historical to the Contemporary* (Oxford University Press 2012).

Calverley, D. J., 'Imagining a Non-Biological Machine as a Legal Person' (2008) 22 *AI & Society* 523.

Campbell, K., 'Fuller on Legal Fictions' (1983) 2 *Law and Philosophy* 339.

Carter, I., 'Value-freeness and Value-neutrality in the Analysis of Political Concepts' in David Sobel, Peter Vallentyne, and Steven Wall (eds), *Oxford Studies in Political Philosophy, Volume 1* (Oxford University Press 2015).

Chapple, C., *The Moral Responsibilities of Companies* (Palgrave Macmillan 2014).

Chin, G. J., 'The New Civil Death: Rethinking Punishment in the Era of Mass Conviction' (2012) 160 *University of Pennsylvania Law Review* 1789.

Chloros, A., Rheinstein, M., and Glendon, M. A. (eds), *International Encyclopedia of Comparative Law, Volume IV: Persons and Family* (Mohr Siebeck 2007).

Chopra, S. and White, L. F., *A Legal Theory for Autonomous Artificial Agents* (University of Michigan Press 2011).

Clutton-Brock, T. H. and Parker, G. A., 'Punishment in Animal Societies' (1995) 373 *Nature* 209.

Coase, R., 'The Nature of the Firm' (1937) 4 *Economica* 386.

Coing, H., *Europäisches Privatrecht, Band II* (C.H. Beck'scheVerlagsbuchhandlung 1989).

Cole, D., 'Are Foreign Nationals Entitled to the Same Constitutional Rights As Citizens?' (2003) 25 *Thomas Jefferson Law Review* 367.

Conard, A. F., *Corporations in Perspective* (Foundation Press 1976).

Cupp, R. L. Jr, 'A Dubious Grail: Seeking Tort Law Expansion and Limited Personhood as Stepping Stones toward Abolishing Animals' Property Status, A' (2007) 60 *SMU Law Review* 3.

Curnutt, J., *Animals and the Law: A Sourcebook* (ABC-CLIO 2001).

Daniels, N., 'Reflective Equilibrium' in Edward N Zalta (ed.), *The Stanford Encyclopedia of Philosophy* (Wint 2013) <http://plato.stanford.edu/entries/reflective-equilibrium/>.

Daniels, N., *Justice and Justification: Reflective Equilibrium in Theory and Practice* (Cambridge University Press 1996).

Dayan, C., *The Law is a White Dog: How Legal Rituals Make and Unmake Persons* (Princeton University Press 2011).

de las Heras Ballell, T. R., *Introduction to Spanish Private Law: Facing the Social and Economic Challenges* (Routledge-Cavendish 2010).

Deakin, S., 'The Juridical Nature of the Firm' in Thomas Clarke and Douglas Branson (eds), *The SAGE Handbook of Corporate Governance* (SAGE Publications 2012).

Dean, R., *The Value of Humanity in Kant's Moral Theory* (Oxford University Press 2006).

Dennett, D., *The Intentional Stance* (MIT Press 1987).

Derham, D. P., 'Theories of Legal Personality' in Leicester Webb (ed.) *Legal Personality and Political Pluralism* (Melbourne University Press 1958).

Dewey, J., 'The Historic Background of Corporate Legal Personality' (1926) 35 *Yale Law Journal* 655.

Dias, R.W. M., *Jurisprudence* (3rd edn, Butterworths 1970).

Dickson, J., *Evaluation and Legal Theory* (Hart Publishing 2001).

Duff, P., 'The Personality of an Idol' (1927) 3 *The Cambridge Law Journal* 42.

Duff, P.W., *Personality in Roman Private Law* (Cambridge University Press 1938).

Duncan, D. G., 'When is a Human Being Not a Legal Person?: Lethal Ramifications at the Beginning of Life' (2013) 8 *University of St Thomas Journal of Law & Public Policy* 82.

Duxbury, N., 'Why English Jurisprudence is Analytical' (2004) 57 *Current Legal Problems* 1.

Duxbury, N., 'Jhering's Philosophy of Authority' (2007) 27 *Oxford Journal of Legal Studies* 23.

Dworkin, R., 'Taking Rights Seriously', *Taking Rights Seriously* (Harvard University Press 1977).

Dworkin, R., *Law's Empire* (Harvard University Press 1986).

Eleftheriadis, P., *Legal Rights* (Oxford University Press 2008).

Enoch, D., 'Reason-Giving and the Law' in Leslie Green and Brian Leiter (eds), *Oxford Studies in Philosophy of Law, Volume 1* (Oxford University Press 2011).

Evans, E. P., *The Criminal Prosecution and Capital Punishment of Animals* (The Lawbook Exchange, Ltd 2010).

Favre, D., 'Living Property: A New Status for Animals Within the Legal System' (2010) 93 *Marquette Law Review* 1021.

Favre, D. S., 'Judicial Recognition of the Interest of Animals—A New Tort' (2005) *Michigan State Law Review* 333.

Fede, A., *People Without Rights: an Interpretation of the Fundamentals of the Law of Slavery in the US South* (Garland Publishing, Inc 1992).

Feinberg, J., 'The Rights of Animals and Unborn Generations' in William T. Blackstone (ed.), *Philosophy and Environmental Crisis* (University of Georgia Press 1974).

Finkelman, P., 'Slavery in the United States' in Jean Allain (ed.), *The Legal Understanding of Slavery: From the Historical to the Contemporary* (Oxford University Press 2012).

Finnis, J., 'The Priority of Persons', *Intention and Identity: Collected Essays, Volume II* (Oxford University Press 2011).

Flynn, E. and Arstein-Kerslake, A., 'Legislating Personhood: Realising the Right to Support in Exercising Legal Capacity' (2014) 10 *International Journal of Law in Context* 81.

Francione, G., *Animals, Property, and the Law* (Temple University Press 1995).

Francione, G., 'Reflections on "Animals, Property, and the Law" and "Rain without Thunder"' (2007) 70 *Law and Contemporary Problems* 9.

Freeman, M.A., 'Measuring Equality: A Comparative Perspective on Women's Legal Capacity and Constitutional Rights in Five Commonwealth Countries' (1990) 16 *Commonwealth Law Bulletin* 1418.

French, P.A., 'The Corporation as a Moral Person' (1979) 16 *American Philosophical Quarterly* 207.

French, P.A., *Collective and Corporate Responsibility* (Columbia University Press 1984).

Freund, E., *The Legal Nature of Corporations* (Batoche Books 2000).

Funkhouser, E., *The Logical Structure of Kinds* (Oxford University Press 2014).

Gaius, *Institutiones or Institutes of Roman Law* (Edward Poste tr. ed., 4th edn, Clarendon Press 1904).

Galanter, M., 'The Modernization of Law' in Myron Weiner (ed.), *Modernization* (Basic Books 1966).

Gallie, W. B., 'Essentially Contested Concepts' (1956) 56 *Proceedings of the Aristotelian Society*.

Gamauf, R., 'Slaves Doing Business: The Role of Roman Law in the Economy of a Roman Household' (2009) 16 *European Review of History: Revue europeenne d'histoire* 331.

Genovese, E., *Roll, Jordan, Roll: The World the Slaves Made* (Random House USA 1976).

Ghestin, J., Goubeaux, G., and Fabre-Magnan, M., *Traité de Droit Civil: Introduction générale* (Librairie générale de droit et de jurisprudence 1994).

Gibson, S., 'The Problem of Abortion: Essentially Contested Concepts and Moral Autonomy' (2004) 18 *Bioethics* 221.

Gierke, O., *Political Theories of the Middle Age* (F. W. Maitland ed., Cambridge University Press 1951).

Gilbert, M., *Sociality and Responsibility: New Essays in Plural Subject Theory* (Rowman & Littlefield Publishers 2000).

Gill, C., 'Personhood and Personality: The Four-Personae Theory in Cicero, De Officiis I', *Oxford Studies in Ancient Philosophy: Volume VI* (Oxford University Press 1988).

Glackin, S. N., 'Back to Bundles: Deflating Property Rights, Again' (2014) 20 *Legal Theory* 1.

Goubeaux, G., *Traité de droit civil. Les personnes* (Librairie générale de droit et de jurisprudence 1989).

Gray, J. C., *The Nature and Sources of the Law* (David Campbell and Philip Thomas eds, Ashgate 1997).

Groot, H. de, *Inleydinge tot de Hollandsche rechts-geleertheyt* (Jan Boom 1738).

Grotius, H., *On the Law of War and Peace* (A. C. Campbell tr. ed., 1814).

Grotius H., *The Jurisprudence of Holland* (R.W. Lee tr. ed., Clarendon Press 1926).

Gunkel, D.J., 'The Other Question: Can and Should Robots Have Rights?' (2017) 19 *Ethics and Information Technology* 1.

Haakonssen, K., 'Natural Law and Personhood: Samuel Pufendorf on Social Explanation', *Max Weber Lecture Series* (European University Institute 2010).

Hallevy, G., 'The Criminal Liability of Artificial Intelligence Entities—from Science Fiction to Legal Social Control' (2010) 4 *Akron Intellectual Property Journal* 171.

Hallevy, G., *When Robots Kill: Artificial Intelligence under Criminal Law* (Northeastern University Press 2013).

Hallis, F., 'An examination of some modern theories of the relation of law and state with special reference to the juristic doctrine of corporate personality: a study in jurisprudence' (University of Oxford 1927).

Hallis, F., *Corporate Personality. A Study in Jurisprudence* (Oxford University Press 1930).

Halpin, A., *Rights and Law—Analysis and Theory* (Hart Publishing 1997).

Hart, H. L. A., 'Are There Any Natural Rights?' (1955) 64 *The Philosophical Review* 175.

Hart, H. L. A., *The Concept of Law* (Clarendon Press 1964).

Hart, H. L. A., *Essays on Bentham. Jurisprudence and Political Theory* (Clarendon Press 1982).

Hart, H. L. A., 'Jhering's Heaven of Concepts and Modern Analytical Jurisprudence', *Essays in Jurisprudence and Philosophy* (Clarendon Press 1983).

Hart, H. L. A., 'Definition and Theory in Jurisprudence', *Essays in Jurisprudence and Philosophy* (Oxford University Press 1984).

Hattenhauer, C., '"Der Mensch als Solcher Rechtsfähig"—Von der Person zur Rechtsperson' in Eckart Klein and Christoph Menke (eds), *Der Mensch als Person und Rechtsperson* (Berliner Wissenschafts-Verlag 2011).

Haupt, C. E., 'The Nature and Effects of Constitutional State Objectives: Assessing the German Basic Law's Animal Protection Clause' (2010) 16 *Animal Law Review* 213.

Hauser, L., 'Chinese Room Argument', *International Encyclopedia of Philosophy* <http://www.iep.utm.edu/chineser/>.

Heaton, J., *The South African Law of Persons* (4th edn, LexisNexis South Africa 2015).

Hegel, G. W. F., *Elements of the Philosophy of Right* (Allen W. Wood, ed., Cambridge University Press 1991).

Hegel, G. W. F., *The Philosophy of History* (J. Sibree, tr. ed., Batoche Books 2001).

Heldrich, A. and Steiner, A. F., 'Capacity', *International Encyclopedia of Comparative Law, Volume IV: Persons and Family* (Mohr Siebeck and Martinus Nijhoff 2007).

Herget, J. E. and Wallace, S., 'The German Free Law Movement as the Source of American Legal Realism' (1986) 73 *Virginia Law Review* 399.

Higginbotham, Jr, A. L. and Kopytoff, B. K., 'Property First, Humanity Second: The Recognition of the Slave's Human Nature in Virginia Civil Law' (1989) 50 *Ohio State Law Journal* 511.

Hobbes, T., *Leviathan* (C. B. MacPherson, ed., Penguin Books 1968).

Hodgson, L., 'Kant on the Right to Freedom: A Defense' (2010) 120 *Ethics* 791.

Hoeflich, M. H., 'Savigny and His Anglo-American Disciples' (1989) 37 *American Journal of Comparative Law* 17.

Hoeflich, M. H., *Roman and Civil Law and the Development of Anglo-American Jurisprudence in the Nineteenth Century* (University of Georgia Press 1997).

Hoff-Wilson, J., 'The Unfinished Revolution: Changing Legal Status of US Women' (1987) 13 Signs 7.

Hohfeld, W. N., 'Nature of Stockholders' Individual Liability for Corporation Debts' (1909) 9 *Columbia Law Review* 285.

Hohfeld, W. N., 'Some Fundamental Legal Conceptions as Applied in Legal Reasoning' (1913) 23 *Yale Law Journal* 16.

Hohfeld, W. N., 'Fundamental Legal Conceptions as Applied in Judicial Reasoning' (1916) 26 *Yale Law Journal* 710.

Holland, T. E., *The Elements of Jurisprudence* (Clarendon Press 1880).

Holthöfer, E. and Baboukis, J. M., 'Doneau, Hugues' in Stanley N. Katz (ed.), *The Oxford International Encyclopedia of Legal History* (Oxford University Press 2009).

Honoré, A. M., 'Ownership' in A. G. Guest (ed.), *Oxford Essays in Jurisprudence* (Oxford University Press 1961).

Hoven van Genderen, van den R., 'Do We Need New Legal Personhood in the Age of Robots and AI?' in Marcelo Corrales, Mark Fenwick, and Nikolaus Forgó (eds), *Robotics, AI and the Future of Law* (Springer 2018).

Hsiao, E. G., 'Whanganui River Agreement: Indigenous Rights and Rights of Nature' (2012) 42 *Environmental Policy and Law* 371.

Hugo, G., *Lehrbuch eines civilistischen Cursus* (6th edn, August Molius 1820).

Iwai, K., 'Persons, Things and Corporations: The Corporate Personality Controversy and Comparative Corporate Governance' (1999) 47 *The American Journal of Comparative Law* 583.

Jääskinen, N., *Historiallisen koulun oikeustiedekäsitys* (University of Helsinki 1983).

Jaworska, A. and Tannenbaum, J., 'The Grounds of Moral Status', *The Stanford Encyclopedia of Philosophy* (Summ 2018) <https://plato.stanford.edu/archives/spr2018/entries/grounds-moral-status/>.

Jhering, R. von, *Geist des Römischen Rechts auf den verschiedenen Stufen seiner Entwicklung, Teil III* (Breitkopf & Härtel 1877).

Jolowicz, H. F., *Roman Foundations of Modern Law* (Clarendon Press 1957).

Jones P., 'Group Rights' in Edward N. Zalta (ed.), *Stanford Encyclopedia of Philosophy* (Sum 2016) <https://plato.stanford.edu/archives/sum2016/entries/rights-group/>.

Kaczor, C., *The Edge of Life: Human Dignity and Contemporary Bioethics* (Springer 2005).

Kant, I., *Metaphysical Elements of Justice. Part I of the Metaphysics of Morals* (John Ladd ed., 2nd edn, Hackett Publishing 1999).

Kelsen, H., 'Zur Theorie der juristischen Fiktionen. Mit besonderer Berücksichtigung von Vaihingers Philosophie des Als Ob' (1919) 1 *Annalen der Philosophie* 630.

Kelsen, H., *Pure Theory of Law* (Max Knight tr. ed., The Lawbook Exchange, Ltd 2005).

Kelsen, H., *General Theory of Law and State* (Transaction Publishers 2006).

Kelsen, H. and Kletzer C. (tr.), 'On the Theory of Juridic Fictions. With Special Consideration of Vaihinger's Philosophy of the As-If' in Maksymilian Del Mar and William Twining (eds), *Legal Fictions in Theory and Practice* (2015).

König, P., 'Das System des Rechts und die Lehre von den Fiktionen bei Leibniz' in Jan Schröder (ed.), *Entwicklung der Methodenlehre in Rechtswissenschaft und Philosophie vom 16. bis zum 18. Jahrhundert* (Franz Steiner Verlag 1998).

Korsgaard, C. M., 'Kantian Ethics, Animals, and the Law' (2013) 33 *Oxford Journal of Legal Studies* 629.

Kraakman, R. and others, *The Anatomy of Corporate Law: A Comparative and Functional Approach* (2nd edn, Oxford University Press 2009).

Kramer, M. and Steiner, H., 'Theories of Rights: Is There a Third Way?' (2007) 27 *Oxford Journal of Legal Studies* 281.

Kramer, M. H., 'Rights Without Trimmings' in Matthew H. Kramer, N. E. Simmonds, and Hillel Steiner (eds), *A Debate over Rights. Philosophical Enquiries* (Oxford University Press 1998).

Kramer, M. H., 'Do Animals and Dead People Have Legal Rights?' (2001) 14 *Canadian Journal of Law & Jurisprudence* 29.

Kramer, M. H., 'Getting Rights Right' in Matthew H. Kramer (ed.), *Rights, Wrongs and Responsibilities* (Palgrave 2001).

Kramer, M. H., 'Rights in Legal and Political Philosophy' in Gregory A. Caldeira, R. Daniel Kelemen, and Keith E. Whittington (eds), *The Oxford Handbook of Law and Politics* (Oxford University Press 2008).

Kramer, M. H., *Moral Realism as a Moral Doctrine* (Wiley-Blackwell 2009).

Kramer, M. H., 'Refining the Interest Theory of Rights' (2010) 55 *American Journal of Jurisprudence* 31.

Kramer, M. H., *The Ethics of Capital Punishment: A Philosophical Investigation of Evil and its Consequences* (Oxford University Press 2011).

Kramer, M. H., *Torture and Moral Integrity* (Oxford University Press 2014).

Kramer, M. H., Simmonds, N. E., and Steiner, H., *A Debate over Rights: Philosophical Enquiries* (Oxford University Press 1998).

Kurki, V., 'Förbudet mot åsamkande av onödigt lidande enligt djurskyddslagstiftningen' (2011) *Tidskrift utgiven av Juridiska Föreningen i Finland* 290.

Kurki, V., 'Animals, Slaves and Corporations: Analyzing Legal Thinghood' (2017) 18 *German Law Journal* 1096.

Kurki, V., 'Legal Competence and Legal Power' in Mark McBride (ed.), *New Essays on the Nature of Rights* (Hart Publishing 2017) 31–48.

Kurki, V., 'Rights, Harming and Wronging: A Restatement of the Interest Theory' (2018) 38 *Oxford Journal of Legal Studies* 430.

Kurki, V., 'Hohfeldian Infinities: Why Not to Worry' (2017) 23 *Res Publica* 137.

Kurki, V., 'Why Things Can Hold Rights: Reconceptualizing the Legal Person' in Visa A. J. Kurki and Tomasz Pietrzykowski (eds), *Legal Personhood: Animals, Artificial Intelligence and the Unborn* (Springer 2017) 61–90.

Lagercrantz, H. and Changeux, J.-P., 'The Emergence of Human Consciousness: From Fetal to Neonatal Life' (2009) 65 *Pediatric Research* 255.

Larenz, K., *Allgemeiner Teil des deutschen Bürgerlichen Rechts. Ein Lehrbuch* (C. H. Beck'sche Verlagsbuchhandlung 1983).

Larenz, K. and Wolf, M., *Allgemeiner Teil des bürgerlichen Rechts* (C. H. Beck'sche Verlagsbuchhandlung 1997).

Law, J. and Smullen, J., *A Dictionary of Finance and Banking* (4th edn, Oxford University Press 2008).

Lawson, F. H., 'The Creative Use of Legal Concepts' (1957) 32 *New York University Law Review* 909.

Lehmann, M., 'Der Begriff der Rechtsfähigkeit' (2007) 207 *Archiv für die civilistische Praxis* 225.

Leibniz, G. W., *Sämtliche Schriften und Briefe, Sechste Reihe, Erster Band* (Berlin-Brandenburgischen Akademie der Wissenschaften/Akademie der Wissenschaften zu Göttingen ed., 2nd edn, Akademie-Verlag 1990).

List, C. and Pettit, P., *Group Agency: The Possibility, Design, and Status of Corporate Agents* (Oxford University Press 2011).

Locke, J., *An Essay Concerning Human Understanding* (Thomas Bassett 1690).

Lucy, W., 'Persons in Law' (2009) 29 *Oxford Journal of Legal Studies* 787.

Lucy, W., *Law's Judgement* (Hart Publishing 2017).

Luig, K., 'Die Privatrechtsordnung im Rechtssystem von Leibniz' in Günter Birtsch (ed.), *Grund- und Freiheitsrechte von der ständischen zur spätbürgerlichen Gesellschaft* (Vandenhoeck & Ruprecht 1987).

Lutz-Bachmann, M., 'Der Mensch als Person. Überlegungen zur Geschichte des Begriffs der "moralischen Person" und der Rechtsperson' in Eckart Klein and Christoph Menke (eds), *Der Mensch als Person und Rechtsperson* (Berliner Wissenschafts-Verlag 2011).

MacCormick, N., 'Children's Rights: A Test-Case for Theories of Right' (1976) 52 *Archiv für Rechts- und Sozialphilosophie* 305.

MacCormick, N., 'Persons as Institutional Facts' in Ota Weinberger and Werner Krawietz (eds), *Reine Rechtslehre im Spiegel ihrer Fortsetzer und Kritiker* (Springer 1988).

MacCormick, N., *Institutions of Law: An Essay in Legal Theory* (Oxford University Press 2007).

Machen, A, W., 'Corporate Personality' (1911) 24 *Harvard Law Review* 253.

Magallanes, C. J. I., 'Nature as an Ancestor: Two Examples of Legal Personality for Nature in New Zealand' (2015) 22 *VertigO—la revue électronique en sciences de l'environnement*.

Maitland, F. W., *State, Trust and Corporation* (David Runciman and Magnus Ryan eds, Cambridge University Press 2003).

Malaurie, P., *Cours de droit civil. Les personnes, les incapacités* (5th edn, Éditions Cujas 1999).

Mauss, M. and Halls, W. D. (tr.), 'A Category of the Human Mind: The Notion of Person; the Notion of Self' in Michael Carrithers, Steven Collins, and Steven

Lukes (eds), *The Category of the Person: Anthropology, Philosophy, History* (Cambridge University Press 1985).

McCord, D. J., (ed), The Statutes at Large of South Carolina. Vol. 7, Containing the Acts Relating to Charleston, Courts, Slaves, and Rivers.

Mele, A. R., *Autonomous Agents: From Self-Control to Autonomy* (Oxford University Press 2001).

Meyerson, D., 'Persons and their Rights in Law and Morality' (2010) 35 *Australian Journal of Legal Philosophy* 122.

Moore, M. S., *Placing Blame: A Theory of the Criminal Law* (Oxford University Press 2010).

Morris, T. D., *Southern Slavery and the Law, 1619–1860* (University of North Carolina Press 1996).

Morss, J. R., 'The Legal Relations of Collectives: Belated Insights from Hohfeld' (2009) 22 *Leiden Journal of International Law* 289.

Muniz-Fraticelli, V. M., *The Structure of Pluralism* (Oxford University Press 2014).

Naffine, N., 'Who are Law's Persons? From Cheshire Cats to Responsible Subjects' (2003) 66 *Modern Law Review* 346.

Naffine, N., *Law's Meaning of Life: Philosophy, Religion, Darwin and the Legal Person* (Hart Publishing 2009).

Naffine, N., 'Legal Persons as Abstractions' in Visa A.J. Kurki and Tomasz Pietrzykowski (eds), *Legal Personality: Animals, Artificial Intelligence and the Unborn* (Springer 2017).

Nagel, T., 'What Is It Like to Be a Bat?' (1974) 83 *Philosophical Review* 435.

Nékám, A., *The Personality Concept of the Legal Entity* (Harvard University Press 1938).

Nesteruk, J., 'Persons, Property and the Corporation: a Proposal for a New Paradigm' (1990) 39 *DePaul Law Review* 543.

Neuner, J., 'Zur Rechtsfähigkeit des Anencephalus' (2013) 31 *Medizinrecht* 647.

Nozick, R., *Anarchy, State, and Utopia* (Blackwell 1974).

O'Donnell, E. L. and Talbot-Jones, J., 'Creating Legal Rights for Rivers: Lessons from Australia, New Zealand, and India' (2018) 23 *Ecology and Society* 7.

Ohlin, J. D., 'Is the Concept of the Person Necessary for Human Rights?' (2005) 105 *Columbia Law Review* 209.

Olivecrona, K., *Studier över begreppet juridisk person i romersk och modern rätt* (Appelbergs 1928).

Orts, E.W., *Business Persons: A Legal Theory of the Firm* (Oxford University Press 2013).

Padovani, A. and others, *A Treatise of Legal Philosophy and General Jurisprudence, Volume 7: The Jurists' Philosophy of Law from Rome to the Seventeenth Century* (2005).

Pagallo, U., *The Laws of Robots* (Springer 2013).

Pagallo, U., 'Vital, Sophia, and Co.—The Quest for the Legal Personhood of Robots' (2018) 9 *Information (Switzerland).*

Palm, U., *Person im Ertragsteuerrecht* (Mohr Siebeck 2013).

Paton, G.W., *A Text-Book of Jurisprudence* (4th edn, Oxford University Press 1973).

Patterson, O., *Slavery and Social Death: A Comparative Study* (Harvard University Press 1982).

Penner, J. E., 'The (True) Nature of a Beneficiary's Equitable Proprietary Interest under a Trust' (2014) 27 *Canadian Journal of Law and Jurisprudence* 473.

Peterson, C., 'Fredrik Schrevelius och den moderna personteoriens upptagande i svensk civilrättsdoktrin' in Yrjö Blomstedt (ed.), *Rättsvetenskap och lagstiftning i Norden* (Juristförlaget 1982).

Pietrzykowski, T., 'Beyond Personhood: From Two Conceptions of Rights to Two Kinds of Right-Holders' in Tomasz Pietrzykowski and Brunello Stancioli (eds), *New Approaches to the Personhood in Law* (Peter Lang 2016).

Pietrzykowski, T., 'The Idea of Non-personal Subjects of Law' in Visa A.J. Kurki and Tomasz Pietrzykowski (eds), *Legal Personhood: Animals, Artificial Intelligence and the Unborn* (Springer 2017).

Pietrzykowski, T., *Personhood Beyond Humanism: Animals, Chimeras, Autonomous Agents and the Law* (Springer 2018).

Pollock, S. F., *A First Book of Jurisprudence for Students of the Common Law* (Macmillan and Co 1896).

Poole, R., 'On Being a Person' (1996) 74 *Australasian Journal of Philosophy* 38.

Pound, R., *Jurisprudence, Volume IV* (West Publishing Co 1959).

Puchta, G. F., *Pandekten* (Verlag von Johann Ambrosius Barth 1872).

Pylkkänen, A., *Trapped in Equality: Women as Legal Persons in the Modernisation of Finnish Law* (Suomalaisen Kirjallisuuden Seura/Finnish Literature Society 2009).

Quine, W., 'Two Dogmas of Empiricism' (1951) 60 *The Philosophical Review* 20.

Quinn, G. and Arstein-Kerslake, A., 'Restoring the "Human" in "Human Rights": Personhood and Doctrinal Innovation in the UN Disability Convention' in Conor Gearty and Costas Douzinas (eds), *The Cambridge Companion to Human Rights Law* (Cambridge University Press 2012).

Radding, C. M. and Ciaralli, A., *The Corpus Iuris Civilis in the Middle Ages. Manuscripts and Transmission from the Sixth Century to the Juristic Revival* (Brill Academic Publishers 2006).

Rattigan, W. H., *The Science of Jurisprudence, Chiefly Intended for Indian Students* (Civil and Military Gazette Press 1888).

Rauscher, F., 'Kant's Social and Political Philosophy', *Stanford Encyclopedia of Philosophy* (Fall 2016) <http://plato.stanford.edu/archives/fall2016/entries/kant-social-political/>.

Rawls, J., 'Outline of a Decision Procedure for Ethics' (1951) 60 *The Philosophical Review* 177.

Rawls, J., *A Theory of Justice* (Belknap Press of Harvard University Press 1971).

Rawls, J., *Political Liberalism. Expanded Edition* (Columbia University Press 2005).

Raz, J., 'Voluntary Obligations and Normative Powers' (1972) 46 *Proceedings of the Aristotelian Society* 79.

Raz, J., 'On the Nature of Rights' (1984) 93 *Mind* 194.

Raz, J., *Practical Reason and Norms* (Oxford University Press 1999).

Redding P, 'Georg Wilhelm Friedrich Hegel' in Edward N. Zalta (ed.), *Stanford Encyclopedia of Philosophy* (Sum 2018) <https://plato.stanford.edu/archives/sum2018/entries/hegel/>.

Reid, K. G. C., 'Patrimony Not Equity: The Trust in Scotland' (2000) 8 *European Review of Private Law* 427.

Reiff, M.R., *Punishment, Compensation and Law: A Theory of Enforceability* (Cambridge University Press 2005).

Reimann, M., 'The Historical School against Codification: Savigny, Carter, and the Defeat of the New York Civil Code' (1989) 37 *American Journal of Comparative Law* 95.

Reimann, M., 'Nineteenth Century German Legal Science' (1990) 31 *Boston College Law Review* 837.

American Law Institute, *Restatement (Third) of Agency* (American Law Institute 2006).

Reynolds, M., 'DeepMind's AI beats world's best Go player in latest face-off' *New Scientist* (23 May 2017) <https://www.newscientist.com/article/2132086-deepminds-ai-beats-worlds-best-go-player-in-latest-face-off/>.

Riesenfeld, S., 'The Influence of German Legal Theory on American Law: The Heritage of Savigny and His Disciples' (1989) 37 *American Journal of Comparative Law* 1.

Rochfeld, J., *Les grandes notions du droit privé* (2nd edn, Presses Universitaires de France 2013).

Ross, A., 'Tu-Tu' (1957) 70 *Harvard Law Review* 812.

Salmond, J.W., *Jurisprudence or the Theory of the Law* (Stevens & Haynes 1902).

Saunders, H. D., 'Civil Death: A New Look at an Ancient Doctrine' (1970) 11 *William and Mary Law Review* 988.

Savigny, F. C. von, *System des heutigen Römischen rechts* (Veit 1840).

Savigny, F. C. von, *System of the Modern Roman law, Volume 1* (William Holloway tr. ed., J. Higginbotham 1867).

Savigny, F. C. von, *Jural Relations; or, the Roman Law of Persons as Subjects of Jural Relations: Being a Translation of the Second Book of Savigny's System of Modern Roman Law* (William Henry Rattigan tr. ed., Wildy 1884).

Schafer, J. K., 'Long Arm of the Law: Slave Criminals and the Supreme Court in Antebellum Louisiana' (1985) 60 *Tulane Law Review* 1247.

Schwitzgebel, E. and Garza, M., 'A Defense of the Rights of Artificial Intelligences' (2015) 39 *Midwest Studies in Philosophy* 98.

Searle, J., 'Minds, Brains and Programs' (1980) 3 *Behavioral and Brain Sciences* 417.

Searle, J., *Making the Social World: The Structure of Human Civilization* (Oxford University Press 2010).

Searle, J., 'Proper Names' (1958) 67 *Mind* 166.

Shammas, C., 'Re-Assessing the Married Women's Property Acts' (1994) 6 *Journal of Women's History* 9.

Sheehy, P., *The Reality of Social Groups* (Ashgate 2006).

Simmonds, N. E., 'Rights at the Cutting Edge' in Matthew H. Kramer, N. E. Simmonds, and Hillel Steiner (eds), *A Debate over Rights: Philosophical Enquiries* (Oxford University Press 1998).

Simmonds, N. E., 'Grotius and Pufendorf' in Steven Nadler (ed.), *A Companion to Early Modern Philosophy* (Blackwell 2002).

Sinclair, J., 'Introduction' in Belinda Van Heerden, Alfred Cockrell, and Raylene Keightley (eds), *Boberg's Law of Persons and the Family* (Juta & Company 1999).

Skopek, J. M., 'Aesthetic Injuries, Animal Rights and Anthropomorphism' (2009) 122 *Harvard Law Review* 1204.

Smith, B., 'Legal Personality' (1928) 37 *Yale Law Journal* 283.

Solum, L. B., 'Legal Personhood for Artificial Intelligences' (1992) 70 *North Carolina Law Review* 1231.

Sreenivasan, G., 'A Hybrid Theory of Claim-Rights' (2005) 25 *Oxford Journal of Legal Studies* 257.

Stein, P., *The Character and Influence of the Roman Civil Law* (The Hambledon Press 1988).

Stein, P., 'Systematization of Private Law in the Sixteenth and Seventeenth Centuries' in Jan Schröder (ed.), *Entwicklung der Methodenlehre in Rechtswissenschaft und Philosophie vom 16. bis zum 18. Jahrhundert* (Franz Steiner Verlag 1998).

Steiner, H., *An Essay on Rights* (Blackwell 1994).

Stone, C. D., *Should Trees Have Standing? Law, Morality, and the Environment* (3rd edn, Oxford University Press 2010).

Stucki, S., 'Rechtstheoretische Reflexionen zur Begründung eines tierlichen Rechtssubjekts' in Margot Michel, Daniela Kühne, and Julia Hänni (eds), *Animal Law—Tier und Recht. Developments and Perspectives in the 21st Century* (Dike 2012).

Stucki, S., *Grundrechte für Tiere. Eine Kritik des geltenden Tierschutzrechts und rechtstheoretische Grundlegund von Tierrechten im Rahmen einer Neupositionerung des Tieres als Rechtssubjekt* (Nomos 2016).

Sunstein, C., 'Slaughterhouse Jive' *New Republic* (21 January 2001) 40.

Sunstein, C., 'Can Animals Sue?' in Cass R. Sunstein and Martha C Nussbaum (eds), *Animal Rights: Current Debates and New Directions* (Oxford University Press 2004).

Sykes, K., 'Human Drama, Animal Trials: What the Medieval Animal Trials Can Teach Us About Justice for Animals' (2011) 17 *Animal Law Review* 273.

Thibaut, A., *An Introduction to the Study of Jurisprudence* (Nathaniel Lindley tr. ed., T & JW Johnson 1885).

Thibaut, A., *System des Pandektenrechts* (Mauke 1803).

Thiel, U., *The Early Modern Subject. Self-Consciousness and Personal Identity from Descartes to Hume* (Oxford University Press 2011).

Thomas, B., 'A Critical Review of Law's Meaning of Life: Philosophy, Religion, Darwin and the Legal Person' (2011) 38 *Journal of Law and Society* 631.

Thomson, J. J., *The Realm of Rights* (Harvard University Press 1990).

Trahan, J.-R., 'The Distinction between Persons and Things: An Historical Perspective' (2008) 1 *Journal of Civil Law Studies* 9.

Tuck, R., *Natural Rights Theories: Their Origin and Development* (Cambridge University Press 1979).

Tuomela, R., *Social Ontology: Collective Intentionality and Group Agents* (Oxford University Press 2013).

Tuori, K., *Critical Legal Positivism* (Ashgate 2002).

Tuori, K., *Ratio and Voluntas: The Tension Between Reason and Will in Law* (Routledge 2010).

Tur, R., 'The "Person" in Law' in Arthur Peacocke and Grant Gillett (eds), *Persons and Personality: A Contemporary Inquiry* (Basil Blackwell 1988).

Vermaas, P. E. and others, 'The Design Stance and Its Artefacts' (2013) 190 *Synthese* 1131.

Watson, A., *Roman Slave Law* (Johns Hopkins University Press 1988).

Wellman, C., *Real Rights* (Oxford University Press 1995).

Wellman, C. H., 'Feinberg's Two Concepts of Rights' (2005) 11 *Legal Theory* 213.

Wenar, L., 'The Nature of Rights' (2005) 33 *Philosophy and Public Affairs* 223.

Wieacker, F., *A History of Private Law in Europe* (Tony Weir tr. ed., Clarendon Press 1995).

Wilson, S. D., 'Animals and Ethics', *Internet Encyclopedia of Philosophy* <https://www.iep.utm.edu/anim-eth/>.

Wise, S. M., 'The Legal Thinghood of Nonhuman Animals' (1996) 23 *Boston College Environmental Affairs Law Review* 471.

Wise, S. M., 'Hardly a Revolution—The Eligibility of Nonhuman Animals for Dignity-Rights in a Liberal Democracy' (1998) 22 *Vermont Law Review* 793.

Wise, S. M., 'Legal Personhood and the Nonhuman Rights Project' (2010) 17 *Animal Law Review* 1.

Zarka, Y. C., 'The Invention of the Subject of the Law' (1999) 7 *British Journal for the History of Philosophy* 245.

Copyright Acknowledgements

We are grateful for permission to reproduce the following material in this volume: First epigraph reproduced from Hohfeld, W. N., 'Some Fundamental Legal Conceptions as Applied in Judicial Reasoning' (1913) *Yale Law Journal* 23(1). Available at: <http://digitalcommons.law.yale.edu/ylj/vol23/iss1/4>.

Second epigraph reproduced with permission from Leena Krohn. Krohn, L., *Tainaron: Mail from Another City* (translated by Hildi Hawkins, Cheeky Frawg Books). Copyright 2012 Leena Krohn.

Index

Note: For the benefit of digital users, indexed terms that span two pages (e.g., 52–53) may, on occasion, appear on only one of those pages.